SOVIET JEWRY AND SOVIET POLICY

BY ALFRED D. LOW

EAST EUROPEAN MONOGRAPHS

DISTRIBUTED BY COLUMBIA UNIVERSITY PRESS, NEW YORK

1990

EAST EUROPEAN MONOGRAPHS, NO. CCLXXXI

To Matthew and Micah

Contents

Books Previously Published by the Author

Lenin on the Question of Nationality, 1958
The Soviet Hungarian Republic and the Paris Peace Conference, 1963
The Anschluss Movement, 1918–1919, and *The Paris Peace Conference*, 1974
Die Anschlussbewegung in Österreich und Deutschland, 1918–1919, and *Die Pariser Friedenskonferenz*, 1975
The Sino–Soviet Dispute. An Analysis of the Polemics, 1976
Jews in the Eyes of the Germans. From the Enlightenment to Imperial Germany, 1979
The Anschluss Movement, 1918–1938. Background and Aftermath. An Annotated Bibliography in German and Austrian Nationalism, 1984
The Anschluss Movement, 1931–1938, and the Great Powers, 1985
The Sino–Soviet Confrontation since Mao Zedong. Dispute, Detente, or Conflict?, 1987

"Any harassment of any nation is inadmissible, criminal, and shameful. The Soviet People's Commissars declares the anti–Semitic movement and the pogroms against Jews to be a catastrophe for the workers' and peasants' revolution and calls upon the working people of socialist Russia to fight against this evil by any and all means."

> Lenin
>
> *Izvestia,* July 27, 1918

It is "thoughtless, despicable, and harmful to ourselves . . . to oppress a people [the Jews], which has given to the world the greatest prophets of truth and justice and which contributes to its enlightenment men of the greatest talent and intelligence to this day."

> Maxim Gorky

Abbreviations

CC	Central Committee
CP	Communist Party
CPSU	Communist Party of the Soviet Union
CYL	Communist Youth League
CASP	Current Abstracts of the Soviet Press
CDSP	Current Digest of the Soviet Press
JAC	Jewish Anti-Fascist Committee
MGB	Ministry of State Security
MVD	Ministry of the Interior
RSDLP	Russian Social Democratic Labor Party
RSFSR	Russian Socialist Federated Soviet Republic

Acknowledgements

I wish to express my appreciation to the *Current Digest of the Soviet Press* (translation copyright by the CD of the SP, published weekly at Columbus, Ohio) for allowing me the use of its files, especially after the Six–Day War (1967). I am also grateful for the assistance given me by the staff of the Library of Congress, of the libraries of Columbia University, the University of Wisconsin, Madison, and the University of Washington, Seattle. As previously, I owe a debt of gratitude to my wife, Dr. Rose S. Low, for numerous kinds of help during my work for this study.

Alfred D. Low
Bellevue, Washington
April 1989

PREFACE

This study is concerned with the history of Soviet policy toward the Jews and of anti–Semitism in the Soviet period rather than with its historical roots in tsarist Russia. But Russian Jew–hatred goes back centuries and is by no means confined to twentieth century developments whether in Russia or elsewhere. Its causes are intricately linked with the development of Greek Orthodox Christianity and its theology. Orthodox Christianity shares hostility to Jews and Judaism with other branches of Christianity as represented in other parts of Europe. The anti–Jewish hostility in Russia is also rooted in the country's peculiar economic and social system and its educational backwardness.

Communists, while not denying the existence of anti–Semitism under the tsars, have strenuously denied its survival in the USSR. They proclaim that they have terminated the practice of Jew–hatred and that they have banished its ideology from the moment they came to power in 1917. They have held that the mere accusation of the existence of populist anti–Semitism was an intolerable offense. Their presumptuous claim, however, of the disappearance of Jew–hatred in the USSR is a complete distortion of reality and of the historic record. Only in its earliest phase has Soviet Communism held high the banner of national equality, justice, and national development and has trumpeted its theoretical opposition to national discrimination and national and racial hatred throughout Russia and the world. As far as religion is concerned, the Soviets from the start have claimed of having also eliminated all religious privileges as well as religious discriminations. Some liberals and socialists in Russia and abroad have tended to focus on religious "equality" rather than on the Soviets' all–out atheistic propaganda and repression of all religions. They have tried to interpret the extremist godless propaganda as an unavoidable temporary backlash to the long intimate relationship between repressive tsarism and the submissive Greek Orthodox Church.

Jews and gentiles, communists, socialists, and many liberals were long unwilling to believe that any threat to the Jews could ever arise from the Left. But Russian and non–Russian experiences since the Enlightenment should have taught a different lesson. The twentieth century has unquestionably demonstrated the threat to Jewish individual and national existence and to Jewish equality from the extreme Right as well as the extreme Left.

The very extent and intensity of Soviet–instigated anti–Semitic propaganda is a most disturbing phenomenon. It has aroused fear among many people, foremost Soviet Jews. In the opinion of some experts on Jewish and Soviet affairs, the denunciation of Israel as a "pirate state," [1] the obvious attempt to delegitimize it and Jews in general, and the "diabolic" anti–Semitic Soviet progaganda at home and abroad is designed to "prepare the ground for a second catastrophe." The Soviets have made "tremendous efforts" in the field of anti–Semitic propaganda and anti–Zionism "to portray Jews as enemy No. 1." [2]

This has stunned students of the Soviet Union and of Communism since it is in crass violation of the professed Communist internationalism and the doctrine of the equality of nationalities as well as of Lenin's views on Jews and anti–Semitism in particular. Lenin denounced tsarism for its political exploitation of anti–Semitism. In his speech on "Anti–Jewish Pogroms" he castigated "the criminal policy of capitalists who deliberately incited hostility towards the Jews in order to divert the attention of workers from their real enemy, capitalism." [3]

> Shame on accursed tsarism, which has been torturing and persecuting Jews. Shame on those who sow hatred toward the Jews, who sow hatred toward other nations. The Communist Party has always waged a merciless struggle against anti–Semitism as a phenomenon profoundly hostile to the Soviet system.

When *Pravda* at a rare moment, in 1965, warned against anti–Semitism, [4] it quoted Lenin! Another time at a gathering of artists and Party leaders Yevgeny Yevtushenko, prominent writer and dissenter, daring to come to the assistance of the Jews, cited Lenin and warned: "We cannot go forward to Communism with such a heavy load as Judeophobia. And here there can be neither silence nor denial." [5] The problem must be resolved by "cessation of anti–Semitism, along with instituting criminal proceedings against the anti–Semites."

Soviet anti–Semitism under Stalin had already shocked Trotsky, outstanding revolutionary leader and Stalin's rival. Trotsky actually was little interested in the Jewish question which "never occupied the center of my attention." He had not even learned "Jewish" and spent his whole life outside of Jewish circles. But he was puzzled by the "very naive" reaction of people to his accusation that there existed anti–Semitism in the Soviet Union. Many, he charged, recognized only that which suited them. To them "the Germany of Hitler was the absolutist Kingdom of anti–Semitism, the USSR, on the contrary, the kingdom of national harmony." [6] He recognized that the Soviet regime initiated a series of new phenomena, which "because of the poverty and low cultural level of the population were capable of generating anew, and did in fact generate, anti–Semitic moods." In the 1920s already he saw clearly the revival not only of the old and hereditary Jew–hatred but also that of the new "Soviet" variety.

Soviet anti–Semitism has long remained relatively little known and has been able to hide its very nature. This was also due to the deliberate isolation of the totalitarian Soviet regime from the rest of Europe and the world at large. The Soviet government has managed to conceal its growing discriminatory practices which ran directly counter to the noble principles which it loudly propagated. Also, for many people unfamiliar with the Marxist–Leninist phraseology, which frequently employs words such as democracy and liberty, and social and national justice, it proved difficult to decode Soviet progapanda and to decipher it down to its anti–Semitic core.

Dedicated Communists and even Socialists have thus remained long insensitive to all manifestations of Soviet Jew–hatred. But Soviet Jews and their friends have become increasingly skeptical, disillusioned, and frustrated over the Kremlin's deceptive domestic and foreign aspects of its Jewish policy.

Contrary to often repeated claims, the October Revolution did not liberate Soviet nationalities, and least of all the Jews. A straight line leads from Russian anti–Semitism of the eighteenth and nineteenth centuries, if not of earlier times, to Soviet Jewish policy and Jew–hatred of the twentieth century. In some aspects the Soviet variety represents a deterioration of the Russian attitude and of Soviet policy toward the Jews. This is especially the case in matters of cultural and religious freedom and national development, the freedom of emigration (which was never an issue int he last decades of the tsarist regime), the attempt at mass expulsion from Soviet Europe in the last days of Stalin, the extent of Soviet propagation of anti–Semitism on a global rather than merely Russian scale, the denunciation of Jewish "racism," and the hostility displayed toward Zionism. Excepting a few short years, the Soviets have voiced no sympathy, but rather opposition toward the concept of a return of the Jews to their historic homeland and to their assertion of national self–determination. As a rule, they have long battled the Jews' establishment of national independence and freedom in Palestine after centuries of expulsion, oppression, pogroms, and the Holocaust. They have shown no hesitation to continue their anti–Semitic policy.

The situation of the Soviet Jews is the more serious since totalitarian anti–Semitism, in contradistinction to its tsarist predecessor, had deprived Jews of the opportunity of fighting back. Both in Imperial Germany, the Austrian Empire as well as in tsarist Russia the Jews were able to strike back propagandistically and politically at their detractors and at pogromists. *Perestroika* and *glasnost*, while perhaps holding out some hope, have so far not substantially improved the situation of Soviet Jewry. Frankness and openness has permitted Soviet anti–Semitism new leeway, but has not given Soviet Jews the right and ability to retaliate against verbal and other assaults by Soviet anti–Semites. If the treatment of minorities and of the Jewish national–religious minority in particular is a barometer of sanity, decency, and true civilization in the world, the twentieth century, rather than showing moral progress, has been a throwback to the darkest epochs in the history of mankind. The Hitlerian holocaust has resulted in the physical destruction of much of Central, East European and even West European Jewry, of a total of about six million human beings. It has reduced Soviet Jewry by more than one million people. Instead of demonstrating good will toward the pitiful Jewish remnants of the Nazi mass murder of Jews, Soviet policy has in the last years of Stalin's totalitarian rule resulted in depriving Soviet Jews of much of what has remained of their cultural, religious, and national existence. Subsequent Soviet policy has inflamed the mind of anti–Semitic extremists and of the Soviet people against the Jews and let loose an almost unprecedented propaganda of hatred and vituperation against them. It has attacked Jewish religion and Zionism as "racism" and has shown no compunction and commiseration for the Jews, though they were only yesterday the primary target of the Nazi mass murder.

Next to the Jewish concentration in the U.S. and Israel, Soviet Jewry constitutes one of the largest concentrations of Jews anywhere. Its fate is clearly of greatest importance to the Jewish people in its entirety, and, in view of past contributions, to world civilization. The cultural, religious, and national survival of Soviet Jewry as a distinct group depends to a large extent on Soviet policy. The policy of deliberate and ruthless assimilation of Soviet Jewry by forcible means, repudiated by Lenin himself, and the continued discrimination and differential treatment of Soviet Jews could strike a mortal blow at the hope of Soviet Jewry to survive as a people into the twenty-first century. Next to the physical extermination of Jews by Nazi barbarism, no policy is more cruel and revolting than the deliberate cultural and national extinction of an entire people by Soviet policy.

Several years after the end of World War II a highly significant *Statement on the Status of the Jewish Community in the USSR* was made public, signed by some leading American pesonalities such as Eleanor Roosevelt, William O. Douglas, Thurgood Marshal, and Reinhold Niebuhr.[7] It has not only historic significance but also great contemporary importance. It drew attention to the discrimination against the Jewish minority in the Soviet Union, the pattern of differential treatment to which the Soviet Jews were subjected as an ethnic-cultural and religious group. This discrimination, the signatories charged, was "in utter contradiction to the ideological background of the USSR" as well as to its constitutional and legal framework. "No less it is offensive to all men of good will and good conscience, concerned with the rights of minorities everywhere." The Statement points out that while Soviet Jews, like other ethnic groups, were specifically recognized as a 'nationality,' they were, nevertheless, the

> only group of this kind which since 1948 has been deprived by official policy of any of the attendant rights accorded to all other nationalities of the Soviet Union. These include schools, newspapers, publishing and theaters in the national tongue, and instruction in the cultural and historic traditions of the people.

Even Soviet national groups which are territorially dispersed enjoyed these rights. Many Soviet ethnic groups smaller than Soviet Jewry were granted basic cultural rights. There existed "no objective reason" why Jews should be singled out for differential treatment.

In the field of religion too, the *Statement* continued, the Jews were subject to a special discriminatory policy. Unlike other indigenous religious cults, however—Russian Orthodox people, Baptists and Moslems—Jews were prevented from having a nation-wide federation of religious communities, the only framework through which religious groups can maintain and construct houses of worship and manufacture religious articles. While churches were being repaired and reopened, synagogues were being closed. And "the ban" on Hebrew language prevented Jewish children from even understanding their religion.

The foregoing *Statement* sharply criticized the "organized campaign of the Soviet press" "inciting" against Judaism as a religion and against individual Jews as "anti–social elements." Such publications were likely to arouse further antagonism, since people will regard them as being "officially inspired." Among the "tragic consequences" of Moscow's policy toward the Jews were the barring of "any contacts, as a group or community, with Jewish cultural and spiritual communities and organizations outside the USSR," even with those in East European countries. This was a "particularly grievous blow" since historically Jews have been virtually unique in their dispersion across the whole world.

A "humane solution" to the Russian–Jewish problem would be, the *Statement* concluded:

(1) A reinstatement of full cultural autonomy for the Jewish minority— which it enjoyed in Lenin's and even Stalin's early days and which existed until "violently dismantled" by administrative measures in 1948.

(2) The undersigned asked for permission to Jewish religious institutions to practice their rites freely and to establish formal contact with each other.

(3) These Jewish religious and cultural institutions should be permitted to establish formal contact with their dispersed kin in Israel and throughout the world.

(4) The Soviets should "end" their anti–Jewish press campaign.

In view of developments int he postwar period and the obvious escalation of Soviet anti–Semitism and anti–Zionist campaigns during the last decades, the foregoing *Statement* needs updating and expansion. Anti–Zionist propaganda especially since the Six–Day War and since the passing of the infamous "Zionism is racism" resolution in the U.N. in 1975 has increased. It has flooded the Soviet Union and taken on a global characer. To establish "normal" relations between the Soviet Union one hand and Israel and world Jewry on the other it would be necessary to completely cease anti–Jewish and anti–Zionist campaigns in the Soviet Union and abroad, erase the shameful "Zionism is racism" resolution in the U.N., resume unconditionally diplomatic relations with Israel, and permit the free emigration of Jews from the USSR. The difficulties of such decisions for the Soviets after decades of pursuing policies of discrimination and vituperative anti–Jewish progaganda are apparent, but no half–way measures will bring about a "normalization" of relations. It might be argued that such "normalcy" between Russia and its Jewry has never existed. But in the era of "restructuring" the time has come for radically uprooting the legacy of past and present prejudices and for rebuilding Soviet–Jewish relations on an entirely new and just foundation.

I. INTRODUCTION

The Soviet Union has fifteen constituent Republics. The largest of these republics is the Russian Socialist Federated Soviet Republic (RSFSR) in which the bulk of the Great Russians but also many of the smaller national minorities live. According to the official statistics of mid–January 1959 the Great Russians make up less than half of the entire population of the USSR. With the two other Slavic nationalities of the Soviet Union, the Ukrainians and White Russians (Byelorussians), however, which since the last days of Tsarism have been recognized as distinct and separate nationalities, the Slavs form a much larger percentage of the Soviet population. As a result of the industrialization of the Soviet Union since the October Revolution, the spectacular growth of new towns and cities in the border regions and the deliberate effort at Russian colonization in these areas, the Slavic nationalities in the USSR constitute a growing percentage of the population in the other Soviet Republics. Though there is no single state language in the USSR, the Russian language and culture is given preferential treatment and prevails in the schools and universities of the Soviet Union and dominates its press, radio, television, and theater.

According to the census of 1959, there lived 2,268,000 Jews in the USSR.[1] However, two years later, in 1961, the Soviet Institute of Ethnography listed a total of 2,469,000 Jews in the Soviet Union. In another official publication it was estimated that in 1966 there were about three million Jews in the USSR. In any case, the Jewish population in the USSR is actually larger than the total population in eight of the fifteen Soviet republics.

The Jews in the USSR, according to the census of 1970 the accuracy and reliability of which have been questioned, constituted about 1 percent of the total Soviet population—a percentage comparable to that of Weimar Germany's Jewish population. They are dispersed throughout all the fifteen Union Republics, the Russian Republic (38 percent), the Ukraine (36 percent), and Byelorussia (7 percent). Fifteen percent live in the Baltic Republics, in Moldavia, Georgia, and Uzbekistan. The Soviet Jews are by no means one of the smallest nationalities in the Soviet Union. Of over 108 principal nationalities they are the twelfth largest national group.

Differently from other Soviet national minorities, the Jews are an extraterritorial ethnic group, dispersed not only over Russia but over the world. Also different from other Soviet nationalities, they had two languages, Hebrew, the language of the Old Testament and of prayer, and Yiddish, a German dialect which they had brought eastward to Poland. Yiddish was printed in Hebrew letters and had numerous Hebrew words. Though the authorities from the beginning had targeted Hebrew for destruction, Yiddish was first encouraged. In the 1920s and even early 1930s the Jews in the USSR had almost one thousand schools in which Yiddish was the language of instruction. There existed then also three teachers' colleges, sixteen technical and five agricultural institutes, 116 libraries, 47 reading clubs, three theaters and a children's theater in Yiddish. There were also Yiddish departments at some universities and institutes of higher education.[2]

In the 1920s there were published in the Soviet Union no less than eighty Jewish newspapers and periodicals. The state supported more than forty Yiddish State Theaters; every large city had its own theater. The Soviets had not yet embarked upon the suppression of the Yiddish language and culture. In 1925 as many as 208 Yiddish books were published in the USSR.[3] Soviet Jews are an educated segment of the USSR, quite different from that of their nineteenth-century ancestors. Cultural and national oppression aside, their social and educational level is relatively high. They also live in large numbers in the most important urban centers of the Soviet Union. Four and a half percent of the population of Moscow are Jews, over 5 percent of the inhabitants of Leningrad, 13.9 percent of Kiev, and 7.6 percent in Minsk. In Kishinev, Riga, Tbilisi, and Vilna, the percentages respectively are 19.9, 5.0, 2.5, and 7.[4a] Numerous demographic specialists outside the Soviet Union hold that the Jewish population of these cities are considerably larger.

The important role of Jews in Soviet life can be further appreciated by taking account of the circumstances that in 1968 14.7 percent of Soviet doctors were Jews, 8.5 percent of all writers and journalists, 10.4 percent of all judges and lawyers, and 7.7 percent of all actors, musicians, and artists.[4b] Among scientists, Jews, about 51,000, are, next to Russians and Ukrainians, the most numerous nationality.

There are about half a million of specialist workers having a higher or specialized secondary education. But since Jews are not a majority in any of the republics, autonomous republics, autonomous regions or even national areas, but live dispersed all over the USSR, they lack representation in the Soviet of Nationalities, the "upper" house of the Soviet Parliament. According to the theories of Lenin and Stalin, they are not a nation. Yet, in strange contradiction, they are repeatedly and officially still considered a nationality, though one in a state of transition to complete assimilation.

The contemporary lack of public appreciation of the Soviet Jews stands in sharp contrast to Lenin's praise of their role in the revolutionary movement. In Geneva, on the eve of the February Revolution, Lenin had remarked: "It should be said to their credit that today the Jews provide a relatively high percentage of representatives of internationalism compared with other nations."[5] Today, however, they are accused by the Soviets of being guilty of nationalism and "cosmopolitanism" rather than being given credit for their internationalism. Lenin's high appreciation of the Jews was testified to by Maxim Gorky even more strongly. As Lenin voiced it: "There are few intelligent people among us. We are, generally speaking, a gifted people, but intellectually lazy. An intelligent Russian is almost always a Jew or a man with Jewish blood."[6] Lenin not only denounced anti–Semitism, but in his own political appointments generally refused to yield to popular biases as anti–Semitism, rejecting such an opportunist attitude. Though yielding to Y. Sverdlov's insistence not to appoint Trotsky as commissar of home affairs,[7] he did not hesitate making him commissar of foreign affairs.

In view of Lenin's uncompromising attitude on anti–Semitism, when and why did the Soviets make a turn–about after his death and why did they subsequently embrace a virulent Jew–hatred? The fledgling Soviet state was involved in a war of survival against the White Russian armies which following the Tsarist example used Jew–hatred as a major weapon; they saw in it not only an instrument of the struggle against the Jews, but against Bolshevik rule. On July 27, 1918, the Council of People's Commissars issued a decree which aimed at destroying "the anti–Semitic movement at its roots.[8a] Lenin himself inserted then the phrase that the pogromists and persons inciting to pogroms be "outlawed." But self–interest rather than philo–Semitism prompted this attitude.

In regard to individual employment and opportunities the Soviet Jewish intelligentsia made large strides in the 1920s as compared to the tsarist period, though the economic transformation brought many a hardship. With the rise of anti-Semitism in Soviet society however, and with the consolidation of Stalin's power the situation began to change. Once again a *numerus clausus* was introduced at some Russian universities. In many economic activities a *numerus nullus*, the total exclusion of Jews, did take place. Jews found themselves excluded from prestigious positions in many fields, referring to themselves as "fifth-rate invalids"—in reference to the fifth item in the domestic passport which listed the nationality of the bearer—a designation which no Jew could escape. In the tsarist era the Russian Jew could embrace Christianity—undesirable as it appeared to the great majority of Russian Jews—and the road at least to personal advancement lay then open before him. This alternative was now closed to Soviet Jews.

In the early years of the Soviet regime Jews were quite prominent in the diplomatic service; among them were Maxim Litinov, Karl Radek, and Adolf Yoffe. In the 1920s and 1930s many of the Soviet diplomatic representatives and consular officers were still of Jewish descent, though under Foreign Commissar Litvinov their number was much reduced. Their very presence abroad was widely noted. A Jew, Konstantin Umansky, was appointed Soviet ambassador to the U.S. in 1939. Ivan Maisky, a half-Jew, was made Soviet ambassador to Great Britain during the war. Litvinov held the post of deputy foreign Minister, a post later occupied by Maisky and Solomon Lozovsky. Boris Stein served as member of the Soviet delegation in the early days of the U N.. though by that time the number of Jews serving in the foreign office and in important overseas posts was already sharply diminished. In diplomatic training colleges there were in this period still Jews both among professors and students.

As far as the Soviet army was concerned, the situation was not strikingly different regarding the overall reduction of the number of Jews in top echelon positions, though military ranks could not be revoked at the end of one's service. Nor could Jews be debarred from lower commissioned ranks. Yet in the 1930s Jews were purged from the posts of highest military command. Many high-placed Jewish military officers had been removed and a few even executed in 1937; one, General Ian Gamarnik, had committed suicide. During the war a larger number of Jews were in supreme command, but during the "black years," 1948–1953, 63 Jewish generals, 111 colonels, and 159 lieutenant-colonels were retired. At the end of this period, there was not a single Jew among the top-ranking officers, marshals, chiefs of staff, and active generals. When Milovan Djilas visited Moscow with a Yugoslav delegation in 1948, he was informed by a proud official of the CPSU that when the deputy chief of staff, General Antonov, was "discovered" to be of Jewish descent he was promptly dismissed.

In the 1930s there was only a single Jewish member of the Politburo, L. Kaganovich. In the Central Committee (CC) in 1939 the number of Jews among 71 members was reduced to 9, and in 1952 at the 19th Party Congress a single Jew was re-elected to this body. Similarly, a single Jew, C. D. Veinberg, was nominated and elected to be a candidate for membership in the Central Committee; he later lost this post. In 1952 approximately seven million Party members of altogether 37 nationalities, 1,192 delegates and 167 candidate delegates were represented in the CC. Among these nationalities were tiny groups such as Yakuts, Ossetians, Mordovians, Udmurts, Komis, Chuvashas, and Buriats, but no Jews!

As far as the Supreme Soviet is concerned, a comparison of the results of the 1937, 1946, and 1951 elections shows that Jewish representation declined sharply in both chambers. In the 1937 elections there were 47 Jewish members out of a total of 801. In the March 1950 elections the proportion of Jews dropped further to 0.4 percent of the total population. While before World War II the percentage of Jewish representatives in the Supreme Soviet was far above that of Jews in the entire population, after the war, when Jews formed about 1 percent of the populace. it was far below it. The war and the Nazi extermination had sharply reduced the number of Jews in the USSR. On the other hand, the Soviet Union had annexed the Western Ukraine, Byelorussia, the Baltic countries, Bessarabia, and the Northern Bukovina—regions where some Jews had survived the Nazi murder.

At the end of the Civil War the Bolshevik regime had tried to combat anti-Semitism vigorously. The Civil Code of 1922 provided a minimum of one year's solitary confinement and death in time of war for propaganda and agitation aimed at arousing national and religious enmities and dissensions. The criminal code of 1927 was even more severe in regard to Jew-hatred. The mere possession of hate literature was subject to these penalties. Party and State organs published about one hundred books and pamphlets against anti-Semitism. It was revealing, however, that *Pravda* blamed the connivance of local Party, Komsomol, and trade union organizations for various "manifestations of anti-Semitism."[8b] The daily pointed out that the anti-Jewish campaign was permitted to go unpunished

for months and even years. Party leaders who sided with Stalin in
the intra–Party struggle against both Zinoviev and Trotsky and their
followers, gave the campaign a deliberately anti–Semitic character,
as Trotsky complained in a private letter to N. Bukharin on March
4, 1926.[9] Though Stalin, as late as January 1931, disavowed anti-
Semitism in the USSR as a "phenomenon profoundly hostile to the
Soviet regime," he actually inveighed against the political opposition not disdaining to use the anti–Semitic weapon himself. Years
later Premier V. M. Molotov called anti–Semitism a "bestiality."[10] He
called attention to Marx's Jewish origin—which was a rarity, hardly
ever repeated in the USSR—and stressed that the Jewish people had
given "many heroes to the revolutionary struggle" and "continues to
produce more and more fine and gifted leaders and organizers" in the
Soviet Union. Such words of praise for Jews have not been heard in
the USSR for decades!

During the 1920s some Soviet leaders, foremost M. Kalinin, then
President of the USSR, realized that the Jewish people, compared to
other Soviet national groups, was in a disadvantageous situation.[11]
Kalinin wanted the Jews to become a full–fledged nation in the USSR.
He wished to turn an urban people toward agricultural activities—
perhaps influenced by the Zionist example—and simultaneously to
improve Soviet policy toward the Jews. He thought highly of them,
calling them "one of the most lively and politically most influential
nations."[12]

Among organizations to assist Jews to return to the land was
the voluntary organization Ozet. Parts of the southern Ukraine were
chosen for this purpose. Altogether three Jewish national districts in
the Kherson and Dnepropetrovsk region and two in the Crimea were
established to promote the return of the Jews to agriculture. Actually,
on the even of World War I the number of Jews in agricultural colonies
was about 90,000. The total number of Jewish collective farms in the
mid–1930s in the USSR amounted to about 500. About 225,000 Jews
lived as agriculturists in the Crimea and in some parts of the Ukraine.

A major goal of the return of Jews to the soil and to agricultural
occupations was not only to counter the increasing urbanization and
to bring about economic normalization. It was also designed to give
Jews a stronger legal footing among the nationalities of the Soviet
Union. Lenin's and Stalin's rigid theories about the Jews not being a
full–fledged nationality but one destined to assimilation and national
death were largely responsible for the refusal to grant them cultural
autonomy,[13] and for discouraging support for the preservation and

cultivation of Hebrew and Yiddish national culture. Soviet practices reminded Jews constantly of their alien character and their pariah status. The persistent attacks on Judaism, Jewish religion, and Zionism spread inevitably fresh anti–Semitism throughout the USSR. All this of course worked at cross purposes with the declared communist goal of assimilation.

In the hour of need the Russian Jews had faced the murderous Nazi hordes virtually alone, without the moral and material support of Soviet authorities and of the Soviet populace. Even after the Holocaust on Russian soil Yevtushenko's poem "Babi Yar" was living testimony to the continuity of Jew–hatred in the USSR and to Soviet unwillingness to concede that Jews had been the special target of mass murder and the most numerous victims. Soviet history and historians were to bury this unprecedented crime, to extirpate Nazi atrocities against Jews, and thus to falsify Soviet and Jewish history.

Jewish territorial concentration, aimed at by the Soviets since the 1920s, has failed to come about. So has turning to agriculture on a massive scale. While almost half of the inhabitants of the Soviet Union live in rural areas, 96 percent of the Jews still reside in towns and cities. But compared to the tsarist era, a great social transformation of Russian Jewry has unquestionably taken place.

A noticeable change in occupations had occurred already after the October Revolution. In 1930 30 percent of all Jews were manual workers, 41 percent employees and members of the liberal professions, 20 percent artisans, and 6 percent farmers. There has been since a considerable further shift of Jewish occupations in favor of administrative posts, white–collar jobs, of teaching, and managerial jobs. Prominence of the Jews in some spheres of Soviet economy was due to their being city–dwellers and to their high educational standards. On the other hand, Jews have been virtually excluded from certain areas of public life, especially Soviet diplomacy and politics. As Krushchev pointed out in May 1956 to an official delegation of the French Socialist Party:

> At the outset of the Revolution we had many Jews in the leadership of the Party and the state. They were educated, may be more revolutionary than the average Russian. In due course we have created new cadres.[14]

While Krushchev has denied any personal anti–Semitism, he has conceded that "anti–Semitic sentiments still existed in Russia" and has made clear that a virtual *numerus clausus* had been established in some fields because of the training of new cadres. As far as the economic and social structure of the Jews was concerned, it was still different from that of other nationalities. The Jewish poor and those without any definite occupation have largely disappeared. But the economic and social life of the Jews still differ from that of other nationalities—a difference that has aroused envy and caused anti–Semitism. But the latter would have had no chance of developing and growing without being constantly fed by Soviet anti–Jewish and anti–Zionist agitation. Moscow has created an atmosphere conducive to the spread of Jew–hatred. Soviet policy has made populist anti–Semitism permissible.

There is a striking discrepancy between the official status of the Jew and Soviet reality. Contrary to all official claims, Soviet Jews do not enjoy genuine equality. While they are at times considered a nationality, at other time this status is simply denied to them. The contradiction is rooted not only in Lenin's various judgments about Jews at different times but, as stated, also in their lack of a territorial base. No other ethnic–religious group in the USSR faces hostility comparable to that Russian Jews face. No other national and religious unit in the USSR is the target of a negative propaganda such as is unleashed against Soviet Jews.

The Jewish nationality is not represented in the Soviet Council of Nationalities, since the latter is elected by citizens voting in Union Republics, autonomous republics, autonomous regions, and national districts. Due to the lack of territorial concentration, there was according to the Soviet statistics of 1959 only one Jewish deputy among 457 in the Ukraine, two out of 407 in Byelorussia, and three out of 209 in Lithuania—all with a large Jewish population. Out of five deputies in Birobidzhan only one was Jewish. Those few Jewish deputies elected in their individual capacity are of course not truly authorized spokesmen for the Jewish population as a collective unit. There exists no internal communal Jewish structure in the USSR. Soviet Jews have neither an elected nor appointed organization to speak in their behalf. They have no cultural or educational institutions satisfying their needs and guaranteeing their survival as a distinct group.

This is in striking contrast even to Soviet policy in the 1920s when the regime still encouraged Jewish culture at least in its Yiddish garb. In the mid–1920s there were 250 Jewish schools in the Ukraine alone[15] which was still a lively center of Jewish creative and artistic culture. In 1935 there existed ten Yiddish newspapers in the Ukrainian Soviet Republic to which Jewish writers and scholars contributed. But after the war, on May 19, 1952, the best Jewish writers of the USSR were executed, among them many Ukrainian Jews. Between 1948 and 1959 altogether only thirteen Yiddish books were published, a negligible improvement over the preceding zero years. There is today no organized Jewish life either in the entire Ukrainian Republic or the RSFSR. There also exists no organized contact between the Jews in the different republics of the USSR or between them and other East European countries, not to mention the West. According to the Warsaw Yiddish newspaper *Folkshtimme* in communist postwar Poland—which had a Jewish population of less than 10,000 people—56 Yiddish books have been published in Poland, 8 in Romania, and only 7 in the much more populous USSR—a population variously estimated, as stated, as between 2.2 and 3 million Jews. In the entire USSR there is currently only one Yiddish publication, a small newspaper in Birobidzhan which appears three times per week.

Though the Soviets' official policy and the Soviet constitution are supposed to provide children with instruction in their native language (article 121), it is a fact that not a single school in the USSR teaches Hebrew or Yiddish.* In contrast with these Jewish languages, 59 languages, of instruction are used in Soviet schools. During the last years of Stalin's life the famous Moscow Yiddish State Theatre has been closed as have been all Jewish publishing houses, magazines, schools, and all Jewish cultural institutions. Again, smaller Jewish communities in communist-ruled countries, such as Poland and Romania, have their own state schools, newspapers, theaters, and other cultural institutions. The Soviet prohibition regarding Jewish institutions must furthermore be judged in the light of the fact that as many as 487,786 Russian Jews gave Yiddish as their mother tongue. In Lithuania the respective percentage of Jews listing Yiddish as their native language was 75 percent, in Moldavia 50 percent, in the Kiev region 32 percent.

The Soviets have claimed that the Jews desired to assimilate and that they have grown indifferent to Jewish culture. The truth is quite different. There has been and is a growing interest in learning Hebrew, Yiddish, and Jewish history.[16] The popularity of Jewish concerts is immense. A report of the Socialist International stressed that Soviet Jews would turn any occasion, even an evening of Jewish songs, into

---

*However, during the last years a few of the higher Soviet educational institutions have apparently introduced the teaching of Hebrew and Yiddish.

a demonstration of national pride. The wrenching war–time experience of Russian Jews, generally repressed, has aroused even many of
the Russian intelligentsia (see Yevtushenko's poem "Babi Yar") en-
graved itself into the historic conscience of Russian Jews, and deepened their national consciousness despite its general erosion through
Soviet policy. The new post–war anti–Semitism under Stalin and
thereafter, the long–standing Soviet anti–Zionism, and the barrage of
anti–Jewish polemics, voiced increasingly in the Soviet press, radio,
and television, have probably strengthened Jewish national cohesion.
Cut off from contacts with the West, Russian Jews, attempting to
obtain the right to emigrate, have encountered momentous obstacles.
Soviet domestic and Soviet foreign policy have conspired to frustrate
them, and Soviet bureaucracy has refused to let them go except in
small numbers, reducing them to the status of being virtual hostages.
It is hardly self–interest, but a mixture of chicanery, spite, and totalitarianism which doom them to the perpetuation of life in what Lenin
called the "Russian prison house of peoples." The Tsarist "prison"
has been turned into a Soviet jail, but escape from it has been made
incomparably harder.

Even traditionally pro–Soviet Jewish communist writers such as
Isaac Deutscher have had to take notice of the "surging up of old and
only half–hidden prejudices of anti–Semitism."[17] The native tradition of pogroms and the population's traumatic wartime experiences
with Nazism, the Soviet policy of deliberately ignoring special Jewish
suffering, and, subsequently, the virtually consistent pro–Arab and
anti–Zionist Soviet stance in the Mid–East was bound to foster hostile feelings toward Soviet Jews. All this has contributed to making
Jews a special target of national and religious hatred and discrimination. The campaign against Judaism has by far exceeded campaigns
waged in behalf of atheism against other religious and ethnic groups.
The persistent link–up of Zionism with dark reaction, "bourgeois nationalism," and even racism, and its denunciation as a mere tool of
U.S. imperialism have raised Zionism and international Judaism in
Soviet propaganda to be major enemies of Soviet communism.

While the U.S. is geographically far away, Soviet Jews are a close
and immediate target—just as German Jews and those in German-
occupied lands were the target of Nazism during World War II. Attacks on Judaism and Zionism have become indistinguishable for the
Russian masses and even for the Russian intelligentsia. Censorship
guidelines, which in general are stricly enforced, have become relaxed
in regard to anti–Semitism. They have almost completely vanished, as

numerous anti–Jewish publications testify to. An example is a book of the notorious anti–Semitic scribbler Trofim Kichko, *Judaism without Embellishment*, which repeated centuries–old anti–Jewish clichés. To Soviet readers the dissemination of such stereotypes is an open invitation to indulge themselves in anti–Semitic propaganda, since these views have received the government imprimatur.

The hostility displayed toward Jews and Zionists has heightened since the Six–Day War. The active diplomatic, propagandistic, and military support given to the Arabs was bound to make Jews fair game. Anti–Zionist campaigns are popular in Moslem–inhabited regions. In 1967 13 percent of the total Soviet population were Moslems; they happen to be one of the fastest growing minorities, comprising several nationalities in the Soviet Union. While the anti–Jewish and anti–Zionist attitude of Moscow has numerous causes, it has been reinforced by the government's expectation that the Moslems in the Soviet Union will be gratified by Moscow's negativist policy toward Israel. In any case, anti–Semitism and anti–Zionism have become permanent features of Soviet propaganda and thought, notwithstanding the major thrust toward internationalism and brotherhood of nationalities inherent in Marxist–Leninist theory.

It is quite apparent that whenever Russian or Soviet nationalism burst forth in the USSR, leading to a sharper confrontation with Western powers, mistrust also of non–Russians and of Jews has gained ground. Stalin, haunted by sucpicion of non–Russians, expelled several nationalities from the Crimea and the Caucasus and Germans from the Volga into Asia, and continued to displace Jews from positions of leadership in Soviet economy and technology. The war years deepened the revival of Russian and Soviet nationalism as well as of anti–Semitism which the populace and broad segments of the Soviet republics eagerly endorsed. The Nazi genocide of Jews as well as the attendant Soviet silence was to make an indelible impression upon them.

In the wake of the Six–Day War, Soviet propaganda at home and in the Soviet bloc began a massive attack upon Zionism and the Jews. A Polish Communist Party ideologist, A. Werblan, accused Jews without exception of "being particularly inclined to revisionism" (then an arch–enemy) and "to Jewish nationalism and Zionism." In 1971, a Soviet writer, V. Blishuklin, declared in *Pravda* that every Zionist was automatically an "enemy of the Soviet people."[18] G. Arbatov, already a very influential advisor to the Politburo, judged that the great bulk of Soviet Jewry, 90 percent, appeared in an "unfavorable

light," since they might become Zionists and thus enemies of the Soviet people, "without being conscious of it." Distrust of Jews became
widely disseminated in the Soviet Union, and crystalized as an article
of faith and indoctrination. The Soviet Jewish refugee Dr. R. Nudelman quotes in his sociological study "Social Progress," V. Mishin
who, abandoning the principle of equality of opportunity, made a
far–going "correction" by postulating the slogan "equalization of the
level of development of all peoples in the USSR."[19]

According to Nudelman, assimilation, which seemed at least formally possible during the first decades of Soviet rule, had become
"absolutely impossible at present,"[20] since both the population and
the government have been for decades deeply infected with morbid
anti–Semitic alertness, suspiciousness, and readiness to expose Jews.
It would be naive to think that he results of such "education" which
has already been inculcated in the second generation could be eliminated by a single decree. Russian anti–Semitism, whatever the impact
of the Nazi example of mass murder of the Soviets and their inadequate response, did of course not originate with World War II or,
going even further back, with World War I and the Bolshevik seizure
of power. Deeply rooted in Russian soil, it destroys the chance of
complete Jewish assimilation.

II. MARXISM, LENINISM, AND THE RUSSIAN JEWS

A Bird's Eye View of Russian Jewish History

From earliest times on relations between Kievan Rus and the Khazars in the southeast of European Russia—who had adopted Judaism—to the "heresy of the Judaizers" in the early modern period were tense and remained part of Moscow's heritage which was to influence subsequent Russo–Jewish relations. Battling Kievan Russia, the Khazar state was destroyed in the mid–tenth century. Jew–hatred also goes back to the rule of Ivan the Terrible and even to the more enlightened regimes of Peter the Great and Catherine II. Though the last–named rulers were more farsighted, their policy toward the Jews showed virtually no changes. Under Catherine's reign, in consequence of the three partitionings of Poland in the last third of the eighteenth century, most Polish Jews came under Russian rule, but remained largely confined to the Pale of Settlement.

It was regulations issued by Catherine II and Tsar Alexander I which laid the groundwork for establishing the Pale of Settlement which lasted until World War I (1915). Russian Jews were thus confined to those parts of the Empire where their ancestors had lived when Poland was partitioned in the late eighteenth century. They were further restricted in the 1880s under Alexander III. Only a limited category of Jews had obtained the right to live wherever they chose and to travel freely in Russia, Jews with university degrees, dentists, pharmacists, and a few others—including some Jewish artisans. The admission of Jews to educational institutions varied in the course of time. Starting in 1887 under Alexander III a quota system limited the number of Jewish students to a specific percentage. The quota determined for Jews in schools within the Pale was 10 percent, outside of it 5 percent, but in St. Petersburg and Moscow only 3 percent. The Pale of Settlement prevented the great majority of Jews from settling in nine–tenths of the area of the Russian Empire.[1a] There were numerous other restrictions in law or practice which hampered Jewish economic activities. Judicial appointments of Jews and their access to professorships were also severely curtailed, the latter most often made contingent on baptism.

The "Tsar Liberator" Alexander II, who emancipated the serfs, had in 1856 tried to "integrate" the Jews into the Russian population but had failed. A combination of religious, economic, political, and more or less conscious racial motives prevented Jews from achieving legal equality. But in May of 1906 the First State Duma adopted unanimously the principle of equality without exception before the law; but the 1905 Revolution had already spent its strength.

The greatest obstacle to Jewish emancipation proved in the end Tsar Nicholas II. A former minister of finance, N. V. Kokovtsev, related in his *Memoirs* that in October 1906 the very conservative Prime Minister Stolypin proposed to his ministerial colleagues to revoke "excessive restrictions" upon Jews—which would also silence "the anti-Russian propaganda on the part of the most powerful Jewish citadel in America"[1b]—but his proposals were rejected by the Emperor, apparently after the intervention by the reactionary and anti-Semitic "Union of the Russian People." It was not until March 20, 1917, several weeks after the February Revolution, that the Provisional Government, facing formidable domestic and foreign policy problems, revoked "religious and national disabilities." With the stroke of a pen it abolished the multitude of restrictive laws, adverse administrative orders, and judicial interpretations which had been in force for more than a century.

The miserable status of the Jews, second-class citizens, was firmly rooted in the Russian mind. Jews had been kept separate from the populace of the Russian Empire, nationally, religiously, culturally, and territorially. Their image was always associated with the most negative stereotypes. It found expression in Russian folklore and literature, though the reaction of the Russian muzhiks, illiterate as they were, was perhaps not greatly affected by this poor perception. The Ukrainian national tradition especially was steeped in anti-Semitism. Though with the accession to the throne of Alexander II some improvements of public opinion and its attitude toward the Jews was noticeable, the new era turned out to be short-lived. A reaction set in after the Tsar's assassination. During the reign of his successors, Alexander III and Nicholas II, Russian chauvinism and imperialism raised their heads. National and social repression grew by leaps and bounds, and Russification and the assimilation of non-Great Russians became state policy.

Intellectual and political movements were shaped by Slavophilism and Westernization; both had their impact upon Russian policy toward the Jews. Despite their different philosophies and approaches, both Slavophiles and Narodniks (Populists), helped to confirm the most unfavorable images of the Jew as an exploiter and parasite. The myth of Jewish domination over the Russian people and the world loomed always in the background.

In his introduction to vol. I, *Anti-Semitism in the Soviet Union*, the Israeli scholar S. Ettinger reached this conclusion: "The populist circles and those of the radical Russian intelligentsia differed on various issues, but shared their attitude toward Jews, reflecting the Slavophiles' negative views."[2] In Slavophile rightist circles "and those connected with official ideology, the whole revolutionary movement was the result of a Jewish conspiracy." Nihilism was a Russian phenomenon, but the secret head of this movement was allegedly the *Alliance Israélite Universelle*, located in Paris, which was working out plans for the "destruction of the world." Russian nihilism was considered only the first stage of the Jewish scheme for world domination. "A paradoxical situation arose toward the end of the 1870s when official policies were somewhat more moderate than policies of radical groups on the right and left."

While the question of integration of the Jews into Russian cultural and social life became a topic of discussion by bureaucrats and newspapers, right-wing-and-left-wing journals viciously attacked Jews. Both held that Jews would never become Russian citizens as long as they did not celebrate the same religious holidays. Following the assassination of Alexander III in 1881 the greater part of the Russian press and of Russian public opinion virtually defended the anti-Semitic outbursts as a justified uprising against Jewish exploiters and parasites. Only a minority of the intelligentsia pointed the accusing finger at the social and political deficiencies of the Russian state and society as the root causes of anti-Semitism. The Russian bureaucrats, Ignatiev Gotovstev and others who prepared the anti-Jewish decrees actually did not create but rather reflected the anti-Jewish sentiments which prevailed in Russian society.

A more favorable shift in the intelligentsia's attitude toward the Jews occurred only in the 1880s and 1890s.[3] It was then that the thought developed that the condition of the Jews could be improved only by a change of governmental policy. In the late 1890s most of the intelligentsia began to relinquish outright anti-Semitism. But they did not acknowledge the right of the Jews to national self-determination. Finns, Poles, Georgians, Armenians, and others could demand national self–determination, but if Jews insisted on these same rights, the Russian Left considered it a manifestation of "Jewish separatism."

Under Constantine Pobiedonostev, advisor to the last two Romanovs, Alexander III and Nicholas II, the discrimination against Jews on religious, national, economic, and social grounds intensified. Pobiedonostev openly revealed his program for Russian Jewry: One third were to emigrate, one third to be assimilated through language and adoption of Russian culture, and through intermarriage and conversion; the last third was to perish. Numerous pogroms were then organized against Jews by the notorious Black Hundreds, at Kishinev in 1903 and thereafter. Most of them were inspired by the Ministry of the Interior and especially encouraged by Tsar Nicholas II and his German–born wife Alexandra Feodorovna. The royal couple strongly supported anti–Semitism, with the police lending a helping hand. Many Russian intellectuals, among them Leo Tolstoy, raised their voice in protest condemning the riots and pogroms. The latter were a direct outgrowth of widespread inflammatory anti–Semitic propaganda, of conspiracy and plots which were aimed against the alleged Jewish domination over Russia and the world.

The concepts of Jewish conspiracy and global subjugation originated in France before the 1789 Revolution. From France they spread to Russia in the late nineteenth century, only to return to the West, especially to Germany in the wake of World War I. It was a tract by Maurice Jolly with its major thrust aimed against the regime of Napoleon III (not against the Jews), which formed the core of the later *Protocols of the Elders of Zion*. Jolly's pamphlet was about an encounter between the spirits of Macchiavelli and Montesquieu. The *Protocols* which turned out to be a gross forgery, climaxed in the accusation of the existence of Jewish conspiracy which allegedly aimed at world domination. But in 1921 it was discovered that three–fourths of the *Protocols* with only minor changes had been lifted directly from Jolly's pamphlet. It was also proven that the chief of the Russian secret police, Rachkovsky, at the turn of the century was deeply involved in this falsification which was designed to influence the anti–Jewish policies of Nicholas II. In his credulity, the Tsar had for a time been fascinated by the *Protocols*.[4]

In 1905, during the Russian Revolution, the journalist Sergius Nilus authored the book entitled *The Great with the Small. The Anti–Christ as an Imminent Political Possibility*; a constituent part of it were the *Protocols of the Elders of Zion.* The tsarist police and Nicholas II himself knew finally that the *Protocols* were a forgery. For this reason they never referred to them during the 1913 Beilis trial in which a Jew was accused of blood libel. This trial had wide repercussions in Russia, all over Europe, and even overseas.

Anti–Semitic Literature of the Early Twentieth Century and Other Voices

In the early years of the twentieth century an abundance of anti–Semitic literature flooded Russia. Special attention was aroused by the books by A. Shmakov, *International Secret Government. The Jewish Problem in World History;* and V. Shulgin, *Pogrom,* Ya. Damienko, *Jewish Strategy and Tactics in the Cause of the Bloodless Conquest of the World,* V. Zalesky, *Mental Inferiority of the Jews,* L. Epifanovich, *Jews, Their Outlook and Social Activity,* etc. The theses elaborated in these writings, reminiscent of the earlier *Protocols of the Elders of Zion,* were involvement of Jews in a plot aiming at the corruption and destruction of society and ultimately at Jewish world domination. This literature was satiated with Jew–hatred, which extended to religion, nationality, morals, and every aspect of Jewish and Russian life. The Soviet anti–Semitic literature of subsequent years and decades linked up in a conscious fashion with anti–Semitic thought of prerevolutionary Russia and with Jew–hatred throughout the ages. While in the early twentieth century anti–Semites accused the Jews of trying to undermine and destroy both Christian society and archconservative political structures like the tsarist Empire, in the recent Soviet period the alleged target of Jews and Zionists was the integrity of the Soviet state and their ultimate goal, anti–Sovietism. Still, Soviet propaganda at times followed closely anti–Jewish pronouncements of the tsarist era, especially the model of the *Protocols* in regard to conspiracy, treason, and, during the last decades, world domination.[5]

After 1917 the *Protocols of the Elders of Zion* were published in both Russian and German translation and distributed in Russia by anti–Semitic groups of the White Guard movement. The *Protocols* were reprinted in Germany by Adolf Hitler and Alfred Rosenberg in millions of copies. Germany's defeat in World War I and the Versailles dictate were, according to both men, attributed to the activities of secret Jewish organizations.

Ever since toward the end of the nineteenth century the socialist movement and its international congresses spread their revolutionary propaganda, social revolutionary radicalism was in the ascendancy. But to many Russian reactionaries the socialist threat appeared too distant to lend itself to full propagandistic exploitation. For Russian anti–Semites the Russian Jew was a more relevant and immediate target and soon emerged as the main enemy. As a matter of fact, the Jew and the revolutionary were increasingly identified. Combatting the Jew, the Jew–haters hoped, would enlist broad popular support in Russia and divert attention from the social and political miasmatic conditions of the country and from the pressing social demands of the Russian people.

The first Zionist Congresses, starting with one in Basel in 1897, seemed to coincide with the rise of unrest in Russia and with increased revolutionary activity, the latter culminating in the 1905 Russian Revolution and the plotting of the Russian secret police. To Russian anti–Semitic circles, this appeared as a proof of a Jewish "plot" against Mother Russia, as a golden opportunity for stirring up anti–Semitic propaganda. This propaganda was intensified in the wake of Russia's war in the Far East in 1904–05 and her military debacle in World War I. The Russian Jew–hatred had become a powerful force.

Of all classes of Russian society the liberal middle class and the Russian intellentsia seemed least affected by anti–Semitism and were often sharply opposed to it. The Russian intelligentsia even displayed a kind of Judaeophilia. In 1901 in a private letter Leo N. Tolstoy wrote: "The Jew is that sacred being who brought down from heaven the everlasting fire and illumined with it the entire world." The Jew was, he asserted, "the religious source," "the pioneer of liberty" and "of civilization," of "civil and religious toleration," the "emblem of eternity."[6] After the pogrom of 1881–82 Tolstoy had joined a hundred other distinguished members of the intelligentsia in a petition to Alexander III, protesting the massacre of Jews. In the early twentieth century he continued to protest the pogroms of Kishinev and at other localities. Maxim Gorky pursued the same course, denouncing not only the pogromists but also the upper classes who approved the outrages as "no less guilty."

It is revealing of the Soviet political and cultural leadership that, according to one estimate about 200–300 pages of favorable utterances on Jews and the Jewish question have been purged from a thirty-volume edition of Gorky's works published by the Soviet Academy of Sciences between 1948–56 and from a later smaller edition which appeared between 1959–1963. In December 1911, protesting the Beilis blood libel case, Gorky castigated the spread of the "false story of the spilling of Christian blood by Jews," this "familiar device of ancient fanaticism,"[7] in a manifesto signed by 150 leaders of the Russian intelligentsia. A major role in the drafting of this manifesto was played by the noted novelist Vladimir K. Korolenko. In his novel *Yom Kippur* in which he portrayed favorably several Jewish characters he held that the Jewish question was not only a Jewish problem but a general Russian problem and that the untruth and corruption uncovered at the Beilis trial was "an all–Russian untruth and corruption."[8] But liberal and leftist public opinion, while holding out hope for the future of Russian Jewry, was by no means entirely free from traditional feelings of alienation from and hostility toward the Jews.

Marx and Lenin about the Jews

Russia's thoughts and sentiments about the Jews have been shaped by numerous factors, for centuries primarily by Greek Orthodox Christianity and for most of the twentieth century by Soviet Marxism. Karl Marx himself had revealed his deep hostility to the Jews, despite or because of his own Jewish ancestry. He wrote the pamphlet *Zur Judenfrage* [*About the Jewish Question*], 1843, at the age of 25, without possessing either any deep knowledge of Jewish history or of the contemporary Jewish situation in the Germanies and in Europe as a whole. Saturated with Jewish self–hatred, the had been converted at the age of five. Marxists, Jews and gentiles, have ever since tried to "explain away" his virulent anti–Jewish attitude and especially his identification of Judaism with capitalism. His brochure on the Jews, though first paid little attention to, has later attracted Jew–haters of all persuasions, including Nazis, and has been quoted at length in their writings.[9] They have found Marx's proclamation that Judaism was identical with "huckstering," that "money was the god of the Jews," and his demand for the "emancipation of mankind from Judaism" to their liking. Though every religion was "opium" for the people, Marx reserved a special repulsion for Judaism.

Lenin himself did not share Marx's hostility to the Jews. To the contrary, he frequently battled anti–Semitism and loudly proclaimed the civic equality of the Jews. Lenin denounced tsarist Russia as the "prison house of peoples" and impressed upon the Great Russians, the leading people among Russia's nationalities, that no nation could be free "if it oppresses other nations."[10] Yet there are substantial elements of his thought, including those on religion and nationality, which were bound to do harm to Russian Jews, more than to any other national and religious group in the Soviet Union. A return of the Soviets to pure "Leninism"—often talked about since Lenin died—would therefore not improve the lot of Soviet Jewry a great deal.

The Russian Social Democratic Labor Party (RSDLP) and the Bund

Before the turn of the century the Bund, the Jewish Workers organization in Russia, had reached a membership of between 30,000 and 40,000. Formed in 1897, it attracted impoverished workers, artisans, and small traders. It preceded the Social Democratic Labor Party, the RSDLP, founded in 1898, which had first only 8,000 members. While Lenin esteemed the leadership of the Bund for its intellectual capacities, major tactical and ideological differences soon emerged between them. Like Lenin's Bolsheviki, the Jewish socialists of the Bund were critical of and opposed to Zionism—the first Zionist Congress was held in Basel in 1898—but not to Jewish nationalism on Russian soil. They also objected to religion and clericalism.

Lenin's theory was that the Jews no longer constituted a nationality, but that they were merely "a caste." Therefore they could not claim any national rights, a thesis that the Bund sharply rejected.[11] As early as 1901, the Bund's convention categorically insisted that the concept of nationality also be applied to the Jewish people. While the Bundists were eager to do battle for the Russian Revolution, they were not prepared to relinquish Jewish national identity and submerge it into the Russian nationality. They demanded complete national autonomy and equality in Russia. Lenin, and later on also Stalin, pointed to the absence of a compact territorial entity of the Russian Jews and to their increasing linguistic and cultural assimilation. Lenin claimed that the majority of Jews were disinterested in fostering a Jewish national identity—a view to which the Soviet leadership still clings. But the Bund had a distinct national objective. While rejecting Hebrew as a spoken language and being anti–Zionist, it wanted to perpetuate and develop Yiddish culture on Russian territory and insisted on national–cultural autonomy, in particular extraterritorial autonomy.[12]

This concept had been developed by socialist theoreticians of Austria's multinational realm such as Karl Renner and Otto Bauer. It provided for national–cultural autonomy also to territorially dispersed national minorities. To Lenin, however, Jewish nationalism was basically a "bourgeois" phenomenon. He rejected the Bund's demand for cultural autonomy, the right to conduct their own education and to carry on other cultural activities such as those in the Yiddish theater and the Yiddish press and to organize publishing houses and have them supported by the state. But in the early postwar period Lenin and the Soviet leadership made far–going concessions to Russian Jewry as well as to other nationalities.[13] The Bund also insisted on being acknowledged as the sole representative for all Jewish labor in Russia. This would have deprived the Russian Social Democratic Party (RSDLP) of full organizational and political control over the entire working class.

Lenin's thinking was always marked by his preference for a tightly knit centralized party organization—as a forerunner of a highly centralized state organization. He also sharply opposed any kind of "federalism" in Party and state structure. In the name of internationalism he demanded the subordination of the Bund to the RSDLP and, closely connected with it, predicted and insisted on the ultimate fusion of all nations into a single society. What was imperative was forging an effective Communist Party, the indispensable instrument of the class struggle against tsarist autocracy and for the overthrow of the political and social structure of capitalism. The Jews in general and the Bund in particular were being sacrificed for the sake of socialism; they were to submit to the need for a centralized party structure. And Jewish nationalism was to yield to internationalism.[14]

Yet despite Lenin's ideological opposition to the Bund and his support of assimilation, Lenin was no anti–Semite. He did not harbor or voice any anti–Jewish prejudices. He did oppose, however, any national "separatism" in the Party structure. While he acknowledged the importance of national languages, he looked at them primarily as necessary and effective instruments of communist propaganda rather than as having independent positive cultural values. After the seizure of power in October 1917, Lenin, as said, made further concessions on the national question. Soviet federalism, which gained his support after the Civil War, was a major concession to minority nationalities. Even the Party structure permitted separate Communist parties for several national minorities.

But the Jews, due to Lenin's preconceived notions and narrow conception of what constituted a nationality, were not to have a separate Party. He did not consider the Jews who lacked a compact territorial base, whatever their own views, to have a right to develop their own national identity, though numerically they were by no means one of the smallest ethnic groups in Russia. At a conference of the RSDLP in Brussels and London in 1903, the attack against the Bundists was led by the "un–Jewish" Jew Leon Trotsky and the former Bundists Julius Martov and Paul Axelrod,[15] Jews by descent, but alienated from Judaism past and present and from the Jewish laboring masses. These men were convinced that Revolution and assimilation were the high roads to the solution of the "Jewish question" and that socialism was the ultimate, inevitable goal, a panacea for all social, national, and all other problems in Russia and elsewhere.

Lenin's struggle with the Bund, primarily over the question of national culture, national identity, and Party organization, continued after the split of the RSDLP in 1903 into Menscheviks and Bolsheviks. The only alternative Lenin saw for the destiny of the Jews was that between "assimilation" and "isolation." Ironically, in his theory on nationality he quoted and relied upon the judgments of Karl Kautsky and Otto Bauer, Austrian social democratic theoreticians, who in turn based their judgments on the outlook and the situation of Central European Jews rather than on those living in Eastern Europe, whom they did not know. The latter showed a much stronger national consciousness than the Jews in Central Europe. Lenin's attitude was the more puzzling since in other important respects he came sharply to oppose and distance himself from Kautsky's and Bauer's democratic philosophy. Yet their observations on nationalism and the Jews proved appropriate and acceptable to Lenin.

Lenin about National Cultural Autonomy and Austrian Theoreticians

Only shortly before the outbreak of World War I, Lenin, while in Cracow, came in contact with Jews who were in many respects different from the assimilated ones in Vienna. According to the book by Lenin's wife, Nadezhda Krupskaya's *Reminiscences of Lenin*,[16] both came to know other Jews more deeply rooted in Jewish culture than those Lenin had previously known. Krupskaya herself wrote sympathetically of the Jews of Cracow, which probably reflected Lenin's own views. She has testified that he had always "hated national oppression in any form" and that on the eve of World War I he paid closer attention than ever to the nationality question, as also seen by the great number of essays he wrote on this topic after 1913 and during World War I.[17] Yet despite all this preoccupation with the nationality question, his conclusions regarding Russian Jewry did not change for the better. In the nationality firmament of Russia after the Revolution, the Jews were foredoomed to be a vanishing star.

Though Lenin spoke highly of the contribution of Jews to the revolutionary movement, he considered Jewish "separatism," as exemplified in his view by religious and national tradition and the Zionist movement, a reactionary force which was bound to weaken the revolutionary movement. He acknowledged that the Russian Jews were the most persecuted national group in the Russian Empire. He also gave expression to his appreciation of the Jewish "contribution" in both Russian and Yiddish "toward creating the international culture of the working class movement.[18-19] But he was primarily interested in this international "contribution" rather than in any which aimed at the perpetuation of a separate Jewish cultural and national life. Assimilation, the disappearance of the Jews, their submergence in Russian culture, was his ultimate goal. Lenin agreed therein with the earlier hostile point of view of Marx. Later on Stalin concurred with this latter point of view. Still, after the October Revolution, the Jewish minority, in accordance with Lenin's wishes, was given numerous facilities to establish its own Yiddish institutions. As an observer held, had Lenin lived longer, he might have proved "a valuable force in Jewish life in Russia."[20] Perhaps, more likely, he might have delayed the process of applying brute force to accelerate the natural assimilation proceeding in Russia.

Since the Bund's concept of the future Russian state was that of a realm based upon a federation of nationalities, the Bund correspondingly also asked for a federalization of the RSDLP at its Second Congress in 1903. When the Party rejected these demands, the Bund withdrew in protest, severing its ties with it. In readmitting the Bund in 1906 at the so-called "Unification Congress," the Bund, as well as the Social Democrats of Poland, Lithuania, and Latvia, rejoined the Party as regional organizations. The Party avoided taking a position in regard to national-cultural autonomy which the Bund had reasserted the previous year. The nationality question and the future of Russian Jewry remained thus a controversial subject among Social Democrats.

Vladimir Medem, a noted pre-war leader of the Bund has pointed to the differentiation in the Russian treatment of the Jews as compared with that of other national minorities, a differentiation to which Soviet policy despite its claims to the contrary has steadfastly clung. Generally, he stressed the Great Russians' national oppression aimed at denationalizing a certain national group and at integrating it with the ruling nation. "With the Jews, however, it is a different story. Not only does anti-Semitism not aim at the assimilation of the Jews,

it turns directly against assimilation. It does not want amalgamation, but fears it and closes the door to it." On this ground it introduced the notorious percentage norms for Jews in Russian schools
that blocked free admission of Jews to educational institutions. While
the government prevented thus the Jews' acquisition of Russian culture, "one does not permit the Jews to develop their own culture.
One closes both roads to them."[21]

According to Medem, the Russian police state cannot tolerate the
development of a Yiddish "national language" and of a "democratic
culture." It "cannot tolerate it" and rudely rejects "every national
claim" of the Jews. It prohibits

> Jewish assemblies, Jewish education—all this is dangerous
> separatism which one wants to extirpate. Thus, the Jew is
> not allowed to become a Russian nor to remain a Jew . . .
> he must be a welcome object of extortion for the police and
> must find therein justification for his existence.[22]

The continuity between Tsarist and Soviet policy in the questions of assimilation and anti–Semitism is striking and indisputable,
notwithstanding the changes from tsarist to Communist ideology. So
is the status for Russian Jews as an oppressed national and religious
minority.

Bolshevik Disputes on Nationality Policy

A good many, including most prominent Party members, maintained serious reservations about the Party's nationality program,
including national–cultural autonomy and the right to secession. The
position of the Right on the nationality question was that of the
Bund, numerous socialists of other national minorities and all others who supported extraterritorial national–cultural autonomy and
federalization of the Party. The Left was formed by those interna-
tionalists who were unwilling to make any concession to nationalism
and rejected self–determination as the Party program. Its leading
spokesmen were Rosa Luxemburg, Nikolai Bukharin, Karl Radek,
and Grigorii Piatakov. The Center was the position taken by Lenin
himself who pleaded for recognition of the reality of nationalism.[23]
He demanded support for the Party program of the right to national
self–determination, meaning to secession, which, he claimed, would
further the proletarian class struggle rather than divert attention from
it. The leftist, internationalist wing of the Party simply tended to disregard the Party's program of national self–determination, while both

the Right and Lenin upheld this right, though they sharply differed in the interpretations of it. Lenin's theory of self–determination was close to the stand of the Second International at its London Congress in July and August 1896.[24] At its own founding Congress in 1898 the RSDLP made in its manifesto no reference to self–determination, but the Second Party conference had embodied it in point nine of its program, which subsequently was repeatedly confirmed. Actual secession of a compactly settled border nationality had always more theoretical and propagnadistic significance than a pragmatic one.

Lenin himself was sharply critical of the Left of the Party for ignoring national oppression—an issue which he thought closely linked with the success of the "proletarian" revolution—and the Right for fundamental concessions to nationalism. The Left had a negative, a "nihilistic" position in regard to the national question; the Right was prepared to meet nationalism half–way. Lenin shared with the Left the international outlook, while he agreed with the Right as to the actual importance of the national movement, which on tactical grounds had to be fully taken account of.

Stalin's Marxism and the National Question (1913)

In 1912 Lenin encouraged Stalin, then known as Koba–Djugashvili, himself a member of the Georgian nationality, to journey to Austria for the purpose of studying the nationality problem in that multinational Empire. His essay *Marxism and the National Question* (1913) established Stalin as a Bolshevik expert on the nationality question and led after the October Revolution to his appointment as Commissar for Nationalities. Some have held that in this treatise Stalin took a harsher line toward the Bund and the Jewish people than Lenin himself[25] The Soviet expert Adam Ulam too found it somewhat surprising that Lenin (whom he basically considered a Russian nationalist himself) did not take exception to Stalin's nationalism which, despite all Marxist professions, already strongly emerged in the foregoing treatise on nationalism.[26] According to both men, Lenin and Stalin, however, the Jewish people was historically destined for complete assimilation.

Stalin held that a nation had definite characteristics, including a common language and common territory. On account of the lack of the latter, Stalin simply denied the Jewish people the right to nationhood. He accused the Bundists of being "bourgeois nationalists" and spouted sarcasm and venom against them and against "their desire to preserve all the national peculiarities of the Jews," even those that are patently noxious to the proletariat;" he criticized their desire to preserve their "isolation." His bias against the Jews, which subsequently became even more transparent, was already flourishing.[27]

As his later life and policies revealed, Stalin's prejudices were aimed against many other national and religious groups in Europe and Asia, including the Chinese neighbors.[28] These biases clearly revealed his "Great Russian chauvinism." But during Lenin's lifetime Stalin had to keep a tight rein on his sentiments and his philosophy.

Lenin and Stalin. "Amalgamation of Nations"

Lenin should have been able to think in terms of the future, of the phenomenon of nationality cleansed of national hatred, jealousy, and chauvinism. Yet he held that under socialism not only national hatred and nationalist tensions and struggles were bound to disappear but also nationalities as such. This unjustifiable optimistic view was rooted in wishful thinking rather than based on clearly noticeable historic trends. But it held Lenin and the Bolsheviks captive as well as a good number of socialists everywhere, primarily those of big nationalities whom Marc's and Lenin's view clearly favored.

Some of the smaller and scattered nationalities and the Bundists, representatives of Jewish workers, favored national–cultural autonomy and opposed, as said, the tight, centralist Party organization, largely because it rested not on a strictly territorial basis, but on a individualistic–national one. The Bund wanted to be recognized as the sole representative of the Jewish proletariat "in whatever part of Russia it lived" and "whatever language" it spoke. If accepted, this would have split the Party along national lines and, in Lenin's and also Stalin's view, would have weakened and destroyed it. Lenin quoted approvingly Karl Kautsky who held that national–cultural autonomy would "strengthen nationalism and neglect internationalism completely."[29] Lenin rejected the "separation" of schooling on the ground that one must strive in general "for the amalgamation of nations," for socialism[30] and for the integration of national proletarian organizations. He hailed physical and cultural assimilation. National–cultural autonomy would only delay this natural process and encourage nationalism.

Unlike many other nationalities, the Jews lived scattered in the USSR and only in some areas, in the Ukraine and Byelorussia, in more compact settlement. Lenin apparently had made up his mind that the Jews would be better off by assimilating themselves. He criticized the

Bundists' demand for the creation of institutions which would "guarantee" the freedom of Jewish national development. Lenin hoped that many nationalities would follow the road leading to assimilation, though he did not recommend it outright as a solution of the nationality problem. In his opinion, Jews in civilized countries were no nationality any longer. In Galicia and Russia they were not yet a nationality; they were there, unfortunately, "still a caste." Thus, if one did not question his ambivalent analysis, his demand for their assimilation was not illogical.

Lenin was neither inclined to resort to force to reduce the number of nationalities for the purpose of compulsory assimilation—the policy of many a chauvinism—nor to further their increase for the sake of ethnic–cultural pluralism. He rather looked favorably upon assimilation of nationalities as the unavoidable historical trend, the inevitable result of the spread of the idea of national equality and of increasing economic and cultural interchange.

From the viewpoint of cultural and national pluralism, the disappearance of any nationality, like that of any biological species, is to be regretted. But Lenin's theoretical opposition to nationalism made him wary of its further growth. A larger number of nationalities meant at least the possibility of more and more intense national movements and national differences. In his rejection of national pluralism and his undissimulated joy over the assimilation of nationalities, Lenin may have been motivated by fear that national strife was not merely the result of economic disputes but also the consequence of innate national differences. On the other hand, the Party's slogan of national self–determination stimulated a concession to nationalism. This implied "approval" of the national state, of self–determination, contradicted of course Lenin's support for the amalgamation of nationalities at any stage of their development.

Genuine self–determination included not only the right to secession—which Lenin conceded theoretically at least—but also the right to federalism and national–cultural autonomy. Thus, the national minority which rejects secession does not remain standing empty-handed. Actually, Leninism "narrowed" down the concept of self–determination so much as to leave the nationalities nothing but the theoretical right to secession. This right was further emaciated by numerous qualifications which Lenin attached to it. E. H. Carr, in *The Bolshevik Revolution 1917–32*, aptly called Lenin's position, giving the nationalities the right to secede, but denying their right to virtually anything else, an "all or nothing" position.[31] Lenin gave the

nationalities the alternative of complete separation or complete submission, complete freedom or "voluntary" and permanent acceptance
of the union. The nationalities, especially those in the interior, which
neither could nor would secede, were faced with a harsh, brutally
stiff ultimatum. Lenin's alternative was not based on real freedom of
choice. Also, Lenin's autonomy happened to be one which was that of
an unfettered government. He spurned the idea of constitutional limitations of the sovereign power. Lenin's and the Soviet government's
postwar thought on federalism—a concept which he had previously
opposed—was simply that the Party, facing after the October Revolution and the Civil War unexpectedly strong national movements,
must make at least theoretical concessions on the issues of federalism
and nationalism. Some concessions in the 1920s to the latter affected
also Russian Jews.

From the 1917 Revolutions to the Civil War

Domestic developments during World War I as well as the Russian army's setbacks led to the February and October Revolutions of
1917. During the eight months of rule by the Provisional Government, the decree signed by the then Minister of Justice Aleksandr
Kerensky proclaimed the equality of residents of the Empire, irrespective of social status, nationality, or religion. When the Bolsheviks
seized power in October, national equality was once again solemnly
proclaimed. According to Leon Trotsky,[32] anti–Jewish laws which
had accumulated during the rule of the Romanov dynasty over three
centuries were eliminated with the stroke of a pen. So were discriminatory laws affecting other national groups. Actually, more than
half of the population of the multinational Russian Empire was composed of minorities, with many living in the outlying border regions.
Communists, as the Bolsheviks soon called themselves officially, were
anxious to gain the loyalty and cooperation of the various national
minorities.

Jews, however, on religious and economic grounds gave far from
enthusiastic support to the Bolsheviks who propagated an intolerant
atheism and an economic program based on social revolution. This
held little attraction for deeply religious people who also practiced
traditional occupations of trade and business. Only few Jews, some
intellectuals and low–class artisans, supported the Bolsheviks. On
the other hand, the prospects of national equality and the end of
discrimination attracted Jews who had long been resolute opponents
of tsarist oppression and created new opportunities for them. As a

result of many vacancies in the Government and in the Party, an increasing number of Jews filled these new posts. However, their visibility far exceeded their actual numbers.

As far as nationalism was concerned, the Soviets have to this day applied different yardsticks to Jews and other Soviet nationalities. Excepting Social Revolutionaries (SR), most of the adherents of the liberal and radical parties which espoused Russian political centralism such as the Cadets (Constitutional Democrats) and the Social Democrats, entertained a negative view of the Jewish national movement and of Zionism and opposed Jewish national demands. Many intellectuals, including liberals and socialists, feared that a further increase of the number of Jewish journalists, artists and actors would only do irreparable harm to Russian creativity. Jewish participation in Russian cultural and social life would do lasting damage to Russian culture and the Russian people. This group, though generally consisting of progressive Russian intellectuals, favored neither Jewish nationalism nor the Jews' assimilation.

The October Revolution brought this dialogue to a standstill. As one observer put it, it created a "thaw" in the relation with the Jews. For a brief moment in 1917 even rightist circles no longer talked against Jewish equality. But the deep–seated anti–Semitism of the Russian populace, not only of the extreme Right but also of moderates and leftist elements, was not thoroughly uprooted. Russians and non–Russian national groups merely bided their time.

The October Revolution seemingly catapulted Jews from perhaps the lowest position in Russian society into the foremost rank. As one student put it, the Jewish people—the "Zhidy"[33]—who had been "nothing" became "almost everything." While formerly living in the "pale of Settlement," they now flocked into the interior and into the big cities. As students they entered the higher institutions of learning, and quite a few became professors at state universities. They entered professions and obtained important positions in the Russian bureaucracy and the Russian economy. This political and social revolution aroused the resistance of the Russian intelligentsia and contributed to the rise of a new anti–Semitism in the 1920s and 1930s. Yet Soviet industrialization and transformation of the Russian economy under the Five–Year plan required the utilization of all human resources to the best collective advantage. It tended to restrain the spreading of anti–Jewish sentiments in the Soviet population.

In the early Soviet period centralizing influences were pronounced, and Soviet Jews were widely employed in Party and state to strengthen centripetal drives in the multinational realm. But with the industrial growth and general economic development of the minority nationalities the need and desire to satisfy the latter and to train their own intelligentsia gained ground. The Communist Party responded to the demands of Soviet nationalities to displace the Jews and put their "own" people into leading positions in Party and state. In the RSFSR the Russian intelligentsia strove to attain the same goal. All Soviet nationalities seemed then agreed that Soviet Jews holding leading positions had to be squeezed out by Great Russians and members of national minorities. A partly open, more often concealed drive aiming at reducing the number of Jews was soon in full swing. Especially in the border republics this ethnic shift resulted frequently in less qualified cadres taking the place of better qualified ones. New domestic nationality developments in combination with Stalin's desire to please Hitler by reducing Jewish "influences" in the USSR produced ominous changes in the economic situation of Soviet Jewry on the eve of World War II.

The bloody Civil War, 1918–1921, had pitted Whites and Reds against each other. While both sides committed atrocities, those of the Whites resulted in the slaughter of nearly a quarter million of Jews, a number far exceeding that of the victims of previous Tsarist pogroms. The Bolsheviks officially denounced anti–Semitism, having come to realize that Jew–hatred was the widely used tool of their enemies. Lenin declared anti–Semitism "barbarism" and Stalin, Commissar for Nationalities since the October Revolution, castigated it as an instrument serving "the exploiters" and as a lightning rod protecting "capitalism from the attacks of the working people." Both appealed to the Communist Party to battle Jew–hatred which they considered "profoundly hostile to the Soviet regime."[34] But it was self–interest rather than any sort of philosemitism which motivated them. Both self–interest and idealism moved also the Jews. They remembered tsarist oppression and dreamt of their own and the Russian people's liberation.

During the Civil War Jews played a major role in the Red Army. Next to Trotsky, its famous commander, such persons of Jewish descent as Yakim, Shtern, Eydeman, Feldman, and Gamarnik played a vital part among Soviet military leaders. Later on, during the purge trials in the late 1930s, prominent military leaders, gentiles such as Marshall Tukhachevsky and prominent Jewish military figures like the foregoing were killed. With the exception of Gregory Shtern, they fell victim to the purges. The latter played in the 1930s a major role in the defeat of the Japanese troops along the Manchurian border.

Soviet Nationality Policy in the Interwar Period and the Legal Status of Soviet Jewry

The Soviets have always prided themselves of having achieved national reconciliation among their different nationalities—a claim obviously belied by their internal nationality disputes—and of having solved the age–old nationality question. They have also proclaimed as their goal the flowering of national cultures. But in practice they have fostered, and are still fostering, national assimilation, especially of small nationalities and also that of Soviet Jews. While, as stated, other nationalities, territorially concentrated in one or the other area, have representation in the Soviet of Nationalities, the Jews, territorially deprived, are no longer represented in this chamber and thus have no voice in the Soviet family of nations. The Soviets claim that the assimilation of Jews to Russian language and culture was the major cause of their failure in national respects, also in regard to the colonization scheme of Birobidszhan in the Far East. They maintain complete silence about the forcible assimilation to which Jews have been subjected. Though after the October Revolution and during the Civil War Lenin himself came out against Russian anti–Semitism, he also left behind the legacy of his struggle with the Jewish labor organization, the Bund.

According to Stalin, to repeat, one of the criteria of nationality was territory—which Jews lacked. According to Lenin, the Jews were in the early twentieth century allegedly "only a caste," destined to "amalgamation" and national death. Since the Jews were one of the most assimilated minorities such assimilation would greatly increase the number of Great Russians. To the latter this was of critical importance in view of the higher birthrate of the other non–Russian nationalities. National self–interest, though not publicly admitted, determined to a large degree Lenin's and the Soviets' interest in the assimilation of the Jews. Assimilation had been a goal also under the last Tsars, as their powerful advisor Pobiedonostev conceded. It has remained such a goal to this day.

Stalin held that cultural rights for the Jews was a reactionary and retrogressive demand. First, the RSDLP supported the elimination of all ethnic restrictions and national inequalities, but did not want to stimulate national culture. However, after the Civil War the Soviet Constitution made greater theoretical concessions to the national minorities. Still, as far as the Jews were concerned, they were hardly meaningful, substantial, or lasting.

The legal position of Soviet Jews in the interwar period showed striking inconsistencies and outright contradictions. Prior to the October Revolution, in 1914, Lenin, drafting a bill on nationality for the Bolshevik delegation in the Duma, specifically provided for "the repeal of all restrictions upon the rights of Jews," clearly considering the Jewish people a nationality. Such lability, if not discrepancy, has marked communist thought and policy toward the Jews to this day. The Bolsheviks have vacillated between considering the Jews a nationality and a mere "caste" on a road to the transition to a non-national entity, to "nothing."[35] Still, a Communist Party resolution adopted at the Tenth Congress in March 1921, specifically listed the Jews as an example of a national minority. In accordance with it, Yiddish was formally recognized in the Byelorussian Republic as one of four official languages. Similarly, the introduction of the "passport" in the USSR, needed for domestic travel and as a document of identification, giving also the nationality of the bearer—in case of the Jews "Evrei"—acknowledged the national character of the Jews!

Soviet law requires that every urban resident, sixteen years or older, has to carry a passport. The introduction of this new regulation was probably due to factors other than Soviet nationality policy, namely to the Five–Year Plan and the growing housing shortage in the cities and towns. Still, the system had broad implications for Soviet nationality policy and especially for policy vis–à–vis Soviet Jews. Every child of a Jewish father and mother is listed in the passport as a Jew. In such cases nationality was of course not voluntarily chosen. Only in case of a mixed marriage, involving one Jewish parent, could the sixteen–year old youngster choose between the nationalities of his or her parents.

A strong case can be made that Soviet Jews on the basis of Soviet constitutional and ordinary laws are entitled to national rights, though they have been withheld from them in practice. Some of these national rights go back to the earliest Soviet proclamations and legislation which have never been repealed. Only a week after the Bolshevik seizure of power, on November 15, 1917, the government issued a formal Declaration of the Rights of Peoples,[36] which pledged the "free development of national minorities and ethnic groups inhabiting the Russian territory." This pledge amounted to more than a mere preservation of different nationalities and their cultures; it solemnly promised their "development." The stress of freedom therein excluded any paternalism based on the alleged superior knowledge of the Great Russians who were soon to dominate the state and the Communist Party! The first Soviet constitution of 1918, on the eve of the Civil War, pledged "not to oppress national minorities or to impose any limitations whatsoever on their rights," since it was contrary to the fundamental laws of the new regime. The 1924 constitution made a point to reaffirm the principle of equality of the rights of nationalities in the constitutions of the individual republics. Though the 1936 Stalin constitution made less reference to the rights of using native languages in courts, administrative bodies, etc., it reaffirmed in article 121 the "right to instruction in schools . . . in the native language." In August 1962 the USSR ratified the UNESCO convention against discrimination in education, which obligated the Soviet Union to maintain schools and use native languages in the education of national minorities.[37] In 1961 the Twenty–second Party Congress had committed itself to the teaching of native languages. Yet despite all these promises, there does not exist today anywhere in the Soviet Union either a Yiddish school or a Yiddish class. Even the few schools open in Birobidzhan were closed down in 1946. The closure of Jewish and Yiddish theaters, schools, libraries, and museums and the earlier suppression of Hebrew was bound to eradicate Jewish culture and accelerate assimilation. Through these measures the Soviet authorities have strangled the promised free development of Jewish national culture.

It was after World War II that occurred the complete and deliberate destruction of Jewish cultural institutions. In November 1948 the Yiddish publishing firm *Emes* was forced to close its doors. Next to *Ainkayt* [Unity], which appeared three times weekly, it had after the war published altogether only ten books. In the same month the *Jewish Anti–Fascist Committee*, which Stalin had created to assist Russia's war effort at home and abroad, was dissolved. Its chairman, the actor Solomon Mikhoels, was murdered by the secret police. In January 1948 other officials of the Committee disappeared from the Soviet scene. For Soviet Jewry cultural life simply vanished, being destroyed as if a natural disaster had completely wiped it out. Theaters were closed and all publications ceased their activities except for a small periodical the *Birobidzhan Shtern* with a circulation of only one thousand. No other nationality was robbed of the solemnly promised cultural opportunities to the same extent as the Jews. Stalin had forgotten his pledge back in 1925 at the University of Toilers of the East that all national cultures "must be given an opportunity . . . to expand and to reach all their potentialities."[38] True, at the same time he had also spoken of "their fusion into a single common culture with a single common language, but the elimination of Jewish culture and of Yiddish has had no comparable development in any other Soviet nationality.

This goal of the fusion—the submergence of the individual national cultures by the Great Russian language and culture—has been affirmed by the "new Party program," formulated in 1961[39] which called for "the effacement of national distinctions . . . including language distinctions" and for speeding the processes of assimilation, of the "drawing ever closer together" of the nationalities of the USSR. M.S. Dzunosov, a Soviet expert on the nationality question, has proudly pointed to the increasing use of the Russian language by non–Russian nationalities and the increasing rate of intermarriages in the Soviet Union.[40] Richard Pipes of Harvard University, however, has drawn attention to a contrary development.[41] Some major Soviet national groups in areas where they have a numerical or administrative preponderance were acquiring "a linguistic hegemony"[42] to the disadvantage of the Great Russians. Along the same line, Soviet army leaders have repeatedly complained publicly about the inadequate knowledge of the Russian language among non–Russian soldiers, with harmful consequences for the efficiency of Soviet troops.

Constitutional guarantees assure equal access of every nationality to housing. Though the top echelons of the Party are out of reach for Soviet Jews, admission to the Party at lower levels, to trade unions, and to the army is feasible. In prestigious areas such as medicine, law, science, and the arts Jews are widely represented, though their role has been sharply restricted compared to the early Bolshevik period. From other important and conspicuous fields such as decision–making and diplomatic service Jews are virtually excluded, due to written or oral directives. Contrary to constitutional provisions, a quota system exists in practice in many areas demanding anti–Jewish discrimination. The high percentage of Jews in the civil service and administrative posts in the 1920s had been sharply reduced in the 1930s and this trend has continued and has further increased after World War II.

In 1957, meeting with a visiting French parliamentary delegation of the French Socialist Party, Krushchev, speaking about non–Russian Soviet Republics, pointed out that "formerly backward and illiterate, these peoples now have their own engineers and professionals. Minister of Culture Y. Furtseva made similar remarks in an interview with the *Manchester Guardian.* While conceding that anti–Semitism was a "remnant of a reactionary past," Krushchev likewise justified the exclusion of Jews from some areas of activity in the republics.[43]

Soviet law as such has proved to be an ineffective weapon against Jew–hatred. Though the Soviet constitution did not permit but rather condemned "agitation and propaganda arousing antional enmity and secession," anti–Semitism has not been specifically prohibited. The Soviets have never made the propagation of Jew–hatred a crime as such. As a matter of fact, Soviet law has turned a blind eye toward anti–Semitism, though it has been one of the worst and most widespread national prejudices directed against a national or religious minority in the USSR.

What Soviet criminal law in 1921 forbade was only "agitation and propaganda arousing national enmity,"[44] and national defamation in general. But during most of their existence, the Soviets have not lived up to their own laws. Soon after the October Revolution, the Council of People's Commissars outlawed "pogromist agitation and attacks on the Jewish working population," but left the interpretation of who was a member of the "working" people to the Russian, Ukrainian, and Byelorussian masses. The latter and the CPSU of course considered the "Jewish bourgeoisie" and "non–working" people fair game. Thus the much touted new equality of Jews was undermined almost from the beginning.

In view of the attitude of the government the Soviet press has already in the 1920s frequently maintained an ominous silence about anti–Semitic occurrences. Yet in those years it permitted Jewish newspapers to report anti–Semitic outbursts. In general, however, the Soviet leaders have denied the existence of anti–Semitism in the Soviet Union, refusing to come to grips with it. This downplaying of Jew–hatred in the first decade after the Revolution differed sharply from the later stages when they virtually embraced it. The Soviets have consistently denied having incorporated Jew–hatred in their propagandistic arsenal. But from earliest times on they have featured anti–Zionism and rejected Jewish nationalism and religion. Some Russian anti–Semites soon after the Revolution have insisted that Jews allegedly hated gentile nations, exploited them, and wished to establish their rule over Russia and the world at large. In the last two decades they have sharpened their propaganda war against the Jews to an extent which was hardly distinguishable from that of the Nazis prior to the start of World War II.

Soviet Policy and Yevsektsiya on Jewish Religion

In the cultural and nationality spheres Soviet Jews after the 1917 revolutions obtained individual legal equality though not national equality. The Soviet government has suppressed the freedom of teaching and learning Hebrew, Jewish religion and all Zionist activities, though they have long encouraged the use of Yiddish as a vehicle of Communist propaganda. Soviet Jews were first permitted to develop an elaborate system of Yiddish schools and build up their cultural facilities. Also, the government, the CPSU, the trade unions, and the Soviet press have first carried on a broad-gauged struggle against anti-Semitism. But in the later 1920s anti-Semitism spread anew and in the following decades the anti-Jewish campaign was permitted free rein. The official struggle against Jew-hatred gradually subsided.

In prerevolutionary days only a small minority of Russia's Jews had joined the Bolshevik party. But they were strongly represented among its top leadership. This small elite consisted of highly assimilated individuals, who showed no interest in the problems of Russian Jewry, whether religious, national, or cultural; none identified themselves as Jews. They were actually alienated from Judaism, past and present, and indifferent in regard to its destiny. Trotsky, once asked by the Bundist leader Vladimir Medem, whether he fought against the Tsar as a Jew or as a Russian, replied: "Neither, I am a Social Democrat, and that is all."[45] Lev (Lyova) Bronstein—Trotsky's original name before he adopted, like many Russian revolutionaries, the pen name under which he became famous—knew neither Yiddish nor Hebrew and as a youngster spoke at home a mixture of Russian and Ukrainian. In his extensive three-volume work *History of the Russian Revolution,* he devoted merely four sentences to the Jewish people. Despite the rising threat of anti-Semitism in the 1930s in Nazi Germany—not to mention Russia and the rest of Europe—he showed no genuine interest in the fate of the Jews as such. This was also the attitude of other Bolsheviks of Jewish descent who did not wish to be reminded of their Jewish origin. They aimed at the liberation of the Russian people in its entirety rather than that of its minorities and of their own people. They seemed convinced that the October Revolution had raised the curtain of a new era for Russian and East European Jews and that, despite Hitler whose rabid anti-Semitism in the 1930s they managed to ignore, socialism, assimilation, and brotherhood were just around the corner.

This policy of early assimilation and ultimate submergence in combination with immediate propagandistic goals was to be implemented by the *Yevkom* in *Yevreysk Kommissariat* [Jewish Commissariat] and *Yevsektsiya* [Yevreyskaya Sektsiya, Jewish Sections] which were set up in January 1918, only a few weeks after the October Revolution. The Yiddish daily *Die Wahrheit* [meaning Pravda, truth] disclosed that Jewish offices would be established side by side with the Workers', Soldiers', and Peasants' Soviets.[46] These announcements aroused a great deal of expectations for the regeneration of Jewish life, but turned out to be quite deceptive. The new organizations proved to be mere vehicles of a Soviet policy which was to treat the Jewish minority worse than virtually all other Soviet national groups. While the national culture of other nationalities was encouraged and developed, Soviet policy regarding the Jews aimed primarily at their speedy assimilation and the elimination of their national–religious and cultural identity. As one student of Soviet Jewish nationality policy observed: "What began with the inspired idea of building a new Jewish life, ended with the annihilation of the old." The *Yevkom* [Jewish Commissariat] was under control of Semen Dimanshtein, its only Commissar. All its officials were under the sway of the CPSU.

The Commissariat for Jewish National Affairs was abolished in 1920 and replaced by Yevsektsiya [People's Commissariat for National Affairs]. In 1923 its staff was reduced to only five people and thereafter to a single officer! After Lenin's death, in the wake of further changes, only a limited number of Sections in the larger cities survived. In 1930 Yevsektsiya simply vanished. Its leaders, though publicly seldom admitting that assimilation of the Jews was their exclusive goal, clearly understood their "mission." Esther Frumkin, a noted former Bundist leader, who joined the C.P., remarked already in 1922 that the purpose of Yevsektsiya was to convert nationally–oriented Jews to Communism and "never pledged to promise eternal life to the Jewish people."[47] Alexander Chemerisky shared her philosophy that Jewish traditions and beliefs had to be sacrificed on the altar of the economic and cultural development of Russia proper. The teaching of Hebrew was finally forbidden, and old Jewish customs and religious instruction looked upon as superstitions and as "bourgeois" evils and merely assisting "counterrevolutionary" goals.

All Jewish communal organizations were dissolved and Russian Jews deprived of any genuine representation. As the early 1920s already revealed, the only purpose of Yevsektsiya was to speed the flow of communist propaganda to the masses, convey the Communist message to its potential victims in Yiddish, and to hide or at least soften the cultural and national death sentence The Communist goal was to make the dictatorship of the proletariat "prevail in the Jewish street." It was not clearly articulated but became soon transparent that the Soviets aimed at the extinction of Jewish religious and cultural education, at the virtual severance of meaningful contacts with their kinsfolk abroad, and at the total obliteration of genuine representation for Soviet Jewry. Russian Jews were thus unable to initiate policy changes in the Jewish sector and even to file complaints about the growing anti–Semitism of Soviet officialdom and of the populace at large.

Under the most repressive tsarist regimes Jews had been permitted to retain their national–religious identity. They were allowed to perpetuate what was at least a miserable social, economic, and national status. But the Soviets aimed at laying the axe to the tree of Judaism and at obliterating the very essence of Jewish national, cultural, and religious existence.

Soviet Jews were not only an ethnic group but also possessed (rather than possess today) all attributes of a common religion. According to Soviet thought, all religion is the "opiate of the masses." Still, the Soviets have displayed special hostility toward Judaism, a hostility which by far surpasses their enmity toward other religions. The Soviets claim that the USSR accords "completely unrestricted freedom of worship to citizens . . . who are believers." They assert, on the other hand, that the Communist Party, "on the basis of the law of freedom of conscience," carries on "a scientific atheistic propaganda" among the population, since "parts" of the Soviet people have not yet abandoned "religious prejudices."

It is in accordance with this derogatory view of religion that the Soviet attitude toward it has grown more hostile. While the earlier constitutions of the RSFSR (1918 and 1925) permitted both "freedom of religious and anti–religious propaganda," a law of April 1929 deprived religious organizations of the right of active religious education. Only "freedom of religious worship" has been retained. On the other hand, opponents of religious "propaganda" and promoters of "anti–religious propaganda" have a free field. Some Communists wanted to go even further, suggesting the prohibition of "religious rites," but were blocked by Stalin. In documents submitted to the U. N., the Soviet government has listed the laws relating to religious and anti–religious organizations and appropriate comments in two major documents, *The Study of Discrimination in the Matter of Religious*

Rights and Practices and *Manifestations of Racial Prejudice and Religious Intolerance.*[48]

Rights guaranteed to recognize religions were spelled out as early as January 23, 1918, in a decree of the Council of People's Commissars which is still valid, and in the order of the All–Union Central Executive Committee and the Council of People's Commissars of the RSFSR on April 8, 1929. A fundamental feature of this decree—as well as of the earlier decree—was the equality of all religions. The decree abolished the privileged status of The Russian Greek Orthodox Church that had existed under the tsars. But scholars of the history of religion under the Soviets, John Curtiss of Duke University and Walter Kolarz,[49] have pointed to the unequal status of Judaism as compared with that of other Soviet religions. According to the foregoing order of April 19, religious communities may set up "religious centers" which are permitted holding congresses or church councils and publishing periodicals and the "necessary devotional literature."

Since 1926 Judaism had no such central structure and was thus deprived of countering the anti–religious campaign of the Party. While the Greek Orthodox Church, the Baptists, and the Moslems have been able to print new editions of the Bible and of the Koran respectively, Soviet Jews have neither published a periodical nor a Hebrew Bible. The number of Hebrew prayer books published since the 1920s—one edition in 1937, another in 1968—appeared together in only 8,000 copies in the entire USSR!

Soviet Jews in different parts of the USSR are unable to establish contact with each other. In view of the absence of "religious centers" Soviet Judaism was also prevented to communicate adequately with Judaism abroad and to participate in international conferences and congresses, all this in sharp contrast to Christian denominations and to Moslems and Buddhists.

The Soviets allow theological students of many faiths to travel and study abroad at foreign seminaries. Jews, however, were not granted corresponding rights. In practice the training of Jewish theological students on Soviet soil has been virtually terminated.[50] Though in 1957 a single Yeshiva was permitted to operate in the Soviet Union, between 1965 and 1967 no students were reported to have attended. The only remaining Jewish institutions, synagogues, are severely restricted and have been repeatedly the target by authorities, assailed by government propaganda and accused of having engaged in illegal activities, in corruption and pro–Zionist agitation. In an official report to the U.N., Soviet authorities referred to 450 synagogues in the

USSR. After about a decade, in July 1972, this number had dropped to only 58, of which about one–third operated in Georgia, the northern Caucasus and the Central Asiatic Republics, far from the traditional centers of Russian Jewry. Jewish religion in Europe or Russia proper, however, has been selected for destruction. While according to Joshua Rothenberg of Brandeis University, the Russian Orthodox Church had one church for about 2,000 faithful, Islam one house of prayer for 10,000 worshippers, Judaism had only one synagogue for 23,400 worshippers.[51]

Between 1958 and 1961 Jews numbered only about 1 percent of the total Soviet population. But the number of books sharply criticizing, if not vilifying Judaism, is about seven times as great as the number of books assailing Christianity. The situation since the 1967 Six–Day War has grown incomparably worse. An old Bolshevik talking in the offices of *Pravda* to an American visitor[52] conceded that an attack on synagogues was an attack against the Jewish community, since the houses of worship, next to religious significance, also constituted an element of Jewish "cohesion" which the government wanted to destroy!

The attack against Judaism is not confined to religion, but has also apparent national and cultural significance. Both religion and national culture are looked upon by the Soviets with hostility. Even secularized Jews observe for instance Pessach and eat Mazzoth (unleavened bread) and many continue, whenever possible, to believe in the ritual of circumcision. As far as passover is concerned, the Soviets have only occasionally lifted the severe restrictions on the baking of Mazzoth and provided adequate supplies of flour. The national core of the Passover festival, its emphasis on historic loyalty to the Jewish people and to Judaism and the clear Zionist emphasis—including the ancient phrase "next year in Jerusalem"—have all unleashed vituperative communist propaganda and reckless attacks.

Despite Marxist–Leninist hostility to religion as opium of the people the Soviet government's constitutional theory has declared religion the private affair of its citizens. A law dated January 10, 1918, prohibited religious congregations from carrying on educational and welfare activities. Another law, passed on April 8, 1929 in the RS-FSR, and subsequently in other Soviet Republics, further restricted the rights of religious institutions and empowered the state to dissolve religious associations and to close houses of worship. In practice, the Commissariat for nationality affairs took charge of the religions of national minorities. In the case of the Jews, it carried on a relentless struggle against their religion.

Throughout the Soviet period times of relative calm in the anti–religious campaign have been followed by a bitter and intemperate struggle. In the late 1930s, rabbis in the USSR were accused of hiding behind the mask of religion to serve fascist secret services. In the postwar period they were confronted with other charges. They were accused of Jewish nationalism and "cosmopolitanism"—contradictory as these accusations were—of wishing to establish contacts with Israeli and Western Jewry, and of being anti–Soviet and anti–Communist.

Soviet polity toward all religions, including Judaism, has in the course of decades undergone many transformations as has also the anti–religious propaganda. Anti–Jewish propaganda, however, attained an excessive degree of hostility. Religious observance and activities have come under sharpest scrutiny by the authorities. Under the Soviets many synagogues were closed, numerous religious Jews put on trial on trumped–up charges, and Jewish cemeteries were expropriated. Frequently, the anti–Semitic campaign started with the adoption of a resolution by a major organ of the Party. Special seminars were organized for propagandists who dealt exclusively with the Jewish religion.[53] Soviet periodicals have given disproportionate attention to the critique of Judaism. A veritable flood of anti–Semitic books and pamphlets has swamped the book market focussing on Jewish religion as a hostile force in Soviet society. The years 1959–1964 saw the closure of numerous synagogues.

There were and are different kinds of Jewish houses of worship in the USSR: permanent synagogues built for the purpose of worshipping, smaller places located in private homes, and temporary prayer groups (minyanim), also privately organized. The last–named operated with the tacit consent of the authorities.

Of the 1,103 synagogues in 1926, there were only 58 still in existence by 1972.[54] Closure of synagogues usually started with accusations in the local press about alleged criminal and illegal activities carried on by the leaders and officers of the synagogue who were charged with being engaged in shady business deals or in subversive Zionist activities. This was usually followed by a flood of letters from all sectors of the public urging the authorities to end the corruption in their midst. Furthermore, the regime by diverse means obstructed the observation of religious rites and ceremonies such as ritual slaughter, religious marriage, and barmizvahs. Authorities liquidated Jewish cemeteries claiming that the sites were needed for public uses. Such a decree applied for instance to the Jewish cemetery in Moscow in 1963. Basically, the authorities realized that the synagogues intensified loyalty not only to Judaism as a religion but also strengthened the national and cultural identity of the Jews. Apart perhaps from Christian sects such as Jehovah's Witnesses and the Uniates, whose followers were and are severely persecuted, the Jewish religion is the most repressed religion in the USSR and the perennial target of vicious accusations. Neither authorities nor the Soviet public at large make any distinction between Jewish religion as such and general Jewish culture, Jewish nationalism and Zionism, all of which were virtually under constant attack. These attacks have reached at critical times frenzied levels.

III. STALINISM AND THE RISE OF NATIONALISM AND ANTI-SEMITISM

Anti-Semitic Literature in the Interwar Era

In the 1920s there had appeared in the Soviet Union numerous pamphlets and books varying in size from fifty to four-hundred pages, all testifying to the existence of a widespread populist Jew-hatred. This veritable flood which inundated Russia recalled prewar anti-Semitism. While this time perhaps not government-inspired, it was certainly government-tolerated. Some of these publications were authored by Jews, who raised their voice in self-defense and denounced Jew-hatred as the tool of Russian reaction.

The populist anti-Semitism of the 1920s took many forms. It was demonstrated by the objection of Russian workers to Jewish co-workers in the factories—from which Jews under the tsars had been barred. Similarly, forced out as middlemen in the towns by Soviet economic policies, some Jews had turned to agriculture. But land-hungry Russian and Ukrainian peasants objected to the "intrusion" of Jews into the countryside. Especially in the Crimea peasants protested against the government's plan to settle Jews on land. Jews were also frequently blamed for numerous problems in many other branches of the economy. They were charged with monopolizing important political and administrative posts and enjoying special privileges. The Soviets themselves frequently embraced anti-Semitic policies as a proven way out of troublesome situations. As in ages past, anti-Semitism became a lightning rod to deflect popular dissatisfaction. Even the Komsomol [Young Communist League], to the surprise of the CPSU, displayed at times strong anti-Jewish feelings.

The growing number of Jews in the Communist Party and bureaucracy may have given anti-Semitism a novel justification. So did the hesitancy of the regime to declare unremitting war against it. Even in the early phase of the Stalinist regime, the government, partly motivated by Stalin's special dislike of opponents of Jewish descent to his policies and by the anti–Semitic legacy of the tsarist period, was reluctant to appear as a friend or defender of Soviet Jewry. Surviving the fall of the Romanov dynasty, Jew–hatred thus reemerged powerfully in the 1920s. Thereafter, the tactical usefulness of anti–Semitism, as demonstrated by the Nazi struggle against the Weimar "Judenrepublik," became also evident to Jew–haters in Russia.

Among examples of the polemical literature of the late 1920s were the following: G. L. Zhigalin's booklet *The Accursed Heritage. On Anti–Semitism* (Moscow, 1927); Nikolai Semashko, *Who Persecutes the Jews and Why?* [Kto i pochemy travit yevreyev], (Moscow, 1926); Y. Kochetkov, *Vragi li nam Yevrei* [Are the Jews Our Enemies?] (Moscow, 1927); K. Y. Maltsev's *Anti–Semitism on Trial* [Gul nad antisemitizmom], (Leningrad, 1928); and Yury Sandomirsky's *The Road of Anti–Semitism in Russia* [Puti antisemitizma v Rossyyi], (Leningrad, 1928). Several of the foregoing writers and other authors emphasized the need to wage vigorous war against anti–Semitism, such as C. Nagorny, *To War Against Anti–Semitism* [N bor'bu a antisemitizmom], (Moscow, 1929) and M. Ryutin's *Anti–Semitism and Party Activities* [Antisemitizm i partinaya rabota], *Pravda*, (August 13, 1926).

In 1926 appeared also Mikhail Kalinin's essay *The Jewish Question and the Resettlement of the Jews in the Crimea*,[1] which attacked the opposition to agricultural settlement of the Jews in the peninsula. Many communists of Jewish descent, unwilling to admit the depth of anti–Semitism in the Soviet Union, simply repeated Lenin's thesis that Jew–hatred was counterrevolutionary. The historian Yuri Larin recorded in *Jews and Anti–Semitism in the USSR* [Yevrei i antisemitizm v SSSR], (Moscow, 1929)[2] numerous instances of attacks on Jews in many different areas of the USSR.

A good number of authors, Jews and gentiles, seemed especially alarmed about the inadequacy of the Party's and the government's countermeasures. In 1929 and 1930 S. K. Bezborodov wrote two books *Signals on Anti–Semitism* and *The Poison of Anti–Semitism in Our Times*, Leonid Radischev authored *Protiv antisemitizm* [Against Anti–Semitism] (Moscow, 1929), and M. Y. Alexandrov published two books *Klasovyi vragy maskie* [Class Enemy Masked] (Moscow, 1929), and *Otkuda Byeriotsaya Vrazba k yevreyam i Komŭ ona vygodana* [Hatred of the Jews. Where does it come from? Whom does it benefit?] (Moscow, 1929).

During the last decades no Soviet publication has drawn critical attention to anti–Semitism in the Soviet Union, though its existence and official encouragement has long been beyond doubt. But after Lenin's demise, in the second half of the 1920s, the number of publications in which the authors expressed great concern over the spread of anti–Semitism in the Soviet Union had become legion. After the October Revolution Lenin himself condemned anti–Semitism. Mikhail Kalinin, while Chairman of the Central Executive Committee, and Anatoly Lunacharsky, the People's Commissar of Education and himself of Jewish descent, freely admitted in *Ob antisemitizma* [On Anti–Semitism] (Moscow, 1929) the revival of anti–Semitism and advocated measures on how to extirpate it. According to Lunacharsky, anti–Semitism was "the mask worn by every counterrevolutionary."[3] Was it only a mask? Did this denunciation of anti–Semites come to grips with the problem of national and religious hatred in the Soviet Union and the problem of Jewish existence after the Revolution?

Settlement of the Land and Birobidzhan

The question of settlement on the land, of a return to agriculture and the "normalization" of the Jewish economic structure in the Crimea, in the Southern Ukraine, and in Birobidzhan has with varying intensity figured prominently in Soviet policy toward the Jews as well as in Jewish thought.

In January 1925 the Soviets set up a new body, the *Society to Settle Working Jews on the Land in the USSR*, known in Yiddish abbreviations as *Geserd*, in Russian abbreviation as *Ozet*. It consisted of leading personalities of the Soviet state and of *Yevsektsia*. The leaders of *Geserd* appealed to world Jewry to raise the necessary funds for the project, and an agreement was signed with the American Joint Distribution Committee for the implementation of this goal; in later years the Joint was destined to be bitterly attacked by Moscow for "anti–Soviet" activities. *Ozet* pointed out that its plan of settling Jews on the land differed from Zionism, still insisting that Jews were not a nation. They disregarded that the settlement was a classic case of national "separatism" which they generally denounced. The Soviet stance was one of many flagrant contradictions. Leading Soviet diplomats such as G. Chicherin, Maxim Litvinov—later to become Soviet Commissar for Foreign Affairs—and L. B. Krassin played a role in the movement for Jewish settlement on the land.

According to Kalinin, the most pro–Jewish of Soviet leaders, this new program of settlement on the land was:

> one of the forms of national self–preservation. As a reaction to assimilation and national erosion, which threaten all peoples deprived of opportunities for national evolution, the Jewish people has developed the instinct of self–preservation, of the struggle to maintain its national identity.[4]

Yet there developed a keen competition for the best land available in the USSR. Despite government sponsorship of the return of Jews to the land, Jew–hatred raised its head. Among the indigenous Ukrainian and Tartar population of the South, anti–Semitic propaganda fell on fertile soil. Soviet authorities were apparently sufficiently deterred by it to look for other available territories in the region of the Azov Sea and in the steppes of northern Kazakhistan.

Another plan for the settlement of Jews on land, this time in Birobidzhan in the Far East, stemmed from the People's Commissariat of Agriculture. It was strongly endorsed, hardly surprisingly, by the Commissariat for Defense which wished to strengthen the country's defenses in the Far East. Opponents of this project, however, suggested the creation of a Jewish republic in the Crimea, though to no avail.

Birobidzhan was a sparsely populated region at the confluence of the rivers Bira and Bidzhan. At the time the territory was offered to the Jews, its inhabitants numbered only 1,192 people, mainly Koreans and Kazakhs and members of a primitive tribe, the Tungus; their numbers, due to harsh climatic conditions, tended to diminish. *Geserd* admitted the need for bolstering the Soviet Union in the Far East as a major motivating force of the Soviet government. A new Jewish territorial unit would ultimately be transformed into a Soviet Republic, and the Soviet project would divert the attention of both Russian Jews and of Jews abroad away from Palestine and Zionism. Aleksandr Chemerisky, the secretary of *Yevsektsia*, extolled Birobidzhan as "the heaviest blow to the Zionist and religious ideology."[5] While battling Zionism, these Jewish Communists had actually fallen under its spell, as expressed in the Yiddish slogan "Tzu a Yiddish Land" [Toward a Jewish state] and paraphrased Thedor Herzl with the latter's slogan "If you want it—then you will achieve it." The authors of the catch phrase had to renounce it since its relationship to Herzl's slogan was so close as to be embarrassing.

Soviet propaganda unleashed in behalf of the Birobidzhan project was well received in the USSR and abroad. Moscow aimed at winning over American Jews to obtain their financial support, but it did not consider the Russian Jewish response satisfactory. As one correspondent to *Emes* observed: "The Jews raise their hands easily for Birobidzhan, but not their feet." Harsh climatic conditions aside, the great distance from the main centers of Jewish settlement in the Soviet Union, its apparent competition with Palestine—which by far surpassed it in historical, religious, cultural, and linguistic attraction—the likelihood of it becoming a staging ground against Japan, were all to work against it. Yuri Larin made the opposition to Birobidzhan public by drawing attention to its negative features: its swamps, the 'gnus,' a kind of Siberian Tse Tse fly, floods, the long winter in which temperatures dropped to minus 40 degrees Celsius; he also pointed to the vast distance of 1,000 km from the Pacific Ocean.[6]

Yet in March 1928 the Executive Committee of the Supreme Soviet approved the request of *Komzet* [The Committee to Settle Jews on the Land] for the development of Birobidzhan with the aim of making it "a national Jewish unit, administratively and territorially." As Lenin had written in the prewar era:

> It is beyond doubt that in order to abolish all national oppression it is extremely important to create autonomous areas even of the smallest dimensions, each with an integral uniform composition of population, towards which the members of a given nationality, scattered in different parts of the country, or even of the world, could gravitate and with which they could enter into relations and free association of every kind.[7]

It is doubtful whether Lenin writing the foregoing had Jews in mind, though the article was primarily a polemic against the Bundists Liebman Hersch and Vladimir Medem. This concept of preserving Jewish nationality was not directly mentioned by the planners of Birobidzhan, though Lenin was constantly quoted. Generally, it ran counter to Lenin's plans for the Russian Jews.

Kalinin and Stalin

The first group of immigrants to Birobidzhan received free passage and a very small amount of pocket money. In 1928 there were 654 immigrants, in 1931, 323, in 1932, 14,000, and in 1933, 3,005.

However, in 1933 more Jews left Birobidzhan than immigrated. By the end of 1935 Jews formed 23 percent of the total population. In 1937 the Soviet government expected to absorb 17,000 people, but only 3,000 arrived in the province. To make the Birobidzhan project more attractive to Jews, the Soviet government in May 1934 proclaimed the area a Jewish autonomous region. The following year Kalinin elaborated on his thesis, sketched first in 1926, on preserving the Jewish nationality through this project. The Jews, he recalled, three million strong, were the "only nationality in the Soviet Union without a state system of their own."[8] The creation of such a region is

> the only [!] means of a normal development of this nationality. The Jews in Moscow will have to assimilate [!]. In ten years time Birobidzhan will become the most important guardian of the Jewish national culture and those who cherish a national Jewish culture must link up with Birobidzhan.[9]

Was this an analysis, prognosis, or an ultimatum?

Kalinin continued: "We already consider Birobidzhan a Jewish national state." Though he admitted the huge problems which Birobidzhan faced, he held out the promise that once 100,000 Jews had settled there, the "Soviet government would consider creating a Jewish Soviet republic." He did not forget stressing the significance of defending the Soviet Far East, attacked Zionism—which had become a Soviet ritual—and acknowledged the help received from the American Jewish Joint Distribution Committee. This stance recalled an earlier slogan: "Down with Zionism, long live Soviet Zionism."

Two years later, however, the promise of Kalinin and the hopes of *Gerserd* were virtually wiped out by Stalin himself. On November 25, 1936, Stalin who had become the ideologist and chief agent of Soviet nationality policy and finally the undisputed boss in the USSR, elaborated a new Soviet nationality policy, virtually dashing Jewish expectations. In his speech "On the Draft Constitution of the USSR,"[10] though not directly mentioning Birobidzhan, he made clear that three conditions had to be fulfilled before autonomous regions were to become constituent Soviet Republics. Such a region must, first, be a border republic and not be completely surrounded by Soviet territory.*

---

* Why were border republics given at least the theoretical right

Second, the nationality giving its name to a given Soviet republic must constitute a more or less compact majority within that republic. Third and most important, the republic must not have too small a population, no less but more than a million people. At the time it was considered quite unlikely that one million, one-third of the entire Jewish population of the USSR, would ever settle in the Far Eastern territory. In any case, Stalin's pronouncement made a sham of Kalinin's pledge. The anti-Semitic atmosphere of the time of the purges and the continuing decline of the influence of Soviet Jewish leaders made this rather apparent.

Stalin, Trotsky, and Anti-Jewish Hostility

The October Revolution abolished the pariah status of Russian Jews, but, according to Trotsky, this did not mean that the Soviets were able to crush anti-Semitism with one blow:

> The battle against national prejudices just as against religion did not change the thought and sentiments of the people or raised their cultural level. The older half of the population has been educated under the Tsars, while the younger half has inherited a lot from their elders. Every thinking human being must realize that national and chauvinist prejudices, especially anti-Semitism, has survived among the more backward elements of the population.[11]

According to Trotsky, the Soviet regime created a number of disturbing phenomena which, if added to the poverty and low educational standards of the population, made possible the creation of a new anti-Semitic climate. The Jews, a people inhabiting towns and cities, constituted a substantial percentage of the urban population in the Ukraine, Byelorussia, and Russia proper. The new regime needed a large number of civil servants and relied to a great extent on Jews in urban centers, especially at lower and intermediate levels. This, Trotsky held, explained the existence of anti-Semitism among the Russian working masses who had always hated bureaucracy.

---

to secession, while other nationalities situated in the interior were not even granted the right to cultural autonomy? The fact that some could "separate" from the USSR, while others were doomed to assimilation and disappearance, was hardly in conformity with the much exalted concept of national equality.

While powerful, the Soviet bureaucrat felt like living in a belea-
guered fortress. He engaged in pseudo–socialist demagoguery: "Socialism has already been reached." He was supported by a broad
segment of new "aristocrats," the "Stachanov" workers and many
others who were beneficiaries of the Soviet regime, such as recipi-
ents of military honors and decorations. Many a bureaucrat shared
"the national prejudices of the backward segments of the population." The Ukrainian bureaucrat in particular tried to prove that he
was "the brother of the peasant." The bureaucracy, bent on preserving its "privileges," abused the "darkest instincts" of the population.
It attempted to divert the dissatisfaction of the masses toward the
Jews.[12] Trotsky saw in the much hated Soviet bureaucracy a major
source of the "new" anti–Semitism in the USSR.

In the struggle for power between Stalin and Trotsky in the
1920s the former made reckless use of anti–Semitic prejudices among
the Russian people and in the Party itself. A whispering campaign,
unleashed against Trotsky on account of his Jewish descent, played
a not insignificant role in the outcome of the domestic in–fighting.
At the same time Stalin made use of two Jewish henchmen, Lazar
Kaganovich and Yemlyan Yaroslavsky—which was to serve as proof
that he did not harbor any anti–Jewish sentiments.

As long as Zinoviev and Kamenev were linked with Stalin as
member of the "troika," "the play on the strings of anti–Semitism
bore a very cautious and masked character." But after they joined
the Opposition, the situation radically changed. Under the direction
of Stalin, Uglanov in Moscow and Kirov in Leningrad carried the
anti–Semitic line systematically. Trotsky quoted a German radical
journalist who compared Stalin's anti–Semitism with that of Julius
Streicher. Though Trotsky had never paid special attention to the
Jewish question, he asserted that "he did not have the right to be
blind to the Jewish problem which exists and demands solution."[13]

In an article "Thermidor and Anti–Semitism" (February 22, 1937)
which was first published in May 1941 in *The New International*, Trotsky accused Stalin that in fighting the Opposition he had exploited
Russian anti–Semitism. He, Trotsky, had received numerous letters
and inquiries from "very naive" and apparently "confused" people
who juxtaposed abstractly Jewish emancipation under the Communist banner to fascist anti–Semitism. Some people paid inadequate
attention to reality and recognized only what suited them. Since in
their view Hitler–Germany was "the kingdom of anti–Semitism, the

USSR is therefore the kingdom of national harmony."[14]

Theoretically Lenin welcomed assimilation, though only on a voluntary basis. Stalin, however, fostered assimilation by every means. Early concessions to the Jews were made while Lenin was still alive, but they were nullified in the late 1920s and 1930s. Trotsky was disinterested in Jewish cultural development, but was sharply opposed to Stalin's course, including his nationality policy. In 1938 he criticized the forcible assimilation of Jews. In a letter to leftist Jewish intellectuals in the USSR in October 1938[15] Trotsky asserted that a workers' government was "obligated to create for every nationality the best conditions for cultural development." This means among other things "to create for those Jews who demand their own schools, their own press, their own theater, etc., a separate territory for self-determination and development." In regard to the nationality question no curtailment should be permitted.

> To the contrary, the cultural needs of all nationalities and ethnic groups must be materially supported by all means. If this or that national group is destined to disappear [in a national sense], then this must be as a natural process but never a consequence of some territorial, economic or administrative [man-made, artificial] difficulties.

On the issue of voluntary assimilation of the Jews Trotsky was closer to Lenin, while opposing Stalin who clearly supported and practiced the policy of forcible assimilation. Between 1923–26 Stalin made sure that Soviet anti-Semitism was still concealed. The Soviet press resorted to the trick to give, next to the names of leading Jewish Party members such as Zinoviev and Kamenev, their original Jewish names, thus underlining that these men of the Opposition were "dissatisfied Jewish intellectuals."[16]*

When the Soviet press deliberately began to call Zinoviev and Kamenev by their previous names, Radomislyiski and Rosenfeld, Stalin played on the anti-Semitic moods of the Russian people. Even in the Moscow factories the agitation took on a distinctly anti-Semitic note. On one occasion, in a private letter to Bukharin, Trotsky recalled that the Bolsheviks used notorious "Black Hundred" methods against the Opposition.[17] In his view, in the latter half of 1927 the anti-Semitic movement assumed an "unrestrained character." The Bolshevik slogan "Beat the Opposition" only replaced the old Tsarist

---

* Kamenev actually was half-Jewish.

slogan "Beat the Jews and save Russia" to establish the continuity of anti–Semitism.

After Lenin's demise, Stalin's prejudices and animosity against the Jews had increasingly free rein. The more firmly Stalin's rule became entrenched and both the Left and Right Opposition was crushed, the more the Vozhd's tyrannical rule and anti–Jewish policies became apparent. Some of his first victims were, ironically, Jewish communists, who actually had lent a helping hand to disseminating communist propaganda among the Jews, to dissolving Jewish organizations, and spreading communist ideas on assimilation and amalgamation. Among the most prominent were Lenin's close associates, Zinoviev, Kamenev, and Radek, all later purged and finally liquidated. Trotsky was exiled until, at Stalin's order, he was assassinated in Mexico. Leading Jewish communists, such as S. Dimanshstein, J. Lieberberg, Chairman of the Executive Committee of Birobidzhan, prominent Jewish writers and poets, officials of Jewish cultural institutions, and every Jew accused "of carrying on Jewish nationalist and Zionist activities," became a Soviet target, destined to being eliminated.

Still concerned with appearances, Stalin, to soften Jewish protests and those of non–Jewish communists abroad, made a point to retain some high–placed Jews in the Party, the government, and the bureaucracy. Occasionally the Soviet government granted prizes to Jewish artists and writers. In January 1931, Stalin, talking to a representative of the Jewish Telegraphic Agency, equated anti–Semitism with cannibalism. In 1936, at the Eighth Party Congress, Molotov castigated Jew–hatred, juxtaposing Nazism and Fascism with the "humanism" of Communism, as allegedly expressed in the Stalin constitution of that year.[18] It was also on this occasion that Molotov himself, married to a Jewish woman whom Stalin later banished into exile, referred to the "Jewish origin" of Karl Marx—a fact which was never since recalled by a Soviet leader. It was less embarrassing for Soviet leaders and the Soviet people to think of Marx "the German," or better the internationalist, than of Marx "the Jew," despite the circumstance that World War I and II were waged against the German invader. German enemies were more acceptable to many Russians than Russian Jews.

In the purges of the late 1930s, which assumed unprecedented scope, Stalin took revenge against all those who had crossed his path or had committed "deviations." He also took "precautionary moves" against those whom he considered potential foes, among them numerous imaginary enemies.

The accusation of being deviationists was also aimed at would-be leaders of national minorities. The foes included those who cultivated "bourgeois nationalism." The charge of national deviationism however, was not hurled against those who practiced Great Russian "chauvinism." The latter were condemned only in the abstract. While eliminating during the show trials and purges Jews along with members of other nationalities and Great Russian "traitors," the number of Jewish victims of the purges was exceptionally high. Next to such prominent Communists as Zinoviev, Kamenev, Radek, numerous Jewish Communists active in Jewish cultural affairs, in Soviet Yiddish Institutes, and Yiddish journalists were arrested, purged, and ultimately killed. In 1937 the last Yiddish newspaper in Moscow, *Emes*, a sister publication of *Pravda* and founded in the early days after the October Revolution, was closed.

According to Maxim Litvinov's *Notes for Journal*, the full authenticity of which had admittedly been questioned, Trotsky held 'Koba" (Stalin) "quite capable of sending his rivals to their death," and "with the help of doctors from our clinic in the Kremlin[!]"! A correct prediction as far as Trotsky's assassination was concerned, though Kremlin doctors were not involved therein. But they emerged later as defendants in the so-called "doctor's plot."

Trotsky had declined Lenin's invitation to become Chairman of the Council of Commissars, pointing to his Jewish origin. The Counter-Revolution would make good use of the slogan "The Soviet Government is in the hands of Jews." According to Litvinov: "Ilich [Lenin] laughed and replied: They say in any case we are all Yids [a deprecatory term for Jews]. And those who are not Jews must be Lithuanians or Chinese." [19]

Stalin's early obsession with Zionists—he referred once to the "Zionist rabble"—can also be seen from his order to "prepare a full list of all Jews in the USSR who were paying a shekel [a contribution of all who voted for the Zionist Congress] "and all these persons should be immediately sent to Siberia." Litvinov, according to his account, warned Stalin of the likely negative American Jewish reaction against such measures. Kaganovich also once told Litvinov that

> Koba [Stalin] had explained to him at length the difficulty
> of making a Jew, even a Jewish workman, into a true Communist and atheist, because the Jews, he said, were typical

petty–bourgeois with the instinct of ownership developed over the centuries.

Of course, Litvinov went on, "Koba's anti–Semitism is the sequel to the support given by the majority of Jews in our Party to Trotsky and the opposition." Still, Litvinov "noted that Koba felt some inherent hostility toward us." He related "jocularly" that he had a "Marxist explanation" for this phenomenon.

> There had been two shoemakers' shops in Gori, one owned by Koba's father and the other by a Jew who had settled in Gori. Competition between the two shoemakers turned Koba into an anti–Semite. . . . Of course this explanation is an oversimplification, but it contains a grain of truth.[20]

While he always saw in Trotsky a rival, Stalin told Litvinov that he "despised" Zinoviev and Kamenev for the alleged lack of principle "in tactics." Theirs was the tactics of "treachery." "We shall have to strike first [!] before they can carry into effect their plan of treason." Stalin indeed struck first.

During the Great Purge anti–Semitism was kept deliberately alive to be politically abused by Stalin. The number of Jews in the Old Guard was always much higher than in the Party as a whole. In the words of Stalin's daughter Svetlana Alliluyeva, "with the expulsion of Trotsky and the extermination during the years of 'purges' of old Party members—many of whom were Jews—anti–Semitism was reborn on new grounds and first of all in the Party itself."[21] A great metamorphosis then took place in the CPSU. While in the days of the Civil War in the 1920s anti–Semitism was considered the enemy, by the late 1930s the Jews had been turned into a main enemy, and Jew–hatred had become entrenched in the very center of Soviet power, the Party itself. Having survived the establishment of the Bolshevik regime, it was now in the driver's seat. Though anti–Jewish animosity was apparent, it was on the whole still muted rather than openly acknowledged. But people abroad took notice of it. At the insistence of Canadian communists, the Comintern in 1939 made an attempt to set up a study commission to ascertain why Soviet authorities had adopted anti–Semitism. Yet at that very time the European war broke out, terminating the inquiry.

Not only Communists and Westerners but also the Nazis had begun to question the Soviets' sincerity in regard to the loudly proclaimed doctrine of national equality and their alleged opposition to anti-Semitism. The high proportion of Jewish victims in the Soviet purges must have made a deep impression upon the Führer. Both Hitler and Ribbentrop wanted to believe that Stalin's pro-Western orientation in the mid-thirties was only the result of Jewish influences such as Litvinov's and of other Jews active in the Comintern, while Russian "nationalists" such as Stalin and Molotov favored an understanding with the Third Reich. In communicating with Berlin, German diplomats in Moscow, to facilitate a Soviet-German understanding, also kept quiet about the Jewish wife of V. Molotov, who had succeeded Litvinov as Foreign Secretary. Such a report, while truthful, would have only made the Führer uncomfortable!

The bulk of Russian Jews had in 1917 supported the Mensheviks and other parties. Still, in the first six months and early years after the October Revolution Jews had rendered useful services for the new Bolshevik regime. But later on they turned out to be a roadblock to further "progress" and had to be removed. After the Hitler-Stalin pact was signed, the Soviet press went out of its way to refrain from criticizing the Third Reich also in regard to the Jewish problem. Trotsky later pointed out that since the German-Russian non-aggression pact, the Soviets uttered "not a single critical word" about the destruction of Czechoslovakia and of Poland, the occupation of Denmark and Norway and in regard to the unheard-of bestialities practiced by Hitler's soldiers against the Polish and Jewish peoples.[22]

In the 1930s growing Russian nationalism extolled the role of the Great Russians as the big brother and role model for all Soviet nationalities. The Great Russian chauvinist attitude was also demonstrated in the linguistic sphere. The Soviet authorities had first imposed the Latin alphabet on several Moslem nationalities in Central and Southwest Asia. They aimed at replacing the Arabic script in order to lessen cultural and religious contacts with fellow Moslems in the south and in the Arabian peninsula and to provide a written language for the primitive tribes of Asia. But subsequently, to tie these peoples closer to the Russian core of the USSR, they abolished Latin, substituting for it the Cyrillic alphabet of the Slavic nationalities.

Jews were not the only people suffering from Great Russian cultural chauvinism and imperialism. A case in point was the Abkhazian people of the Abkhazian Autonomous Republic of the Caucasus. The Abkhazian writer Gregory Gyula has revealed in his book *Spring in Sakem* that in 1937 all Abkhazians under the policy "The Correct Regulation of Cadres" were removed from leading posts in the Abkhazian Autonomous Republic. After the war all Abkhazian schools were closed and all Abkhazians were told instead to decide whether to become Georgians or Russians.[23] Gyula was informed by Moscow that there was no such thing as an Abkhazian nationality and to declare that "assimilation" was the key to paradise for small nationalities— which he refused to do. But the Abkhazian Prime Minister, using the name of Dimitri Gyula, son of Gregory, wrote a pamphlet "proving" the need for Abkhazians to disappear as a nationality! This Soviet view on small nationalities, as proclaimed in this case, was by no means unique, but was rather generally upheld.

The Great Fatherland's War

The Stalin–Hitler pact delayed the outbreak of the Nazi invasion of Russia by less than two years after the German onslaught against Poland and the war against the Western Powers. But after the fall of France, Russia was in an incomparably worse military and geopolitical situation than it had been in the summer of 1939. This was due especially to Stalin's blind faith in Hitler's pledges and the official policy of neutrality between them, to the Soviet material deliveries to the warring Third Reich and to the lack of Soviet military alertness in 1941. Soviet Jews were obviously shocked by Stalin's policy of support for Nazi Germany and the growing rapprochement with German fascism. They questioned the durability, morality, and the ideological justification of the link–up with Berlin. In May 1940 *Bezboshnik* [The Atheist] carried an article by a Soviet correspondent who had recently visited Germany, hailing the Nazi attack on Jewish religion as the "principal achievement of the Third Reich!"[24] He held it to be the duty of Soviet atheism to help its new political ally in his struggle against religion. Mark Gallai,[25] considered by many Russians the leading Soviet test pilot, wrote in 1960 that the twenty–two months following the signing of the Hitler–Stalin pact and prior to the Nazi invasion of the Soviet Union were for his generation "strange and incomprehensible."

> The fascists were no longer fascists. . . . What we had been taught to abhor as hostile, evil, and menacing from our Komsomol, nay Pioneer days, suddenly became, as it were, neutral. . . . We looked at photographs of Molotov standing next to Hitler or read reports of Soviet grain and oil flowing into fascist Germany or watched the Prussian goose–step being introduced at that very time into our armed forces.

Faced with the "treacherous" Nazi invasion of Russia, Stalin, hiding in the Kremlin for two long weeks, finally recovered from the apparent mental paralysis which had seized him and tried to rally the Soviet people for the defense of Russia. In the hour of sorely needed help from his people and the West, Stalin permitted Soviet Jewry to establish the Jewish Anti-Fascist Committee. On August 24, 1941, prominent Soviet Jews in Moscow were allowed to proclaim their pride in belonging to the Jewish people, a primary target of the Nazis. The Moscow meeting adopted an appeal "To our Jewish Brothers all over the World,"[26] linking Soviet Jews with fellow Jews beyond the country's borders. The brotherhood of all Jews was suddenly recognized, since at that very moment it was in the Soviet interest to acknowledge it.

During the war and thereafter the Russian press buried Nazi atrocities against the Jews and, prior to their own involvement in hostilities, the massacres of Poles and others, trying to avoid embroiling the Nazi regime. The willful suppression of Nazi mass murders left Soviet Jews extremely vulnerable, once Nazi hordes, bent on genocidal killings, descended upon the Soviet Union. Had Russian Jews been warned in time, many more of them might have succeeded in escaping into the interior and saving their lives. A foreign correspondent of the *Manchester Guardian* and the *The Times* later revealed from personal experience that many Russian Jews had been completely unaware of Hitlerian atrocities in German–occupied Western Poland.

Hitler's war against Russia, strangely enough, took Stalin by complete surprise. It resulted in a radical turn–about of Soviet foreign policy, making Great Britain and the U. S. Soviet allies. It necessitated for a time greater Soviet tolerance toward many—though not all—national and religious minorities, including Jews. Though Stalin's enmity against the latter had a brief respite, it did not lead to any permanent change of Soviet policy toward them. Stalin's continuing hostility was shown in the killing of the leaders of the Polish Bund. The Bund, the Jewish labor party in pre–war Russia, though anti–Zionist, had, nevertheless, retained its national and Yiddish outlook. Its leaders, Henryk Erlich and Victor Alter before World War I had crossed swords with Lenin and Stalin. Following an agreement in World War II between Moscow and the Polish Government–in–Exile in London, both Erlich and Alter, after the German destruction of the Polish state, had been deported to Russia. There they had closely cooperated with leading Soviet Jews in the formation of the *Jewish*

Anti-Fascist Committee. But in December 1941, they were arrested and shot,[27-28] probably without a trial. Stalin vengefully remembered the Bund against which in 1903 he had declared war and with which he again had polemicized in 1913. While Moscow remained tight-lipped about this murder, in 1943 M. Litvinov, Soviet ambassador to the U. S., revealed the execution of the above two Jewish leaders.[29] According to the KGB, the two men were accused of entertaining relations with Nazi leaders—a spurious change but one of which Stalin himself was of course not innocent.

The Nazi war unleashed against the Soviet Union, hit also many Polish Jews who had found refuge in the USSR. When Polish-Jewish survivors returned to Poland after the war, they revealed that, while having encountered assistance and even friendship among some natives of Central Russia and the Southeast of European Russia, Soviet authorities had made them less welcome. Ilya Ehrenburg[39], popular war correspondent, has testified in his diaries that in the Ukraine and Byelorussia he had found very few Jews who had been saved "by their noble neighbors." Though Polish anti-Semitism of the prewar and wartime period was much alive, one British journalist reached the conclusion that "proportionately" more Jews were rescued by Poles than by Russians in the occupied region. Many Polish Jews who had spent the war years in Russia were greatly shocked by their experiences in the USSR. The unfriendliness they encountered in the Soviet Union was the result of the failure of the Soviet government to effectively combat anti-Semitism in the prewar and wartime periods. The Soviet population was unprepared not only for the "treacherous" Nazi military attack, but also for the divisive Nazi propaganda, especially anti-Semitism. Anti-Jewish hatred which had been propagated in the Tsarist era and had been tolerated in the Soviet period had survived in the USSR. In combination with the anti-government sentiments in the wake of collectivization, starvation, terror, and purges, it had provided a fertile soil for the most virulent form of murderous racist anti-Semitism, as displayed by the invader, especially the Einsatztruppen and SA units.

While East European and Soviet Jews in Nazi-occupied regions were the chief victims of the Nazi policy of extermination, numerous other Soviet Jews played a significant role in the defense of the Soviet Union and contributed to the final military collapse of the Nazi regime. Among them was the famous actor Solomon Mikhoels—later to be murdered by the Soviets—and others who lent their names to awakening the sympathy and help of Western Jews and of the Western Powers for the Soviet struggle against the Nazi invasion. The Jewish Anti–Fascist Committee published a report on "Jewish Heroes of the Soviet Union," proudly listing 1,500 Jewish heroes of the USSR and 10,000 Jews who had received orders and medals for bravery.

In the late 1930s many high–ranking Russian officers had been executed on spurious charges of treason. When war engulfed Russia in 1941, the opportunities for military advancement of officers whatever their nationality were thus thrown wide open. In 1943, forty–nine Jewish generals were listed as being in command of Soviet military forces. But news of the patriotism and military bravery of Russian Jews was generally suppressed the same way as all other positive news affecting Soviet Jewry. What was widely disseminated were rumors spread by Nazis and some Russian anti–Semites, that Russian Jewry, not Hitler, was responsible for the war and that the Jews were shirkers—this despite the fact that about 500,000 of them faithfully served in the Soviet army. Such negative views were also widely held among officers and men of the Red Army. Jewish partisans who joined Russian units also played a vital part in the war effort, continuously harassing German military units. But even there clashes occurred between Russian and Jewish partisans, the latter often being betrayed to the Germans. Jews who survived the war bitterly complained about the little friendship and humanity they had encountered among Russian partisans and peasants.

A major source collection of the "ruthless murder of Jews by German fascist invaders throughout the occupied regions of the Soviet Union" and in the death camps of Poland had been *The Black Book*.[31] The editors Ilya Ehrenburg and Vasily Grossman unquestionably identified closely with the Jewish victims, but were compelled to repress the extent of the indifference of the Soviet peoples to the Nazi annihilation of Jews. Their elimination, carried out with sadistic violence on the part of criminals and murderers, was undertaken in preparation of the planned German settlement of the "eastern areas."

During the occupation of Poland, the Polish underground had appealed to the Polish population to assist Jews, offer them safety, and refrain from participating in the Nazi extermination of the Jews. The Polish underground weekly *Gwardzista* described the massacres of Jews, exhorted Poles to "render shelter and help" to the Jewish survivors, and appealed to them to accept Jews into partisan units. Though some Poles cooperated with the Nazi invaders, others heeded this appeal. The Soviets, however, kept silent about Jews being the special target of the Nazi murderers. Soviet Communists, operating clandestinely in Lithuania and Byelorussia, while denouncing Nazi atrocities, consistently ignored the special victimization of the Jews. They continued to do so after the war, as if acknowledging the mass murder would arouse among Soviet citizens sympathy and compassion for the Jews. That, however, was never Soviet intention.

As stated, the lack of timely warnings aimed at the special peril faced by Soviet Jews and the failure of direct appeals to their own people to shun cooperation with the Germans in the mass murder of Jews constitutes a sorry page in Soviet history. Both the Nazi extermination of Jews and the discriminatory Soviet treatment of them prior, during, and after World War II are largely non–events in Soviet history. Maltreatment of the Jews allegedly never occurred. The Nazi annihilation of Jews in the USSR is buried in the general account of Nazi atrocities committed in the occupied regions of the Soviet Union, without special mention or mere inclusion of its Jewish victims. These omissions amount to an outright falsification of the history of the war. They could never have occurred without the deliberate, fraudulent Soviet attempt to rewrite history and without the widespread anti–Jewish climate of Soviet public opinion. Distorting events, the Soviets have tried to expunge unprecedented massacres and unparalleled atrocities in Russian and world history from the consciousness of Jewish and Russian contemporaries and future generations. All this has made the Soviets accomplices in lying about the mass murder of Jews on Russian territory.

After the aggression against Russia in June 1941, Stalin, considering the massacres on Soviet soil, could have reversed the policy of maintaining complete silence on these atrocities, but he refrained from doing so. He was probably restrained from changing course in view of the widespread anti–Semitic sentiments of the population of the border regions which he had acquired only two years earlier, not to mention the anti–Jewish feelings of the peoples of the Soviet border republics. His own anti–Jewish sentiments were bared in wartime meetings with Polish leaders such as General Sikorski and later with President Roosevelt at Yalta when he disclosed his low opinions of the fighting abilities of Jewish soldiers.

According to the prominent dissident Y. Yevtushenko, to whom anti–Semitism had "always been repulsive," Stalin bore the main responsibility for the rise of Jew–hatred. In his view, anti–Semitism was "not in the least natural to the Russian people any more than it was to any other people: "it was just artificially stirred up at various times under Stalin."[32]

This Soviet attitude which has created a "memory hole" was intended to rob the Jewish victims of even a mere footnote in history. No monument commemorates the dead Jews. While the foreign press has taken increasingly note of the atrocities, the Soviet press and media have kept silent, burying the Jewish tragedy under the distorting heading of Nazi crimes "against the Soviet people" and Russian sacrifices. Only in the official statements of Foreign Minister Molotov in early 1942 were Jews included among the victims of German atrocities, without mentioning, however, that they constituted the great majority of the murdered populace. While the Jewish anti–Fascist Committee disseminated in the West the tragic news about the fate of Soviet Jewry, the Soviet press and radio studiously kept their silence, suppressing the anti–Jewish crimes committed by the Nazis.

The formation of the Jewish anti–Fascist Committee during the war, welcomed by Soviet Jews as a major concession by Stalin, strengthened their hope that after the war the USSR would abandon its anti–Jewish policies. This hope was soon to vanish. The formation of the Committee was primarily a shrewd move to enlist Soviet Jews in the life–and–death struggle against the Nazi invader and to boost help in the West for the sake of the Soviet people.

IV. STALINISM, 1945–1953, ISRAEL, AND THE "BLACK YEARS" OF SOVIET JEWRY

Soviet Anti–Semitism and Anti–Zionism

What in the Soviet view is anti–Semitism? Do communists admit the importance of national, religious, and racial biases and hatred in the course of history? Or do they attempt to reduce Jew–hatred solely to economic and social causes and seek a common denominator in the class struggle? Their primary interest clearly does not lie in objective analysis but in offering a concept useful in their tactical struggle to gain power and to hold on to it. The Jews as such, the target of anti–Semites, were and are of little or no concern to them. Their attitude toward them was never determined by any sympathy or compassion on account of past tragedies but only by what they interpreted as the interests of the Revolution and of the Soviet Union at any given moment.

Soon after the Bolshevik seizure of power in October 1917, on July 27, 1918, the Council of People's Commissars issued a decree which bluntly declared that the "anti–Semitic movement and anti–Jewish pogroms" were "fatal" to the cause of the workers' and peasants' revolution and directed the Soviets to "effectively destroy the anti–Semitic movement at its roots." In combating anti–Soviet propaganda, anti–Semitism was defined as "spreading hostility toward Jews," but also characterized as "an adversary tactic of capitalists and landlords in Russia and abroad . . . to divert their ire from the real enemy, capitalism."[1] *The Great Soviet Encyclopedia* pointed out that Jew–hatred arose as a result of competition in the market, but became "an instrument of government policy." After the victory over the Nazis, the *Encyclopedia* emphasized the racial component in anti–Semitism and that its hostility included "legal limitations, expulsions, massacres, and extermination."[2] *The Small Soviet Encyclopedia*, 1958, claimed that the victory of socialism in the USSR "destroyed the ground under anti–Semitism. The Jews, with all other

Soviet nations and races, enjoy full equality."[3]

While the Nazis have viciously attacked Jews and Judaism time and again, including the Zionist movement, the Soviet anti–Semitic propaganda of the 1930s and 1940s, before Israel's birth, had not yet gained the particular anti–Zionist coloring which it was to acquire after the War of Independence in 1948–49. Anti–Semitism had never been entirely absent from the Soviet Union after the October Revolution. Excepting perhaps the period of World War II, outright anti–Semitism and anti–Zionist propaganda has steadily escalated since.

During World War II the Nazis in Russia superimposed their racial–biological anti–Semitism upon traditional Russian Jew–hatred and the more recently created populist anti–Semitism which was also alive among many Soviet national minorities. Thus, even after the Nazis' defeat and their expulsion from Russian soil, the invaders had left a lasting impression upon the mind of the population of the occupied regions of the USSR. The Soviets had had the option of combatting the indigenous Jew–hatred effectively, but they had never done so. They had chosen the road of embracing rather than battling traditional Russian anti–Semitism.

A great deal of information about the prewar and wartime Russian anti–Semitism can be gleaned from the *Harvard Project on the Soviet Social System.*[4] The extensive interviews with Russians and Ukrainians who had left the USSR either during the war or fled immediately thereafter, revealed that the people involved looked upon the Jews a stereotypes—which recalled similar practices in the 1920s. Jews were pictured as aggressive, money–minded, dishonest, and people who shirked their military obligations. In the Ukraine, where there were more Jews and deeper anti–Jewish hostility than elsewhere in Russia, the war had even been called a "Jewish war." After the reconquest of the lost territories the Soviets had been wary of avoiding the appearance of "bringing back the Jews."

The war increased hatred of the German invader, of his treachery and atrocities. Yet, strangely, rather than burying anti–Semitism, it deepened anti–Jewish sentiments. The "Great Fatherland's War" strengthened Soviet patriotism as well as Great Russian nationalism, the former a unifying, the latter a divisive force. Instead of stressing the equality of the diverse Soviet nationalties as having contributed to Soviet victory, it bestowed in the end special credit upon the Great Russians. Stalin toasted the latter as the most loyal of Soviet nationalities and encouraged Great Russian chauvinism. The latter reached a climax in the early postwar years when for a time Russian nationalism made extravagant claims regarding numerous Russian inventions which allegedly had preceded and surpassed in importance those of other nations. Great Russian cultural chauvinism flourished especially under A. Zhdanov, then a favorite of Stalin. It was to counter intellectualism and Soviet intellectuals who looked admiringly to the West and wished to transplant Western ideas and institutions to Russia. Stalin was dead–set against such a course and feared its social, economic, cultural, and political consequences. Soviet Jewry on the other hand was a strong pro–Western force and hoped for increasing cultural ties with the West and for national–religious links with Jews abroad.

After the war, Soviet policy toward the Jews was marked by striking ambiguities. While the return of Jews to their former homes was not outright forbidden, it was discouraged, and employment and cultural opportunities were largely denied to them. Their darkest period began, however, in November 1948, after the dissolution of the Jewish Anti–fascist Committee (JAC). Stalin's suspicion vis–á–vis the Jews had grown by leaps and bounds during the first decades of the Soviet period. The more totalitarian his regime became and the weaker the resistance toward his dictates grew, the more ruthless his policies grew and the stronger his resolve to banish Russian Jews to the East of the Empire, to Asia. A virulent anti–Semitism, no longer concealed, turned paranoic. It replaced the policy of growing Soviet discrimination of the 1930s when he had crushed Jewish political opposition, which was always more imaginary than real, and had started to deliver deadly blows against Jewish cultural institutions.

Milovan Djilas—before his abrupt fall from his position as the second in command in the Yugoslav communist hierarchy—while in Moscow in 1948, frequently conversed with Russians about anti–Semitism. Stalin once asked him why, apart from Pijade, there were no Jews "in your C.C." due to the purges and a policy dating back to the prewar period they had disappeared from the Soviet C.C. and other bodies. As Djilas wrote, in the USSR

> Jews are citizens of the lowest order. The same policy is now being applied in Eastern Europe against that handful of martyred people who survived fascist extermination. And this was, is , and will be done regardless of whether the Jews are bourgeois or socialists.[5]

The contemporary Prague trial, Djilas continued, "exposes—as always with Stalin—in a concealed form a conscious organized anti-

Semitic course. Here anti–Semitism is concealed behind the struggle against anti–Semitism—absolutely in style of Stalinist absurdity."

Anti–Semitism has already become routine in Eastern Europe. It is assuming monstrous forms which would be gro- tesque if they were not bloody and anti–Socialist. The Hungarian leadership is most anti–Semitic in its propaganda today for the simple reason that it is composed of Jews. This leadership desires to prove in this way that it has freed itself from the "Jewish cosmopolitan mentality" and how it is faithful to the very end to Stalin and his great Russian "socialist" imperialism. It strives not only to flatter Stalin but attempts to guess the hidden, secret desires of the master. History teaches us that a regime was always reactionary when it began to become anti–Semitic and that pogroms against he Jews were always a sure sign of the most sinister social reaction. Russian bureaucratic capitalism has become not only nationalistic but racial too. And it must inevitably become—and already is—anti–Semitic also.[6]

Once the Ukraine was liberated, a paper drafted by a committee headed by Solomon A. Lozovsky[7]—a prominent Communist of Jewish parentage and long a confidant of Stalin—and addressed to the Vozhd, contained the proposal that the Crimea after the deportation from it of the Crimean Tartars be turned into a Jewish Soviet Republic within the Soviet Union. But Stalin charged that the Committee members were "agents of American Zionism" and aimed at wresting the Crimea away from the Soviet Union to establish

an outpost of American imperialism on our shores, which would be a direct threat to the security of the Soviet Union. Stalin let his imagination run wild in this direction. He was struck with maniacal vengeance. Lozvosky and Mikhoels were arrested. . . . Investigation of the group took a long time, but in the end almost all of them came to a tragic end. Lozovsky was shot.

Zemchuzhina, Molotov's Jewish wife, was exiled. Stalin actually became furious when Molotov in the crucial session of the C.C. only abstained from voting on her fate!

Though Krushchev later on allegedly agreed with Stalin's assessment of a Jewish Republic in the Crimea being a threat to Soviet security, in his *Memoirs* he took a different tack when he wrote: "There was no excuse for what, to my mind, was a major defect in his character—his hostile attitude toward the Jewish people." Krushchev apparently did not think that his own attitude toward the Jews was comparable to that of Stalin. He continued with great perception:

> As a leader and theoretician he [Stalin] took care never to hint at his anti–Semitism in his written works or in his speeches. And God forbid that anyone should quote publicly from any private conversations in which he made remarks that smelled sharply of anti–Semitism. When he happened to talk about a Jew, Stalin often imitated in a well–known exaggerated accent the way Jews talk . . .; he was very good at it.

Stalin, however, "never permitted anti–Semitic remarks in Kaganovich's presence." Stalin would "have strangled anyone whose actions would have discredited his name, especially with something as indefensible and shameful as anti–Semitism."[8]

To fully understand Soviet Jewry's postwar outlook and Stalin's opportunist and wavering policies, we have to turn to a brief discussion of the immediate postwar situation of Russian Jewry, to the birth of Israel, as well as to the beginning Cold War between East and West. A factor first to be dealt with, however, is Stalin's personal relationship with Jews and Jewish acquaintances which affected Soviet policy.

Stalin's Personal Relations with Jews

Stalin had never liked Jews. But until he consolidated his power in the 1920s he took care not to disclose his aversion against them. Yet he did so blatantly after World War II. Among Jews related to him by inter–marriage was a daughter–in–law, the wife of his oldest son Yakov. When Yakov was taken prisoner by the Nazis, Stalin concluded that someone had betrayed him and that it had been "his wife" who had been "dishonest."[9]

In the winter of 1942–43, Stalin's daughter Svetlana Alliluieva met Alexei Yakovlevich Kapler who later became one of the recognized masters of Russian film making.[10] It was only a brief encounter between a schoolgirl of seventeen and a man of forty whom she greatly admired and who became her first seemingly platonic love. On the pretext that he had numerous contacts with foreign correspondents, he was arrested, sent to Vorkuta and then to work in mines for ten years, to be released only after Stalin's death. Challenged by his daughter, Stalin burst out calling Kepler a "British spy." He had torn up his letters to her and ridiculed her claim that Kepler was a Russian writer. "Apparently the fact that Kepler was a Jew was what bothered him most of all."[11]

In the spring of 1944 Svetlana got married to Gregory Morozov, a student like herself at the Institute of International Relations. "He was Jewish and my father did not like it." While not outright prohibiting the marriage to Morozov, Stalin denied both of them a real family relationship, forbidding Morozov to ever "set foot in his house."[12] Three years later the couple broke up, according to Svetlana, for reasons of a personal nature. Stalin had accused his son-in-law even of shirking military service. He met Svetlana's and Morozov's son Joseph first when he was three years old and, to her surprise, was taken by him. She had been scared though about his reaction to the Georgian-looking boy with his "huge shiny Jewish eyes."[13] In any case, Stalin had several half-Jewish grandchildren. At various periods Jews were part of his enlarged household, as the daughters of Jan Gamarnick and Solomon Lozovsky. The latter, a high-placed Foreign Ministry official, was arrested in 1949 and, as mentioned, executed three years later.

About two years after Svetlana's divorce from Morozov, when many Jewish intellectuals were arrested being accused of Zionism, Stalin remarked to her: "That husband of yours was thrown your way by the Zionists." He also observed: "The entire older generation is contaminated with Zionism and now they are teaching the young people, too."[14] On the other hand, at the time of the "doctors' plot" when Stalin's personal physician V. Vinogradov was arrested, Stalin was supposedly very distressed. He refused to see another physician and remarked that he did not believe the doctors were "dishonest."[15] Perhaps he made this remark only to divert Svetlana's suspicion from his own responsibility for hatching the doctors' plot and playing a major role in this sordid affair.

Leo Mekhlis, of Stalin's personal staff, also held the post of State Controller. He lost his political clout several years before Stalin's death. When he died in February 1953, only a few weeks before Stalin himself passed away, he was given a state funeral. Of Jews squeezed out from significant posts in Party and state were Party propagandists, lecturers, directors of seminars and journalists. Among the latter was David Zaslavsky who lost his key position on *Pravda*. The anti-Jewish purges also affected the Soviet judiciary, judges, prosecutors and defense counsels. These changes were closely connected with the mounting accusations against Jews who were charged with political and economic crimes and of being embezzlers and swindlers. In spite of the anti–Semitic purges extended to a majority of different fields of activities there remained some areas in which Jews were permitted to function such as sculpture, painting, music, ballet, and others. Notwithstanding the campaign against theater critics and cosmopolitanism in general, Jews were also well represented in Russian and Soviet literature, the exact sciences, and in technological fields.

Other Causes of Stalin's Jew–Hatred

Among the roots of Stalin's anti–Semitism may have been his early absorption of the teachings of the Greek Orthodox religion, of traditional Russian Jew–hatred, as well as Karl Marx's quite different source of distinct anti–Semitism, as expressed in his youthful pamphlet *Zur Judenfrage* (1843).[16] Also, Stalin, though himself a member of the Georgian national minority—he was never able to shed his accent—had become, like many a convert to a new cause, a Great Russian chauvinist who mistrusted most non–Russian nationalities. During World War II when Hitler's armies had invaded the Soviet Union, Stalin, exaggerating, if not inventing, alleged dangers from some Soviet minorities, suspected some of them of making common cause with the Nazi aggressors and resorted to virtually unprecedented countermeasures. He uprooted several Caucasian and Crimean minorities and the Volga Germans, banishing them wholesale to Asia. In 1956 Krushchev charged that Stalin had entertained expulsion schemes also in regard to Ukrainians[17] and had relinquished them only because there were too many of them.

In the postwar period Stalin's mistrust of non–Russian nationalities extended to Soviet Jews. Their treatment as second–class, if not third–class citizens, was part and parcel of his policy of repression of numerous Soviet minorities and revealed the bankruptcy of Soviet nationality policy. During the war he had tried to take advantage of international Jewry, of the Russian Jews' ties with Western European and American Jewry, but in the postwar period these very same ties made Soviet Jews suspect to him.

Some observers and students of the Russian scene have ascribed Stalin's anti–Semitic acts, especially those of his last years, to the deterioration of his mental capacities. Such deterioration cannot be observed in most other endeavors of his, though his obsession with anti–Semitism cannot be excluded. Others have tried to find a convenient scapegoat in Beria. Politically overambitious, he was not destined to survive Stalin for long. Litvinov himself, of Jewish descent,

who was steering a pro–Western course in the 1930s and again during the war, had in *Notes for a Journal* testified to Stalin's personal
Jew–hatred,[18a] though the authenticity of some of the Notes written
between 1926 and 1939 has been questioned. According to Litvinov,
Stalin revealed that at the insistence of Rabbi Schechtmann* —rabbi
of the largest Moscow synagogue—he had pleaded with Stalin. The
Vozhd, however, reacted "furiously" and allegedly said: "I don't think
we are shooting enough of that Zionist rabble." Stalin claimed that
the majority of Jews in the Party still supported him and that he
"understood the absurdity of anti–Jewish measures." Stalin's daughter Svetlana Alliluiva revealed in the *Letters to a Friend* that she had
frequently encountered her father's dislike of Jews. Yet for a long
time he had not bared his hatred for them as openly as he did after
World War II.

After World War II, Stalin, the government, and the Party which
he headed had moved with startling speed against the cultural and national aspirations of Soviet Jews, though the Soviet constitution had
promised to preserve and develop national cultures and languages.
His anti–Jewish moves after 1945 against what was left of the Yiddish language and culture, were, in view of the Russification and
assimilation which had taken place in the meantime, based on crude
anti–Semitism. The Jew was declared to be an alien and was to be
humiliated and stigmatized. Stalin apparently seemed to be largely
insensitive to charges that, after defeating Hitler, he was emulating
him, being driven by the same anti–Semitic obsessions as the latter.
He rejected the pleas of Solomon Mikhoels,the leading personality
of the Jewish Anti–Fascist Committee, who intervened in behalf of
Jews trying to return to their farms in the Crimea. Stalin, who during the war had ejected numerous national minorities because of their
suspected cooperation with the German invaders, did not trust the
Jews either. While he had considered them useful during the Great
Fatherland's War against German fascism, he turned against them
in the postwar era. After a striking reversal of Soviet policy toward
Zionism, they had become again the enemy—both in the Middle East
as well as on Russian soil!

According to the eminent Soviet expert Adam Ulam, the Jews appeared to Stalin eternal trouble–makers, critics, dissenters, and even

---

* Stalin "did not like to interfere" in questions concerning the Jewish religion and even threatened to bring this matter to the attention
of the Central Control Commission (pp. 94–5)

spies. The younger bureaucrats, the class created by Stalin's Revolution, owed their very careers and rapid rise to Stalin and his purges. They had imbibed traditional Russian anti–Semitism which Stalin's policies encouraged rather than combatted. They firmly held that some negative aspects of Soviet rule—which had found widespread disapproval, such as the forcible collectivization, the rise of Trotskyism, the purges, and the creation of security agencies—were all the work of Jews.[18b] Jews also, they claimed, dominated the intellectual and cultural life in the USSR. After the start of the Cold War Stalin and the bureaucratic elite accused Soviet Jewry of being the ally of imperialism, admirers of Western civilization, and alleged denigrators of Russian culture. Only Jewish "rootless cosmopolitans," Stalin became persuaded, could adopt a cultural and political line, which was as hostile to Russian nationalism.

Stalin, inclined to suspect dissension and outright treason around himself, bore of course the main responsibility for creating an atmosphere of terror and suspicion in the Kremlin and all over the country. He was convinced of the existence of a widespread conspiracy against himself throughout the USSR. He insisted that his henchmen find culprits among the Jews and other Soviet citizens. Woe to the security man who was unable tor too squeamish to find Jewish spies. That individual put his job, his life, and his security on the line!

Stalin's early animosity against the Jews and mistrust of them grew by leaps and bounds. He magnified his bizarre suspicions against them, turning them into sinister plots and shameful treachery and treason. He was fortified in this view by the Leninist conception that entire classes were guilty of a lack of loyalty and deserved severe punishment, if the Revolution was to survive! He cherished the notion that other groups at critical junctures of history, entire professions and nationalities, could play a traitorous role, and therefore preventive countermeasures were imperative and patriotic! A perverse logic had seized Stalin and he shaped the mind of the ruling elite in his image.

Soviet Patriotism and Internationalism versus Jewish Nationalism and "Cosmopolitanism"

At a meeting with the other heads of the Allied states, Stalin is supposed to have voiced his displeasure with the Soviet Jews who had failed to develop their own territory in Birobidzhan. Just as Zionism, in his view, had always clashed with internationalism, similarly Jewish nationalism was also juxtaposed to Great Russian patriotism, fostered especially during and after the Great Fatherland's War. Still, during this War Russian Jews were encouraged to establish closer contacts with their kinsfolk abroad and thus to strengthen Soviet–Western ties. In this period the Soviet attitude toward Zionism changed somewhat from hostility to neutralism and even temporary support of it, as demonstrated by the Soviet stance toward the partitioning of Palestine in 1947 and by the prompt official recognition of the new state of Israel when it was proclaimed on May 14, 1948. But later in that year, with the growth of the Cold War sentiment, the alienation of Tito's Yugoslavia from the USSR, and the internal changes accompanying Zhdanovshchina and its intolerant chauvinism, there occurred also a change in the attitude toward Israel and Russian Jews.

According to Ilya Ehrenburg's *Memoirs, Pravda's* editor invited him to write an article about Zionism and Soviet Jews.[19] Ehrenburg denied therein the existence of <u>one</u> Jewish people spanning the globe and condemned Jewish nationalism. He also denounced Israel as a bourgeois state and as a tool of Anglo–American capitalism. A solution of the Jewish problem was only possible within the common order of the USSR. It was hardly an accident that soon after the publication of this article the Jewish Anti–Fascist Committee was dissolved and the Yiddish paper *Aynikayt* [Unity] shut down. Remaining Jewish schools were closed and Jewish writers and intellectuals arrested and deported. This was followed by the hardly disguised anti–Semitic campaign against "cosmopolitanism," a purge in Birobidzhan, and the execution of leading Jewish writers. All this climaxed in the infamous doctors' plot in January 1953. The last–named accusation was not dropped until three months later, several weeks after Stalin's death. During this time the authorities attacked individual Jews, charging them with all kinds of crimes, of divulging secrets, of fraud and embezzlement, of irregularities in their University careers, of bourgeois nationalism and Zionism, and of the falsification of records and dissipation of state funds. The latter accusations were intensified in the campaign against economic "crimes" of Jews in the 1960s.[20]

A major source of irritation and confrontation between the Kremlin and Soviet Jewry was rooted in the assertion that Russian Jews did not constitute a nationality, though numerous much smaller nationalities and ethnically less conscious groups and those with fewer claims of having made significant contributions to world civilization have been recognized by Moscow as constituting national units. While some of the primitive and little developed ethnic groups in the USSR were even given an alphabet and their cultural development encouraged to an unrealistic extent—which has puzzled even many Westerners and a leading Soviet scholar such as E. H. Carr[21]—the Russian Jews' ties with their kinsfolk abroad were generally criticized. As stated, the existence of a Jewish nationality was denied on the ground that Soviet Jews did not live on a compact territory. What was totally ignored was the strong national consciousness of the Jews, their religious and historic tenacity and survival under most adverse circumstances, the persistence of the Yiddish language, and the renascence of Hebrew in Israel and elsewhere.

On the other hand, in the 1920s and thereafter the Jews were frequently recognized in the USSR, rather inconsistently, as a national group. In the post–Stalinist era the practice of classifying Jews in their internal passports as "Evrei" has continued. On numerous occasions Soviet Jews have been widely considered a nationality, though the Soviets disavowed this stance whenever it suited them. Excepting a brief pro–Zionist phase after the war, the post–World War II years were a time of bitter disappointment for Russian Jewry. The anti–Jewish policy of the prewar era—seemingly discontinued during the war, though never fully abolished—soon ushered in an era of unrelenting anti–Semitism. During the war more than a million Soviet Jews were terminated by the Nazis, while at the front Jewish soldiers fell in battle making the ultimate sacrifice. After the war Jews were returning to their homes in the Ukraine and Byelorussia from the front lines or other parts of Russia, to which civilians had fled at the approach of the German soldiery. But they often found their homes occupied by their neighbors who were unwilling to vacate them. Nor were Soviet Jews permitted to settle in the Crimea and to rebuild their cultural institutions anywhere. Soviet authorities prohibited their reestablishing Yiddish publishing houses and theaters and the publication of Yiddish newspapers. At the end of the war, the Jews' great expectations which had been aroused during the Fatherland's War were once again shattered.

The Cold War and the War against "Cosmopolitanism"

The leaders of the totalitarian state wage a ruthless war against real and presumed enemies, spurning any sentimentality. In the era of the Cold War the enemy par excellence turned out to be the U. S. and those states allied or even merely sympathizing with it. Characteristic of Soviet propaganda during the Cold War era was its complete disregard for truth, its inclination toward exaggeration, and its vacillations from one extreme to the other, while ignoring its own blatant contradictions. After defeating the Nazi foe, the Soviet government tried to prepare its war–weary peoples for another onslaught, one imagined by yesterday's allies, the Western Powers, led by the U. S. Stalin therefore was bent on extirpating any friendly feelings of the Soviet populace toward the West. He warned his peoples against the sinister plans of "capitalist encirclement" and the danger of "kowtowing" to the West, even if only in cultural affairs.

The leader of the frenzied anti–Western drive became Andrei Zhdanov. Zhdanov started out by vilifying the West's cultural preeminence and boosting Russia's cultural leadership. This was rather similar to the Nazis' earlier attempts to extol German cultural dominance. Russian leadership was claimed in fields as diverse as literature, biology, technology, mathematics, science, and medicine. Those who tried to uphold traditional views which gave full credit to Western science, literature, and inventive genius were declared guilty of "fawning" on Western culture. Zhdanovism was the expression of extreme Russian nationalism and of cultural isolationism. It revealed fear and envy of Western culture, technology, science, and of the West's military superiority at the end of the war.

Soviet Jewry with numerous ties to the West and to fellow–Jews, with their deep sympathies for Western individualism, political freedom, and democracy were denounced as "cosmopolitans" and became a primary target of the Zhdanovshchina. In a series of speeches beginning in September 1946 Zhdanov appearing before conferences of writers, scientists, and philosphers criticized "cosmopolitans." He first targeted gentiles, not Jews specifically, and made it clear that the critique was aimed at the failure of the Soviet intelligentsia to provide their country with "a new powerful ideological weapon" in the struggle against the West. But the campaign against "cosmopolitanism" soon took on a distinctly anti–Semitic character. The number of Jewish "cosmopolitans" shown in cartoons with the unavoidably Jewish hook nose—following closely earlier Nazi anti–Semitic patterns—spread throughout the USSR. This anti–Semitism was designed to arouse greater support for the Russian nationalist movement, to serve as a means of uniting Russians against all aliens, foremost against Jews. The Soviet Jews were described by epithets such as "homeless," "rootless," "passport–less wanderers," "strangers to the Russian people and its national culture," "tribeless vagabonds," none of these heartless descriptions and blatant distortions testifying

to the professed faith of international brotherhood. The often russified names of Soviet Jews were in the Soviet press regularly followed in
brackets by their original typically Jewish names. About 60 percent
of all the "cosmopolitans" denounced and vilified were patently Jews.
When Jewish cultural institutions were closed, they were accused also
of crimes such as "Americanism." Soviet Jews were thus treated as
an accomplice of America, as the ally, at best a potential friend, of
the U. S., which had suddenly become the Soviet archenemy.

The occasional charge of "internationalism" was levelled at Jewry
and Zionism long before the Six–Day War, though with special intensity thereafter. It made sense when mouthed by chauvinistic Nazis.
But it was a strange accusation coming from a consistent champion
of all sorts of international goals and endeavors, primarily of international socialism and of the international proletariat and revolution.
Milovan Djilas, long the second in command of Yugoslav socialism
until dethroned and jailed, had observed in the Belgrade *Borba*[22]
in 1952 that the Jews were international–minded because they were
scattered all over the globe. He also considered them "doomed to
be persecuted" wherever a region "isolates itself." It was indeed a
new isolationism and extreme nationalism which fuelled the postwar growth of anti–Semitism in the Soviet Union and its East European satellite empire. Lenin himself had praised the "progressive
attributes," "the internationalism" found in Jewish culture.[23] He had
also assailed Russia's great power–chauvinism.

But Stalin and the Soviet ruling clique not only radically altered
the outlook and attitude of Russians but also perverted the nomen-
clature calling the internationalist Jews "cosmopolitans." He thus invented a new allegedly bad label, while baptizing Russian and Soviet
nationalism as "patriotism"—a term shunned by Marxist luminaries
and revolutionaries such as Marx, Engels, and Lenin. Stalin also belied national equality when after World War II he called Russians the
"leading" nationality"[24] among the peoples of the USSR.

In the past Lenin had denounced Russia as the "prison house of
peoples," as had similarly the leading contemporary Marxist Soviet
historian M. N. Pokrovksy. But under Stalin Pokrovksy was posthumously dethroned,[25] since his critical view of Russia's past, of Ivan
the Terrible and Peter the Great, of Russia's maltreatment of other
nationalities, and of the glorification of her military heroes was replaced by new theories. One of these new theories was that "Mother
Russia" had been a benevolent ruler over other nationalities and the
related notion that the Russian nationality was a "genius." It was

unavoidable that extolling primarily the Great Russians went hand in hand with minimizing if not negating the role of the West and in particular with deprecating the Jews. The general xenophobia intensified especially Soviet anti–Semitism. The latter could not be associated with Lenin or Communism in general, though it might be linked to Karl Marx's hostility toward his own origin and the Jewish people. It also fitted closely Stalin's dislike of the Jews which he had been compelled to suppress for a long time.

Nor was Krushchev a friend of the Jews. Though trying to reduce Stalin to human size and pointing at many of his errors, he never repudiated his anti–Semitism which had become so apparent especially in his last years. Krushchev, speaking once about alleged Jewish shortcomings, mentioned that they were "prone to scrutinize every occurrence and manifestation": "They take an interest in everything, and end up by holding divergent views."[26] Such a frame of mind clearly did not fit into the totalitarian thought process, but was likely to burst it wide open. "Divergent" views were likely to turn into deviationist thought—which totalitarians had to stamp out.

This inclination of Jews toward criticism obligated a totalitarian regime to take "precautionary" measures such as Stalin had taken toward several other social and national groups. Totalitarians and docile individuals and peoples unquestioningly obey authority rather than challenge it. Stalin even tended to mistrust submissive individuals and groups, since those seemingly loyal at the moment might become dangerous in the future. Anyone with a sort of Jewish "character" or disposition was a potential risk. The macchiavellian or schizophrenic ruler does not wait until the peril has arisen; he rather tries to extinguish it before it has become threatening. Stalin concluded that the Jews were a potential enemy of the Soviet regime and were likely to become a Fifth Column. This threat had not yet appeared on the horizon when the USSR was invaded by the troops of the Third Reich. But there existed in Stalin's mind such a peril in the event of a Soviet–American conflagration.

The battle against "cosmopolitanism" started in earnest with a criticism in *Pravda* late in 1948 by Anatoli Safronov of "an anti–patriotic group of theater critics," listing by name several Soviet Jews and criticizing them as "homeless cosmopolitans" who had "lost all sense of responsibility towards the people" and to whom national pride was "alien." Soon thereafter Konstantin Simonov, deputy secretary general of the Writers' Association, accused "cosmopolitans" of being "prone to degenerate and sell out to the enslavement by

American imperialism." The attack against "cosmopolitans," primarily Jews, was a broad–gauged assault in the most diverse fields of cultural activities,such as art, architecture, literature, the world of cinematography, sports newswriting, historical research, philosophy, jurisprudence, etc. "Cosmopolitans" were pictured as people not only hostile to the Soviet Union as a whole but also as persons despising the national culture of specific nationalities, notably Ukrainians. They had muddied the "pure waters" of Soviet culture by infiltrating everywhere in literature, politics, and science, touted reprehensible concepts of world Jewish unity and Zionism, and combatted the Soviets' stringent measures against Jewish culture. The Soviet campaign against "cosmopolitanism" revealed itself as rabid propaganda directing its shafts both against Jewish "nationalism" as well a Jewish "cosmopolitanism." These currents were considered by most people flowing in opposite directions. But the Soviet creators of an entirely new vocabulary have held on to it to this day.

How did the situation of Soviet Jewry strike Western and Israeli observers at the time of the inception of the campaign against "cosmopolitanism"? An Israeli diplomat in the Soviet capital, M. Namir, reported in October 1949 to Foreign Minister Sharett that

> the animosity toward the Jews had grown. Low–ranking officials cracked down on them on the pretext that the Jews are a disloyal element, suspected of espionage, while at their places of work they are told "Go to your state, to Israel." The courts pervert justice, passing deliberately severe punishments on Jews. Many have been thrown this year into prisons and sent to camp for pro–Israel sympathies or for manifesting a desire to emigrate to Israel or taking part in the street demonstrations last year in honor of our Legation. Heavy depression and fear of the future are weighing down on the Jews here.[27]

Namir continued:

> The dismissal of Jews from places of employment is increasing without reason or on insignificant pretexts, especially from managerial posts; the purge is continuing of cosmopolitans who are considered by the public as a whole to be Jews. Anti–Semitism from below is growing. The general atmosphere is heavy. The central authorities do not apply any restraining hand openly or secretly. They too determine who is a criminal and to be deported. The Jews have a very

heavy feeling, fearing dismissals, deportations, confiscation of property. It sometimes appears that the authorities have an interest in making people afraid.

An Anti–Semitic Purge in Czechoslovakia

In 1948, an overflow of the nationalistic and anti–Semitic Zhdanovshchina into the East European satellites, Romania, Hungary, Czechoslovakia, Poland, and Albania, resulted in the dismissal of numerous high–ranking officials. The Cominform journal *For a Lasting Peace, for People's Democracy* charged that national bourgeois deviationism was still alive in these countries to demonstrate that Western imperialism was intent on undermining these states and to recruit traitors. Of these trials, the one in which anti–Zionism played the most prominent role, was that of Rudolf Slansky, the Czechoslovak Party Secretary General. An investigation carried out years later, in 1968, by the Piller Commission in the archives of the Czechoslovak C.P. has drawn attention to the special position of Soviet advisors who had "enriched" the interrogation with "new techniques."[28] Before and during the Slansky trial the openly anti–Zionist and anti–Jewish line became pronounced. In a letter to Klement Gotwald in July 1951 Stalin himself wrote about "incriminating material" he had received in Moscow on Slansky and Geminder and invited Gottwald to Moscow. Two months later Slansky was arrested apparently after renewed Soviet intervention, to be followed by the arrest of other leading Czechoslovak Party members and diplomats.

Slansky and others were charged with engaging in conspiracy, espionage, sabotage, and anti–state activities, with the training of "terrorists against the Czechoslovak people." He was accused of scheming to shorten Gottwald's life, of having "selected physicians for him" among hostile elements. In addition to Israel, the American Jewish organization "The Joint" and American imperialism were all involved in these criminal activities, as were also British, French, Yugoslav, and Israeli intelligence. Of the fourteen accused, eleven were sentenced to death, and the executions were carried out on December 3. The previous day the Czechoslovak ambassador in the USSR, Karel Kreibish, protested in a letter to the party Secretariat against the racism and anti–Semitism of the judgment in Prague. Gottwald countered this accusation by asserting that the struggle against Zionism had nothing to do with anti–Semitism. The latter was simply a protection from American espionage! The Slansky trial with its pronounced anti–Zionism and anti–Semitism, vigorously pushed from the outside by the Kremlin, was to become the model for the persecution of Zionists and Jews in the Soviet Union itself.

The Rise and Fall of the Jewish Anti-Fascist Committee (JAC)

The JAC was founded in 1942 and was expected to mobilize Soviet Jewry, to arouse sympathy and support at home and abroad for the Soviet Union in its struggle against the Nazi invaders and perhaps to speed the opening of a second front. For the Soviet Jews the Committee offered the possibility of rebuilding the organizational structure which the CPSU had destroyed in 1930 when it abolished the Jewish Sections of the Party. Though in the midst of the war the Soviet government and the Party made substantial concessions to the JAC, they were apparently resolved that the dissolved Jewish institutions should not be rebuilt. The Party's unwillingness to make lasting concessions to Soviet Jews was revealed in the case of the two leaders of the Polish Bund, Henryk Erlich and Victor Alter who had succeeded in fleeing from the German-occupied part of Poland to Soviet-occupied Polish territory. Erlich and Alter were first imprisoned by the Soviets but were released after the intervention by the reopened Polish Embassy in Moscow in September 1941. Both men were then approached by the Soviets to organize and head a worldwide Jewish Committee to support the struggle against fascism. They subsequently negotiated with L. P. Beria, People's Commissar for the Interior and head of the NKVD. Both men, along with other diplomatic missions and foreign news agencies, were transferred from endangered Moscow to Kuibyshev. Yet a memorandum of theirs addressed to Stalin outlining their plan for the reorganization of the JAC, and containing suggestions for restoring Poland's rights to reestablish its freedom and sovereignty, was never dignified with a reply. On December 4, 1941, they were again arrested and soon thereafter shot.

Why were Erlich and Alter killed? Did Stalin take revenge for their opposition as former Bundist leaders to the Bolshevik Party and later for their sharp criticisms of the Moscow trials of the late 1930s? Or for their subsequent proposal to grant general amnesty to prisoners throughout the Soviet Union? They had undertaken most extensive worldwide activities in behalf of the JAC, which, according to their plans, was to comprise members from different countries all over the world. Stalin, however, had no intention of creating an organization which was to embrace Soviet Jews and Jews from abroad, the latter beyond his reach. According to Stalin, the JAC was to help the Russian war effort and to win over public opinion for the USSR by painting an idyllic picture of the relationship between the Soviet peoples and the Jews under his "enlightened" and "tolerant" leadership.

Though the Soviet government's and Soviet Jews' immediate goals seemed congruous, their ultimate intentions differed substantially. The JAC appealed to Jewish national pride and worked for a Jewish cultural revival in the USSR, not for ultimate assimilation and disappearance of the Jews as a national–religious unit. It aimed at national and individual equality of the Jews, not for second–or third–class citizenship. The JAC under actor Mikhoels' leadership was basing its appeal at home and abroad on restoring the concept of one Jewish people in many countries, a concept which Stalin and his regime had long battled. Besides, the JAC was bent on becoming the nucleus of a national central organization for Soviet Jews. Speaking in Russia and abroad, Mikhoels made a point of addressing "our Jewish brethren the world over" and of Soviet Jewry being "part of a world entity." All this ran counter to the main thesis of Soviet thinking on Jews. In JAC rallies and in its publications emphasis was placed on the special tragedy faced by Soviet Jews, apart from that which had befallen the entire Soviet populace. The JAC stressed that the "Jewish nation"[40] would appear as a prosecutor at the anticipated war–crimes trial. The ideas expressed in these utterances and proclamations exceeded by far the limited concessions that Stalin was prepared to grant to the JAC in the first place.

While the Soviet leadership regarded the JAC as a temporary wartime agency, others hoped to turn it into a new permanent center for the entire Jewish population of the USSR. Soviet Jewry would thus obtain national representation which, in striking contrast to other Soviet nationalities, it lacked. And the JAC would become its spokesman! But Stalin had no intention of restoring Jewish autonomy and elevate a transitory committee, created primarily to further Soviet rather than Jewish interests and purposes, and give it a permanent status.

Jewish expectations abroad—as the extended tours of Mikhoels and Feffer to the West demonstrated—point also in the same direction. The English Chief Rabbi made it clear that support for Soviet Russia was not only designed to "smash Hitlerism but to bring Russian Jewry to the fold of Israel." Jews everywhere, including the JAC, hoped that the comradeship–in–arms of Russians and Jews would in the postwar era create a new type of relationship between them. This was the background which beginning in September 1941 prompted talks between Jewish political leaders, including Ben–Gurion, with Ivan Maisky, Soviet Minister to Great Britain. Maisky, who later visited Palestine sent a glowing report about Jewish achievement in Palestine to Moscow. In 1942 Mapai, the largest and most influential political party of Palestinian Jews, seemed full of opitimism concerning future Russian–Jewish relations. The V League, a non–party organization though controlled by Histadruth, expressed the hope that Russia would respond to foreign help with a more positive policy. Zionist representatives and Soviet officials exchanged friendly messages both in London and Constantinople. On the other hand, though Mikhoels and Feffer on their extensive missions abroad passed through the Lydda airport, they, apparently curtailed by Soviet restrictions, did not meet with any Jewish representatives in Palestine.

To establish a meticulous record of Nazi atrocities on Russian soil, an agreement was reached by the JAC with Soviet authorities to publish a *Black Book* simultaneously in the Soviet Union (in Russian and Yiddish), in the U. S. (in English), and in Palestine (in Hebrew). In his *Memoirs* Ilya Ehrenburg revealed later that Albert Einstein was showing interest in the publication of the *Black Book*.[29] In was planned that this publication would consist of a collection of documents, letters, diaries, and eyewitness accounts, all testifying to the Nazi murders. But the book was never published in the USSR. The typeset galleys were destroyed in late 1948, though nothing in the projected publication was damaging to the interests of the Soviet Union. In the unpublished preface of the *Black Book* Einstein made clear that an international organization dedicated to safeguarding the sanctity of life should not limit itself to protecting countries against military attack "but also extend its protection to national minorities within the individual countries" and that the Jewish people must be given "special consideration in the reorganization of peace." The fact that the Jews "possess no country and no government ought to be no impediment." This view was one to which Moscow, given its constitution, its ideology, and its obsession with sovereignty, was bound to object. Though Einstein's preface was suppressed,[30] the Soviet edition of the *Black Book* was never brought out.

During the war the official Soviet attitude toward the JAC underwent notable changes. For a while the authorities, hard–pressed, permitted some manifestations of Jewish nationalism. But the attempts of the JAC to publish jointly with the American Committee of Jewish Writers, Artists and Scientists Yearbooks in Yiddish never bore fruit. Similarly, the collections of its Historical Committee were never allowed to be published. The emphasis the JAC placed on the concept of the unity of the Jewish people irrespective of its countries of residence, and its activities in behalf of Soviet Jews in regard to jobs, apartments, and general welfare[31] aroused Soviet suspicions and resulted in accusations of their entertaining "nationalist views."

Mikhoels' mysterious death proved to be one of the heaviest blows at Soviet Jewry in the postwar era. It was claimed that he had been killed in a road accident in "tragic circumstances." The report was widely disbelieved. But he was given a spectacular funeral. Tens of thousands filed past his coffin and he was honored by most laudatory eulogies. It was believed that he had always had access to the Kremlin and for a time had even enjoyed Stalin's friendship. Having become a spokesman for Soviet Jewry, he had in 1944 in presence of other prominent Jewish leaders appealed to Stalin himself to suppress Soviet anti–Semitic manifestations.

The Zionist Phase of Soviet Policy

Soviet Policy toward a Jewish state in Palestine was in the early post–World War II era not always hostile, as had been the case in the interwar period. Following the British Government's call for the convening of a General Assembly special session of the U. N. in April 1947 until adoption of the partition resolution on Palestine by the Assembly's Second Regular Session on November 29, 1947, the government of the USSR adopted a positive policy favoring the emergence of a Jewish state in the Mideast. Moscow's motivation was hardly altruistic. It aimed at the termination of the British Mandate, the withdrawal of British troops and the evacuation of British military bases from Palestine and at securing a vital strategic position in this region for itself. In Soviet opinion, the interests of the Jews in Palestine, the latter's partitioning into two parts as embodied in the U. N. resolution, coincided with their own self–interests. The Soviet policy announcement in favor of partition, which was made public by the Ad Hoc Committee on the Palestine Question, was preceded by favorable policy declarations by the U. S. and by Poland and Czechoslovakia.

The Soviet delegate reiterated the main points made already in May 1947, especially the need

> to take into account all the sufferings and needs of the Jewish people whom none of the states of West Europe . . . had

been able to help during the struggles against the Hitlerites
and the allies of the Hitlerites for the defense of their rights
and their existence.[32]

Countering Arab criticism, the Soviets made clear that their motivation was anti–British rather than anti–Arab. Moscow's Arabic
broadcasts recalled Soviet past support of the British and French
withdrawal from the Levantine countries and its insistence on the
evacuation of imperialist forces from Egypt, Palestine, Greece, In-
donesia, and Korea. The Israeli Foreign Minister Moshe Shertok
(Sharett) dealt then directly with Soviet representative Tsarapin and
Shtein who inquired about the military equipment the Jewish settlers
lacked, disclosing their apparent sympathy for the Jewish position
and a viable partition plan. But American diplomats made clear
their reservations concerning ultimate Soviet intentions.

On November 26, 1947, Andrei Gromyko laid down the major
Soviet thesis that the partition solution corresponded to the fundamental national interests of Jews and Arabs. Rejecting the Arab
claim that the partition was "an historic injustice," he stated: "After
all, the Jewish people has been closely linked with Palestine for a considerable period of history. Apart from that, we must not overlook
the position in which the Jews are still without a country, without
homes."[33] Partition finally corresponded, he asserted, to the principle of national self–determination of peoples. Gromyko censored the
British refusal to cooperate with the implementation of partition and
subsequently accused them of fanning Arab–Jewish enmity. He also
charged Americans of making common cause with Arab "reaction,"
even after the partition resolution was passed on November 19, 1947.

A recurrent Soviet accusation was the charge that numerous German army officers and soldiers were in Egypt calling for a "holy war"
against Palestine's Jewry. While President Truman seemingly retreated from his earlier strong position for partition to one proposing
a provisional trusteeship for Palestine, the Soviets insisted on the
prompt and effective creation of two states in Palestine. This view
was also expressed by the Israeli Communist Shmuel Mikunis in the
Cominform journal *For a Lasting Peace, for a People's Democracy*,
when he praised, as expected, the Soviet position as against that of
Great Britain and the U. S.[34] Ukrainian, Byelorussian, and East European delegates in the U.N. voiced then likewise pro–Jewish views
in the same body.

In 1945 the USSR had looked favorably upon the concept of an
international trusteeship for Palestine. But when it became apparent

that the Western Powers would reject the idea of the USSR becoming a partner of the Anglo–Saxon Powers in the Mideast, and that the U. S. was vacillating on the partition of Palestine, the Soviet Union insisted on partition, thus aligning its position for a brief moment with that of Palestine's Jewry, which opposed altering the partition resolution.

In the subsequent Palestine War the Soviets, while in their press and radio propaganda criticizing the Western Powers' assistance to the Arabs, committed themselves to support the Jews in their struggle for independence. Radio Moscow, describing the invasion of the newly proclaimed state of Israel in May 1948, pointed out that the Arab ranks were filled with "fascist elements" of different nationalities![35] The Soviet Jewish journalist David Zaslavsky accused the British Labor government of preparing "cold-bloodedly the ground for the wholescale extermination of the Jews—a new Oswiecim" (Auschwitz).[36] Britain's refusal to meet its obligations regarding Jewish immigration and the infiltration of Arab armed bands into Palestine from neighboring countries which were to help in the fighting against Palestinian Jews encountered Soviet opposition.

The Soviets encouraged the emigration of Jews from East European countries to Palestine rather than from the Soviet Union itself. Czechoslovakia provided military facilities for the training of prospective Jewish immigrants. The Soviets themselves facilitated the training of Israeli pilots in Eastern Europe, and Władisław Gomulka also offered Israelis military training in Poland. The Jewish communist leader Shmuel Mikunis made frequent journeys to East European countries for the purpose of obtaining military supplies for Israel. In Romania, Anna Pauker disclosed in talks with the Israeli envoy M. Namir the Soviet bloc's interest in aiding Israel. But Vyshinsky in a conversation with the Israeli Foreign Minister Sharett pointed out that Romania and Hungary, fighting reaction at home could not permit free emigration from these countries, since the Jews were the most loyal elements of the new regimes. Such emigration as was permitted from East European countries caused friction in the Arab world, being bound to strengthen the human and military potential of the emerging Jewish state. The feelings of Soviet Jewry in 1948 were best expressed by Ilya Ehrenburg. His hostile attitude toward Zionism and Israel generally reflected his own close ties with Stalin and the ruling Party. But in the interview with Alexander Werth, *Hopes and Fears* (1962) Ehrenburg revealed not only the Soviets' and his own still favorable attitude in 1948 toward Israel, but

also cast a realistic light upon the Jewish situation in the Soviet Union
as well as the links between the fate of Israel and the destiny of Soviet
Jewry. He expressed the view that

> Jews did not allow themselves to be exterminated by the
> Arabs as they were in the Hitler days. If the Arabs, fol-
> lowing in Hitler's footsteps, would have started massacring
> the Jews, the infection would have spread; we [in the Soviet
> Union] would have here a wave of anti–Semitism. Now for
> once, the Jews have shown that they can also kick you hard
> in the teeth. There was now a certain respect for Jews as
> soldiers.[37]

Arms supplies from the Soviet bloc constituted a most significant
part of help to Israel. Ben Gurion, not inclined to give much credit to
the USSR concerning Jewish policy, revealed later that the arms pur-
chased in Czechoslovakia had "saved the young state of Israel."[38]
Czechoslovak arms would never have reached Israel without prior
agreement between the Czechoslovak communists and military leaders and Foreign Minister Vyshinsky. The first Czechoslovak shipments
arrived in Palestine in March 1948. When Israel proclaimed its independence, it did not yet possess a single plane! Ben Gurion's diaries
are an eloquent testimony to the importance of the dispatch of planes
and tanks from Eastern Europe to Israel at the very birth of the state.

It is ironic that U. S. Ambassador Laurence Steinhardt officially
appealed to the Czechoslovak government to stop arms delivery to
Israel! Yet in December 1949 the U. S. State Department was aware
that Czechoslovak arms by making devious detours were still reaching Israel. In early December 1949 the U. S. chargé d'affaires James
Penfield reported, however, to Washington a "radical restructuring"
of Czechoslovak aid and saw therein a "new turn in overall Soviet
policy."[39] Soviet motives in extending aid to Israel during a crucial
period, after its coming into existence, were of course not selfless. The
USSR pursued its own strategic and political interests in the Mideast.
Despite the cherished communist thesis that Jewish emigration was
ideologically necessary only for Jews from capitalist states, the encouragement of young Jews to emigrate from Eastern Europe and to
participate in the struggle for Israel's independence as well as arms
deliveries to Israel were of immeasurable help for the young state at
a critical moment. For a brief period the USSR tried to demonstrate
friendship to Israel and to win the sympathy, if not gratitude, of
Western Jewry.

Soviet postwar support for Palestine's Jewry and for the creation of a Jewish state and the consolidation of Zionism did not wait for the actual establishment of the Israeli state. Against those who raised doubts about the wisdom, justice, and viability of the U. N. partition resolution of November 1947, the Soviets gave support to the new state to help it withstand the military onslaught by numerous Arab states. The Russian press and radio adopted a sympathetic attitude toward Israel and identified with it. Arab armies were portrayed as aggressors. The Cominform journal *For a Lasting Peace, for People's Democracy* pointed out that "five British–controlled Arab states" had declared war on Israel and reminded the Soviet public of the participation of British officers in the Arab invading armies. It accused the Egyptian command of ordering its troops "to exterminate the Jewish civilian population on their way."[40] When in May 1948 the Egyptian delegate in the Security Council declared that the Egyptian and Arab intervention in Palestine was designed only to restore order, the Ukrainian delegate V. R. Tarasenko countered that according to the rules of the international community each government had the right to restore order "only in its own country,"[41] a point of view which Gromyko seconded on May 20 Andrei Gromyko also voiced reservations about the appointment of Swedish Count Folke Bernadotte as U. N. mediator, disputing that he had greater authority than the Security Council in which all the Great Powers had the veto power. The Soviets later accused Count Bernadotte of ignoring the partition resolution. The Soviet delegation tried by all means to exonerate Israel from any blame for "the fate of the Arab refugees"[42] and rather placed blame on British strategists and U. S. oil companies for having sacrificed "the tranquility of half a million Arabs who have been forced to leave their homes as a result of hostilities instigated from abroad." The Soviet position on Arab refugees was virtually identical with that taken on August 19 by the Israeli spokesman Abba Eban in the Security Council.

Beginning in late summer and fall of 1948, the Soviet media attitude toward Israel underwent notable changes. Less coverage of occurrences in Palestine aside, the identity of the Soviet and the Israeli points of view gradually vanished. The critical, pejorative meaning of the term "Zionist," which since Gromyko's May 19, 1947 address in the U. N. General Assembly had disappeared from the Soviet press and other media, made a return appearance. Just as the Soviet press began to distinguish between "Arab reactionaries" and the anti–imperialist, national–liberation movement of the Arab peoples, it made a similar distinction between the interests of the Zionist bourgeoisie looking toward London and Washington and the "democratically–minded mass" of the Jewish people in the Middle East—first indications of a Soviet change of attitude and leaning toward neutralism and even toward discord between the Soviet and Israeli points of view. Still in early September Golda Myerson (Meir) had friendly talks with both Foreign Minister V. Molotov and his deputy V. Zorin. The Soviets strongly supported Israel's application for U. N. membership as did also the U. S., which caused sharp criticism by Arab delegations.

Articles published in Moscow in December 1948, one in the prestigious *Voprosy istorii*,[43] pointed to the Anglo–Saxon powers' common anti–Soviet policy, their interest in and preparing of Palestine as a bridgehead for a new world war and their joint opposition to the national–liberation movement of the oppressed peoples of the Middle East. The Cold War began to cast its shadow on Soviet–Western relations and to influence a new Soviet orientation toward Israel.

Upon the occasion of Israel's first independence day anniversary, held by the Israeli delegation in Moscow, Soviet Foreign Minister Zorin summed up the positive developments of Israel during this period: the driving out of the British and their inflicting a military defeat on Arabs. On the other hand, Stalin's increasing domestic anti–Semitism split his entourage and had an unavoidably negative impact upon Soviet foreign policy toward Israel. Though, according to Vyshinsky, Israel was the most genuine democracy in the Mideast and played a major role in the Peace movement—which the Soviet Union championed—the USSR began to develop a positive attitude toward the colonial and semi–colonial world and simultaneously assumed an increasingly anti–Western, anti–imperialist and anti–Israeli policy.

The Soviet Union's policy in the Mideast was of course part and parcel of its global strategies and policies. Its temporary pro–Zionist stance in this region was partly based on the dim prospects of the Arabs becoming Soviet allies against the United Kingdom and the West in general. The Soviet change of attitude toward both Arabs and Zionists was due to a reevaluation of the Mideast prospects after the end of the Palestinian war early in 1949.

The USSR was especially apprehensive of the possible inclusion, of the Mideastern states in the Western military framework of alliances, of the U. S. penetration of the Arab world, and of the Anglo–American establishment of a glacis to be used against the Soviet Union. In 1950 the USSR was exploring the possibility of rapprochement especially with Syria and Egypt. Some Arab voices were then raised suggesting that the Arab states turn toward the USSR, if the Western camp continued to refuse to render justice to the Arabs. the Tripartite Declaration by the U. S., Great Britain, and France of May 25, 1950, promising aid to any country which rejected aggression against any other state in the region, was sharply criticized in Moscow. The USSR feared the emergence of a Middle Eastern alliance, one linked with NATO. While the Western Powers wanted the Arab states to align themselves with the West and rejected neutralism on their part, Stalin, on the other hand, vigorously pursued the strengthening of the Peace Movement to counter Western ambitions and further Soviet policy goals. In Israel the Peace Movement showed special strength in the extreme Left and in Mapam, the left wing of the Israeli Labor party. Israel's "progressive" circles comprised several political groups, the Communists (the Maki), and the left–wing socialist Mapam. The Soviets were not unappreciative of the efforts of both, though they contemplated no favors toward them and no change of policy toward Soviet Jewry and of Mideast policy.

But Moscow became increasingly concerned about Israel's role in promoting strategic and military dependence on the U. S. and its alleged economic subservience to it. A *New Times* article, "Toady of the American Aggressors," castigated Israel[44] for its position on Korea, though Ben Gurion had not pledged the dispatch of Israeli soldiers to the Far East. The journal ignored his criticism of Moscow's policy toward Soviet Jews.

A lack of response on the part of Arab states toward Soviet attempts of rapprochement after 1949 is the more startling as the Soviets' growing domestic anti–Jewish and anti–Zionist propaganda became undeniable. Still, in this period the Soviets did not object to Israel's right to Jerusalem. In regard to Arab refugees they accused Britain, and only to a lesser extent the U. S., of creating this entire issue. Like the Israelis, they asserted that large numbers of Arabs had fled from their homes before the termination of the Mandate.

In December 1949 the Soviet journals reporting the establishment of UNRWA (U. N. Relief and Works Agency) condemned it as a foremost means for further penetration by Anglo–American imperialism. Apparently aware of its limitations of power in the Middle East, the USSR demonstrated great caution in taking specific positions and rather tended to be non–committal and evasive on several issues. During the last years of Stalin's rule the Soviet Union followed a policy of wariness and ambivalence towards both Arabs and Israelis. It took a negative position toward Western views and stands on the Mideast. It was prepared to frustrate them, but not ready to follow a clear–cut policy. This was a reflection of Stalin's cautious policy and

of his awareness of the Soviets' impotence in the Mideast, in contrast
to its strong stand in Europe and its determination in the Far East.

Birobidzhan after World War II. The Crimean Affair

The Birobidzhan project of settling Jews in the Far East had
from the start evoked different responses from Soviet Jews. It must
have been puzzling to them that the plan emerged after considerable
investment of moneys and effort had been made in the Crimea and
elsewhere in the Ukraine. On the other hand, the pledge in 1934,
short-lived as it turned out to be, to establish an autonomous Jewish
Republic in Birobidzhan, aroused, despite natural suspicions as to the
Soviets' ultimate purposes, genuine hopes among Jews in the USSR
and even abroad. These expectations were somewhat abated by fears
that the shift of Jewish population to the Far East, thousands of
kilometers from the main centers of Russian Jews in Europe, might
turn out not being a voluntary one. Toward the end of his reign,
Stalin after all entertained the idea of a forcible transplantation of
Soviet Jewry to Asia. Can it be seriously held that some ideas along
this line were completely absent from his mind in the mid- or late
1930s?

In the immediate postwar period, in January 1946, the Council
of Commissars of the RSFSR and that of the entire USSR passed
official resolutions in behalf of Jewish settlement in Birobidzhan. The
reasons for the renewed Soviet interest in the project were identical
with their motives in the 1930s. An additional consideration, however,
influencing the Soviet decision, was the problem of the future of Polish
Jews who during the war had found refuge in the Soviet Union. Many
of them later returned to Poland. With the rise of postwar anti-
Semitism there they emigrated, largely to Israel.

Between 1946–49, 6,326 Jews arrived in Birobidzhan.[45] Yet the
entire Soviet atmosphere, having become satiated with anti-Jewish
hostility, worked at cross purposes with the Party's plan for the development of Birobidzhan. The 1959 census in that territory showed
only 14,269 Jews out of a total population of 162,856 inhabitants or
a mere 8.8 percent. Though for years Yiddish culture was allegedly
fostered in Birobidzhan, between 1932 and 1948 less than a dozen
Yiddish booklets were printed there. Yet about 40 percent of the
Jewish settlers had given Yiddish as their mother tongue. For a few
years a paper and until 1948 a Yiddish theater survived. In 1947
a synagogue was erected which a few years later burned down. A
cantor and a ritual slaughter served the religious needs of the Jewish
settlers.

According to an interview of Krushchev with the correspondent of the Parisian *Figaro*,[46] the Birobidzhan project failed because Jews were incapable of working collectively: they were individuals and not inclined to engage in agricultural work. In reality, they had scored successes in agricultural undertakings in other parts of Russia. Basic reasons for the failure in the Far East were, the harsh climate aside, the contradictions of Soviet policy concerning the Jews, the perennial mixture of hostility, autocracy, at best paternalism, and the lack of genuine governmental support. The entire project, politically motivated, was imposed on the Jews without eliciting their genuine and spontaneous approval. It was designed to make them forget Jerusalem and Zionism. In the meantime, the growing anti-Semitism in the USSR undermined the confidence of the Jews in Soviet projects and intentions.

Soon after the establishment of the Soviet regime and especially after the Civil War, both the government and Jewish organizations had put forward various ideas for settling Jews on the land.[47] These plans had caused widespread debates between the authorities as well as Soviet Jews. Both of course were motivated by a varied complex of ideological, economic, social, and political ideas and by the apparent need to develop a counterplan to Zionist agrarization and colonization in Palestine. Despite the later hostile Soviet attitude to America and Jews, the Soviets first did not object to philanthropic assistance by overseas Jewish organizations. After the establishment of Komzet (the Committee for Rural Placement of Jewish Toilers) it was attached to the Presidum of the Council of Nationalities.

One of the most prominent Jewish settlement schemes in the 1920s had been the Crimean project.[48] Yuri Larin, a leading Jewish Communist, argued that the Crimea had enough land for everybody. Another Jewish Communist, M. Litvakov, enthusiastically embraced the project by saying: "The Crimea is our Palestine . . . for surely you can't compare the Jordan to the Dnjepr." He also claimed to know that "our" Moslems (the Crimean Tartars), unlike their Palestinian co-religionists, did not oppose Jewish settlement—an assessment which turned out to be quite false. Mikhail Kalinin, as pointed out, had strongly supported this agricultural settlement project. Though the rival Birobidzhan plan was commenced in 1928, the activities in regard to the Crimea continued in the 1930s. In 1928 Komzet accepted a five-year plan which provided for the settlement of 15,000 families in the Crimea and of 12,000 families in Birobidzhan. Two years later both regions were destined again for new Jewish settlement. As late as 1937 the Soviets decided on a new plan to settle 500 Jewish families in Crimean collective farms. But between 1933 and 1939 the number of Jewish farmers in the Crimea declined, with the next generation leaving for the towns for work or study. Among the reasons for the ultimate failure of the settlement movement in the Crimea were, similar to the failure in Birobidzhan, the absence of a genuine Soviet Jewish national renaissance, the lack of national content of Soviet cultural autonomy, and the lack of support by the authorities. To it must be added the growing resistance of the Crimean Tartars and others, who accused the CPSU of giving the best land to the Jews.

Actually, large parts of the Crimean peninsula had poor soil and an inhospitable climate and were widely devastated as a consequence of damages wreaked by the fighting during World War II. To some Jews the postwar settlement in the Crimea still appealed as a kind of rehabilitation and compensation for their past sufferings. To the Communists the Crimean settlement was a partial retreat from their activities in Birobidzhan, which the authorities themselves increasingly acknowledged as a failure.

But the Crimean project had also turned out to be an illusion. With the start of the anti–Jewish campaign in 1948 accusations of disloyalty and outright treason were levelled at the Jews regarding the alleged planned secession of the Crimea from the USSR as a Zionist state.

In the trial against the "twenty–five" in Moscow in July 1952, one of the accusations hurled at the defendants was the fantastic charge that they had plotted to sever the Crimea from the Soviet Union and to create there a bourgeois–Zionist republic, to serve as an American imperialist springboard for waging war against the Soviet Union. Clearly it was a hair–brained scheme rooted in the Soviet paranoia of the Cold War. The U. S. was alleged to have embraced this scheme while the USSR was still her wartime ally. Mikhoels and Feffer, leaders of the JAC during their wartime touring of the U. S., had met with representatives of the American Joint Distribution Committee (JDC) and had already laid the groundwork for their anti–Soviet conspiracy! In 1956, Krushchev, while receiving a visiting delegation of the Canadian Progressive Labor Party (communist), had stated that he was "in agreement with Stalin that the Crimea," depopulated at the time in consequence of the war against Germany, "shall not become a Jewish settlement center, since in the event of war it would be turned into an American base against the Soviet Union.[49] Actually, the Soviet Union had inherited a large number of Jewish settlements in the south and west, many of whose inhabitants claimed that their ancestors had settled there centuries ago. These settlements had prospered long before Zionism had become a significant political movement. The U. S. had never developed an interest in the Crimea.

Toward Cultural "Genocide"

It became clear in late 1948 that the attack against Yiddish culture was a massive one and that it had been planned to the last detail to liquidate Jewish culture in the Soviet Union in all its aspects. Among the papers closed down were *Aynikeit*, the organ of the JAC which had appeared three times weekly since February 1945. The *Emes* Moscow publishing house was also closed down. The bimonthly *Heimland* and the Kiev *Shtern*, both having started their publications in 1947, were discontinued in 1948. The latter journals were accused of having "fostered nationalistic tendencies and small-town psychology" and having gone "so far as to presume to draw a comparison between Soviet Jews and the Jews abroad."[50] The only Yiddish paper which was permitted to continue publication was the *Birobidzhaner Shtern*, apparently to demonstrate that Jewish culture was not completely destroyed. But after 1948 the paper was printed only in one thousand copies for the entire country, usually ran only to two pages, and was hardly available outside Birobidzhan. Most importantly, it could not be considered a paper of Jewish content and interest. When the *Emes* publishing house and the foregoing journals were shut down, the Jewish type was completely destroyed.

While old publications were suppressed and no new ones permitted, old Yiddish books were removed from public access. Jewish libraries were shut down. Other public libraries removed Jewish books entirely. Some books were withdrawn to a special section (Spetsodel) which was not accessible to the reading public. Thus, about twenty years after banning Hebrew literature Yiddish literature suffered the same fate. The campaign against Jewish culture was thus brought to a "victorious" end, showing the truly totalitarian and anti–Jewish character of the regime. Schools too became the target of the Soviets' destructive cultural struggle against Russian Jewry. In 1949 the last two Jewish educational institutions, schools in Vilna and Kovno (Kaunas), and all Jewish professional theaters in major Russian cities as well as in Birobidzhan were closed. In January of the same year, the Department of Jewish Culture of the Ukrainian Academy of Sciences in Kiev was also shut down. The climate of Soviet opinion grew so inhospitable and beset with fears that owners of Yiddish books or of any book on Jewish topics discarded or burned them to prevent the authorities from accusing their owners of engaging in nationalistic pursuits!

The vicious Soviet campaign against Yiddish culture was unleashed not only against institutions, journals, books, theaters, etc., but also against authors who contributed to the papers and wrote for the theater, and directors who staged the plays. The campaign's purpose was plain and simple: it was to "decapitate"[51] the creative Yiddish intelligentsia. This campaign was unique in its ruthlessness even in the annals of Soviet "cultural" history.

The Soviets' cultural and physical annihilation of the intellectual elite of Jewish society did not stop even at the borders of Birobidzhan, though the latter had been singled out by them for the flourishing of Jewish culture. By the end of World War II there lived about 25,000 Jews in Birobidzhan, approximately one–fourth of the entire population of the region. Not long after the war, the anti–Jewish campaign flooded also Birobidzhan. The Kaganovich theater, the *Birobidzhan* magazine, and the Jewish publishing house were all shut down. The Sholem Aleichem Library which in early 1948 had enclosed about 130,000 volumes, including works in Hebrew, was simply destroyed; some books were enclosed in the library's vaults. What remained accessible were, among other books, Stalin's works translated into Yiddish and other communist literature.

Among the victims of the purge in Birobidzhan were also numerous writers, artists, and communal leaders. Some of them were sentenced to death, but their sentences were commuted. The defendants were accused of having engaged in nationalistic activities, of having cultivated Jewish endeavors in an area with a largely non–Jewish population, and of having resorted to espionage activities. While in the 1930s Jews had been charged with spying for Japanese imperialism, in the 1950s leading Jews were accused of "plotting" with and spying in behalf of Washington. Thus the Jews of the region—who continued to receive food and clothing parcels from the U. S.—were considered agents of America. Migration to this area from any part of the Soviet Union was therefore stopped. Yiddish ceased to be a language used by the local administration and the legal status of the "Jewish Autonomous Province" was all but forgotten. Within the decade after the start of the anti–Jewish campaign the Jewish population of Birobidzhan declined by more than half, sinking to about 14,269 people, according to the census of 1959. Many of the Jews who left the area moved to the larger cities in the Northeast such as Khabarovsk.

The Soviets, however, did not abolish outright the "Autonomous Jewish Province." Propaganda needs, constitutional considerations, the hesitation to admit failure, all contributed to preserving the fiction of the autonomous status of the Jewish "province." But the accusations against leading Jews in the region left a trail of shattered existences and hopes. Prominent Jews, writers, artists, and communal leaders had been charged with chauvinistic tendencies, with nationalistic egocentricity, and with being disinterested in the Soviet brotherhood of nationalities. Actually, Jews of the province had complained about rising anti–Semitism. This very accusation, directed against Soviet officials, was considered "proof" of their ideological and practical betrayal of the Soviet Union and its interests.

The battle to erase Jewish history and culture from the memory of Jews and gentiles extended to all Soviet publications, including Soviet encyclopedias. The editors of the *Soviet Encyclopedia* showed an increasingly contemptuous attitude toward Jews in the USSR and toward Jewish history, culture, literature, and religion. The second edition of the *Encyclopedia* listed in all its fifty volumes not a single Yiddish writer. Among Jewish writers, who were totally ignored and omitted, were for instance Scholem Asch, Achad Haam, as well as the Jewish historians H. Graetz and S. M. Dubnow.

In the field of politics and socialism numerous distinguished names were completely omitted, such as Aaron Liberman, one of the fathers of Jewish socialism, Maxim Vinover, one of the leaders of the Russian Constitutional Democratic Party, Ber Borochov, prominent theoretician of Socialist Zionism, and numerous others. Not a line was dedicated to Theodor Herzl, the founder of political Zionism. Chaim Weizmann, the readers were told, had joined "the reactionary, nationalist–bourgeois movement, Zionism" and had become a tool of British, later of American imperialism.[52] The noted Hebrew poet Chaim N. Bialik always remained "a bourgeois nationalist and cosmopolite." The Austrian socialist leader Victor Adler, was, in contrast to the first edition of the *Soviet Encyclopedia*, painted in a very critical manner. It kept completely silent about his Jewish descent. His son Friedrich Adler, long a hero of Communists after assassinating during World War I Count Stürgkh, Austria's Premier, was now accused of being an "agent" of U. S. imperialism and declared guilty of "cosmopolitanism"—probably because after World War II he opposed Austria's independence. A former member of the American Communist Party, Howard Fast, long admired by the Soviets, was excised from the *Encyclopaedic Dictionary*, Vol. I (1953), apparently because his books dealt to a large extent with Jewish subjects. He himself denounced the new Soviet treatment of Jews as an attempt to rob them of their past. Indeed, the Soviet attempt to diminish the image of Jews and even to eradicate them from the pages of world history had become indisputable.

The accusations against the Soviet Jews differ significantly from those levelled against the Kalmyks, Balkars, Chechens, and Ingushis–Caucasian peoples ejected by Stalin in the midst of World War II. These peoples were collectively punished for alleged traitorous acts by some of their members. The treatment accorded to the Jews in the postwar period had no connection with war and an alleged traitorous role by the Jews. It was rather a "prophylactic punitive campaign."[53] Undertaken with the intent of preventing a "foreseeable" crime, this "punishment" was in accordance with the twisted Stalinist logic of "looking ahead." This policy was designed to bring about the liquidation of Jewish culture, and was in complete disregard of the contribution of Jews to Russian achievements and to world civilization, not to mention of elementary justice. It worked not only against contemporary Jews, but turned Jewish history upside down.

For a considerable length of time, Soviet authorities treated some Jewish sects and dialects more liberally than the Jewish Ashkenazi communities. Among those less discriminated were the Bokharan, the mountain Jews, the Georgian Jews, and the Krimchaks (indigenous Crimean Jews). Far removed from the greater Jewish centers in the USSR, they were held to be less influenced by adverse modern trends affecting the bulk of Soviet Jews.

In the early Soviet period the CPSU had proudly pointed not only to the encouragement of proletarian Yiddish literature, but had also drawn attention to the development of a number of languages or dialects such as the Jewish–Tadzhik language, a language existing among Oriental Jews in the USSR, and the Tati–Jewish language or "Mountain Yiddish," as referred to by the Soviets. The latter was an ancient Persian dialect, spoken mainly by Jews in the mountain regions of the northern Caucasus. Considering Soviet Jewish policy in general, this encouragement of some Jewish dialects or local languages was not motivated by Soviet support for Jewish culture and languages, but had the goal of splitting the unity of Jewish language and culture.

After Stalin's death Soviet spokesmen, once again ignoring the special discrimination, hardships, and total cultural liquidation which had befallen Soviet Jews, pointed to the victims of other nationality groups who had suffered at the hands of "Beria's gang" and to violations of "socialist legality." Fear of impending national and individual tragedy had haunted many of the Jewish writers who actually became victims of the mad persecution. On the other hand, only a month before tragedy struck, the acting editor of *Aynikeit* tried to assure its readers that anti–Semitism had been totally eradicated in the USSR,[54] that equality was undisputed, and that national brotherhood flourished in the Soviet Union as nowhere else in the world!

The Nazi Holocaust and Soviet Silence

The Soviets' long silence about the Holocaust and Jewish suffering in Russia during the war was as shocking as it was puzzling.

There can be no question about the sacrifices and hardships suffered by all Soviet nationalities during that time. Yet the deepest roots of the strange reaction of the Soviet peoples to the government's suppression of Jewish wartime experiences are two–fold: the traditional Jew–hatred of Russians, Ukrainians, Byelorussians, Baltic peoples, and others, which gripped even the CPSU, and the complicity of Soviet citizens in the Nazi slaughter. There was also the fear of Stalin and the Party leaders of appearing to their peoples as the ally, friend, and protector of the Jews. Hitler's diabolical propaganda that all Jews were Bolsheviks and all Bolsheviks Jews, had spread fear among the Kremlin leaders. As far as Soviet Jews were concerned, Lenin's "internationalism" and his "solidarity" with the Jewish working class were quickly drowned in the stormy sea of Russian Jew–hatred. The Soviets thus downplayed the special suffering of the Jews, that Nazis had singled them out as a special target for genocide. They have displayed indifference and lack of compassion toward Jewish martyrdom. In the postwar era the Communists have encouraged anti–Zionist, anti–religious and generally anti–Jewish propaganda to a shameful extent. They have generally refused to extend recognition to their Jewish fellow–citizens who were mass–murdered by the Nazis on Russian soil, and to erect monuments to perpetuate their memory. In some localities they erased inscriptions in their honor. During the Krushchev era few trials were conducted against Nazi criminals or against Russians, Ukrainians, Byelorussians, or members of Baltic nationalities who had taken part in the extermination of Jews. The Soviets have deliberately kept silent about the heroism of Jewish soldiers and partisans who valiantly struggled against the Nazis. Even when listing thousands of unquestionably Jewish names, they have consistently refused to identify their national and religious origins.

Soviet Reversal about Zionism. Against Jewish Intellectuals and Western Imperialism

The hopes of Soviet Jewry for an improvement of their situation had risen during World War II, but had soon been dashed. The unexpected and, in view of past opposition, puzzling Soviet support in the U. N. for the creation of the state of Israel turned out to be transitory. After the proclamation of the new state, an article by Ilya Ehrenburg, repeating Lenin's and Stalin's earlier critical points of view, asserted that the Jews had no right to call themselves a nation. Even though Israel now existed and Jews had obtained, according to Communist doctrine, the much needed territorial base, admittedly one beyond Soviet borders, they were allegedly still unlike any other nation. Israel was not truly independent. It merely showed the encroachment of

Anglo–American capitalism in the Mideast—a phenomenon which the Soviets apparently had not discovered earlier. Israeli "ruling classes" were ready to betray their own interests to foreign interests for the sake of the dollar. "Jewish working people" in the USSR were like all other working people "strongly attached to the soil" and "must look to the Soviet Union which alone leads mankind towards a better future." This was a clear warning to Soviet Jews on occasion of the visit of the Israeli Ambassador Golda Meir to Moscow. The very warm reception of Golda Meir by Russian Jews had shocked the Kremlin leaders. They had to demonstrate that Zionism was still a forbidden fruit and that the idea of a Zionist movement in the USSR was unacceptable. Moscow's support of Israel for a fleeting moment in the U. N. notwithstanding, the Soviets objected to Russian Jewish ties with their kinsfolk either in Israel or the U. S.

In 1948 the secret police arrested the most prominent Jewish officials in Party and government and the most widely known Jewish writers, poets, and musicians. According to one student of Soviet Jewry, "the entire elite was eliminated, leaving the Jewish minority leaderless and helpless."[55] Of the Jewish intellectuals who were arrested 217 were writers and poets, 108 actors, 87 artists, and 19 musicians. The majority of these people perished in concentration camps. After spending several years in such camps, they were secretly tried and on August 12, 1952 executed. Years later the government rehabilitated them posthumously, officially apologized to their widows, and granted them a state pension.

A single person only, Lana Shtern, who was tried together with 24 writers, had escaped the firing squad. Among those executed were Itzig Feffer, a few writers with worldwide acclaim for their contribution to Yiddish literature, and other well known Jewish personalities. Feffer was tortured, broke down, and "confessed." The accused individuals had been charged with being "nationalistic, bourgeois Zionists" and , worse, "agents of American imperialism." The latter accusations—Zionism and being tools of American imperialism—were repeated *ad nauseam* and became standard practice in Soviet printed propaganda, on radio, and television.

The widow of the Jewish writer, Moshe Broderson, herself of Polish origin, revealed subsequently[56] in a series of articles that in their secret trial which lasted from July 11–18, 1952, the defendants showed obvious signs of having been subjected to torture. She accused the Soviet Union of Writers, particularly Konstantin Simonov, of complicity in fabricating the charges against them.

Accusations of having engaged in nationalist endeavors were nothing new in the Soviet Union. Such charges had been frequently levelled against members of other national minorities, including Ukrainian and Byelorussian writers. But Colonel Feffer and his associates were charged with conspiring "rebellion and dismemberment of the Soviet state." At the Twentieth Party Congress in 1956 Krushchev revealed that the accused were allegedly "plotting against the integrity" of the Soviet state. The foregoing Jewish writers were found guilty and hanged.[57] Posthumously, however, their honor and prestige was restored and their work published or republished, but ever since the authorities have refused to give full details of the trial.

Lazar Kaganovich was the only member of the Jewish Anti-Fascist Committee who survived. He had long been a member of Stalin's inner circle in the Kremlin. Ilya Ehrenburg, himself also of Jewish descent and popular wartime correspondent, appears to have played a dubious role in this affair.[58] Feffer had sharply opposed Ehrenburg, particularly his attacks on the denigration of Israel. A valuable Soviet propagandist, Ehrenburg's work, however, was greatly appreciated by Stalin. After the war he still pleased the Vozhd for supporting the Russian Jews' complete assimilation and his attacks on Zionism, while at the same time maintaining numerous useful contacts in the West. But even Ehrenburg felt threatened by his being "Jewish" and for a time stopped writing for the Soviet press altogether. In a letter to Stalin he dared pleading for a clarification of his own labile status.[59]

"The Doctors' Plot" and Stalin's Expulsion Scheme

Stalin's last years and months were marked by anti-Jewish plots the execution of which was only prevented by his timely death. Foremost among Stalin's monstrous schemes was the doctors' plot. On January 13, 1953, Tass, the official Soviet News Agency, reported that the night before the MVD had arrested a group of nine physicians who had plotted to kill high-placed Soviet leaders.[60] Six of them were Jews, as their names clearly indicated. The names of the non-Jewish doctors were not given! Tass also claimed that some prominent officials in the government and administration—such as A. Zhdanov and A. Shcherbakov, a colonel in the Red Army—had already become victims of these despicable schemes. The plot was discovered by a woman doctor Lidya Timashuk who had worked with the physicians thus charged in Moscow hospitals. As Krushchev later disclosed, Timashuk was an agent of the MVD. At the time *Pravda* hailed her as a patriot and as a *Russian* woman; she was soon to receive the order of Lenin. The authorities charged that the plotters had acted at the express instructions of "Jewish, American as well as British imperialist forces." *Pravda* informed its readers about the doctors who were linked with the international Jewish bourgeoisie, especially the American Joint Distribution Committee (Joint). The latter were established, they claimed, by U. S. intelligence and other subversive foreign organizations, all being part of a world Zionist conspiracy.

The "saboteur–doctors" were accused of cutting short the lives of active public servants of the Soviet Union. The group was charged with having sought to "undermine the health of leading Soviet military personnel" and to conduct espionage, terrorist and other subversive work in socialist countries, including the Soviet Union. The arrested individuals had received orders "to wipe out leading cadres of the USSR."

On the same day, January 13, *Pravda* printed the Tass report about "Foul Spies and Murders in the Mask of Doctors and Professors," "depraved bourgeois nationalists," professed spies of the Joint. The exposure of the "band of poisoner–doctors" was "a blow at the international Zionist organization."[61]

> Feverishly preparing for a new world war, they were sending more and more of their spies into the USSR and the people's democracies, trying to succeed where the Hitlerites failed—trying to create a subversive Fifth Column.

Pravda appealed for greater vigilance on the part of the Soviet people and blamed the remnants of bourgeois ideology and "living persons, secret enemies of our people" as well as the agencies of State Security which had not discovered "the doctors' wrecking, terrorist organization of the time."

At the end of January 1953 the weekly *Novoya Vremya* published an article "Zionist Agents of the American Secret Service."[62] Zionism was pictured as the enemy, a close comrade–in–arms of "cosmopolitanism." Following the official communiqués in *Pravda* and *Izvestia* on the doctors' plot, many other articles in the Soviet press were urging Soviet citizens to avoid being gullible and to be on the alert. The anti–Semitic campaign lasted about three months during which time rumors of the alleged plot were kept alive. The humor magazine *Krokodil* spoke of the "adepts of the Zionist Kahal" and its "breed of outcasts."[63] The rumor of a worldwide Jewish anti–Soviet plot reached frenzied heights. Only Stalin's death brought the accusations to an abrupt end.

The plot concocted only two months before Stalin's death was unquestionably the most sinister scheme against the Jewish physicians allegedly involved in the affair. Beyond it, it threatened to blacken the reputation and patriotism of Soviet Jews in general and to cast doubts about their place in Soviet society.

In an editorial of January 13, *Meditsinsky rabotnik* enlarged upon *Pravda's* denunciation of Zionism of the same day, calling upon the authorities "to bring murderer–doctors to strict account." The Joint, "this international Jewish Zionist organization, which represents nothing but a gang of terrorists and murderers, has now appeared before the whole world in all its horrifying nakedness." [64] It represented "our homeland's enemies." On January 27 the same journal welcomed the exposure of a group of terrorists who operated "in the guise of professors and doctors;" it focussed upon other criminals, one of whom, M. Z. Izrailist, was not even a doctor! On February 13, in answer to a reader's questions the journal continued pillorying "the Zionist agency of the dollar," the *Joint.* It was "not only savage hatred of everything progressive, democratic, and socialist" which united "numerous bourgeois nationalist Jewish organizations in cringing to the dollar." "The most important basis of such unification is the reactionary bourgeois nationalist movement, Zionism." There followed several paragraphs of a brief, completely distorted "history" of Zionism and its "true bestial face" and a reminder of the recent "criminal act of the fascist–like Zionist bands" against the Soviet Legation in Tel–Aviv.

More or less coincidental with the doctors' plot was the deterioration of Soviet–Israeli relations. Early in February 1953 *Pravda* and *Isvestia* had reported a bomb explosion on the premises of the Soviet Legation in Israel, a "vile crime" which allegedly had been preceded by an "unbridled slanderous campaign against the Soviet Union" with the participation of Israeli officials.[65] These officers, the journal asserted, had kindled hatred of the Soviet government and had incited hostile acts against the USSR. Taking advantage of the incident, the Soviet government used it to break off relations with Israel. The Soviet press turned thus from the domestic doctors' plot to attack against Israel and Zionism abroad and claimed that even Soviet borders were threatened.

On February 13, 1953, *Pravda Ukrainy* reprinted an article on Soviet Transcarpathia claiming that American intelligence had for many years attempted to plant agents in this region, to transform it "into a military springboard against the Soviet Union" and had used the Joint and local Zionist organizations to penetrate it and carry out its sinister program.[66] Even long past history was rewritten by the Ukrainian paper. In 1938 Hitler had selected Austria as a target, and with the assistance of the American–British imperialists who in turn had used Zionist organizations! Hitler thus had the support of Zionist leaders and their followers. Little surprise that Trotskyites too had found a "common language with the Zionists"!

On February 17, O. Prudkov in *Literaturnaya gazeta* continued the assault against Israel claiming that the speeches of its rulers with regard to the Soviet Union bore "a clearly provocational character," but they cringed before American imperialism.[67] By faithfully serving the American government, "they help to unleash a new world war."

A few Russian leaders such as the rigid Stalinist theoretician K. Mikhail Suslov called the doctors "the most despicable creatures."[68] The men surrounding Stalin may have fed at various times his suspicions against Jews; they were now anxious to avoid any defense of the Jews, anything which might threaten their own political and physical survival. Nothing was easier in the totalitarian Soviet environment than to place the label of "traitor" and "enemy" on any group, whether they were Jews or pursued divergent political lines. The members of the Politburo who feared for their own positions and their very lives, were hesitant to cross Stalin's path. They could not forget the purges of the late 1930s when he had been prosecutor, judge, and jury in one.

The Russian Jews themselves were terror–stricken, feeling as if Hitler's soldiery were once again at the gates of Moscow. The "doctors' plot," some analysts held, was designed as a "final solution," a Russian "solution" of the Jewish question, transporting them to Asia. Was Stalin in full control of all his mental capacities because of his shocking extremism and incredible vagaries?

That Jews could be plotting the death of Communist and East European leaders, was not an entirely new and unprecedented accusation. In 1952, in neighboring Czechoslovakia, Rudolf Slantsky, General Secretary of the Czechoslovak Communist Party and a Jew by descent, was—with twelve others, ten of them Jews—hanged in the Prankrac prison in Prague. They had been accused of having jointly with a Freemason physician schemed to shorten the life of President Klement Gottwald. In the following trial they were charged with having been "spies, traitors, and embezzlers" and "Zionist agents."[69] After the war, Russian anti–Semitism had been partly voluntarily copied by the satellites, partly forced upon them, and had ultimately ricochetted in more anti–Jewish measures in the USSR. Anti–Semitism had travelled from the East westward and, thus reinforced, had returned to the Russian homeland. Instead of internationalism and brotherhood, international anti–Semitism and the international of anti–Zionism had come to luxuriate in the Soviet Union.

In his famous anti–Stalin oration at the Twentieth Party Congress on February 24 and 25, 1956, Krushchev disclosed that Stalin himself had given personal advice on how to conduct the interrogation of the accused and how to obtain admission of the alleged crimes. To intimidate even members of the Politburo, he had bluntly warned against lack of vigilance.

As far as Soviet Jews were concerned, the atmosphere was saturated with poisonous fumes. Jews were dismissed from their jobs without any reason being given. Some marriages broke up as a result of the pressures exerted upon the gentile party. Differently from tsarist times, when some prominent Russian intellectuals spoke out against the pogroms, Soviet intellectuals were cowed into silence by the very intensity of the hate propaganda which spread throughout the country. In their despair, some Jews committed suicide. Many others were preparing a suitcase or bundle in case of sudden arrest or deportation. The announcement of a plot of doctors–murderers having been discovered was reported by the *New York Times* correspondent from Moscow thus: "It chilled my blood."

Plans for deportation were apparently drawn up by the MGB agencies and in Stalin's personal office. Several large–scale factories passed resolutions favoring eviction of the Jews. An appeal to the Jewish people, that several distinguished scientists and cultural leaders of Jewish nationality were forced to sign, "requesting resettlement," was promptly prepared. In several districts of Kazakhstan barracks for Jews were hurriedly erected. Diplomatic observers in the Soviet Union had long been convinced that the "doctors' plot" was a complete fraud, worked out to the last infamous detail to besmirch Russian Jews and to offer to Stalin and his henchmen an excuse for staging a mass expulsion of Jews to Siberia and the Far East. Of course, other minorities, as mentioned, had been brutally expelled from their homes during World War II, prompted by a paranoic fear that the Volga Germans, the Crimean Tartars, and various Caucasian peoples were betraying the Russian "motherland" to the Nazi invaders and making common cause with them. But in 1953 no war psychosis gripped the Russian people. Soviet Jews, only the day before the target of Nazi assassins, had, in Stalin's distorted vision, in an unbelievable turn–about, become the new suspects. "Zionists" were proclaimed to be spies and traitors and the chief enemy!

Stalin seems to have presented the deportation plan to the Presidium of the Central Committee.[70] When at a meeting held at the end of February 1953 the scheme was disclosed to it, some members of long standing raised questions which revealed the depth of their concern over the unprecedented scope of the anti–Jewish measures contemplated and their clearly punitive character. Some of the members of the Presidium may have been fearful of their negative impact on Soviet life, its economy, and nationality policy and on foreign relations, and their likely adverse consequences for communist propaganda. Unquestionably, the reaction of the world to Hitler's atrocities, the memory of the early Bolshevik tradition of equality and internationalism, as well as fear for their own personal safety may have motivated them. Of those who raised substantive or mere technical questions—all revealing their inner doubts—were Kaganovich, himself a Jew, Mikoyan, Krushchev, and Marshal Voroshilov. Kaganovich was reported to have thrown his Party card upon the table and having said: "If you deport Jews, you must also send me to the concentration camp."[71] According to a later conversation of Krushchev with members of the Polish C.P., it was due to his own resistance as well as that of other members of the Politburo, that the expulsion measure against Jews was cancelled.[72] Marshal Voroshilov, married to a Jewish woman, reportedly called the plan "terrible" and dared recalling the Hitler phenomenon. Stalin supposedly became enraged and suffered a stroke from which he was never to recover. He died a few days later. If the foregoing accounts are accurate, Stalin himself had become a victim of his own anti–Semitic obsession.[73] After having produced "eighty–two days of anxiety," the official annulment of the doctors' libel came on April 4. But the fear that had seized Soviet Jews was never quite forgotten, having become embedded in their Soviet experience. The list of persons exonerated did not include two professors, M. B. Kogar and Y. G. Ettinger, who apparently died in prison, most likely victims of torture.

The "doctors' plot" was no novelty in Russian history. It recalls the fifteenth century ruler Ivan III having killed Master Leon the Jew, his court physician, after accusing him of murdering his son. Soviet progress since the October Revolution could hardly be demonstrated by renewing accusations against Jewish doctors half a millennium after the foregoing event!

It was on April 3, after Stalin's death, that both *Pravda* and *Izvestia* first published a full retraction of the accusations against the Kremlin doctors. Both dailies disclosed that the charges against the arrested doctors were "false" and the documentary sources on which they were based were "without foundation."[74] The testimony of those arrested had been obtained by the officials of the investigatory department of the former Ministry of State Security through the use of "impermissible means of investigation," strictly forbidden under Soviet law. All those arrested had been "completely exonerated" of the charges against them of sabotage, terrorist activities and of espionage and had been freed from imprisonment. The physicians concerned were permitted to resume their practices and, with some exceptions, were given their former positions. The widows of all victims received an official apology. But to avoid further embarrassment to the authorities, they were warned not to discuss the affair with anyone. The police agent, Dr. Timashuk, who had made the false charges, was penalized by the withdrawal of the order of Lenin which she had received as award for her "patriotic" role as police informer. But even after the retraction of the vicious accusation against the Jewish physicians, Soviet public opinion was reluctant to accept the doctors' innocence. As Yevtushenko related in his *Precocious Autobiography*, "the general public by and large had believed in their guilt."[75]

According to the British author Max Hayward who lived in Moscow for two years during the darkest days of the Stalin regime, the fears of Soviet Jews on occasion of the doctors' plot and the rumored penalties were similar to those that had seized them during the days of the German occupation. Their anxiety exceeded that of people during the purges of the late 1930s. In those years well known individuals had been arrested, tried, and shot. This time suspicion fell upon all Jews. Such was the climate of opinion that, beginning in 1949, some Soviet Jews even tried to get rid of their passports which disclosed their nationality, though the loss of these documents carried no minor risks. The anti–Jewish and anti–Zionist campaign unleashed even protests by the Israeli government which, in view of past dependence on arms deliveries especially from Czechoslovakia, was compelled to pursue a cautious line. Yet in speaking for his government, Israel's foreign Minister Moshe Sharett sharply denounced the Moscow doctors's libel, comparing the accusations to medieval charges of Jews poisoning wells and murdering Christian children for ritual purposes. Even at the time of the Beilis trial in 1913, he recalled, the tsarist regime had not coerced the accused into confessing his "crime" and he had been able to defend himself with the help of the best Russian lawyers.

There seems to be ample evidence that Stalin in his last months plotted not against Jews alone. The Soviet regime has always needed internal "enemies" to divert the people's attention and criticism from its own faults and shortcomings. The very men closest to Stalin, his friends, confidants, members of the Politburo, became as Krushchev related in his "secret" speech at the Twentieth Party Congress, the targets of his insane suspicion and ruthless scheming. Stalin suspected Voroshilov of espionage for England and laid plans against Molotov and Mikoyan. He evidently wanted to lessen the power of the members of the Politburo, as its expansion from twelve members to twenty–five a few months before his death indicated.

Beria, a fellow Georgian, Director of the NKVD, had since 1938 quickly risen in the Stalinist hierarchy.[76] He played an important part in the anti–Jewish drama which unfolded in 1948 and thereafter. After the war he had concentrated in his hands the Ministry of the Interior (MVD) and that of State Security (MGB). By controlling numberless prisoners, he exerted further influence in regard to manpower and the development of the national economy. Stalin, though bestowing numerous honors and powers upon him, never trusted him fully. It appears that a dossier had been compiled on Beria by Mikhail Ryumin and Semyon Ignatiev of State Security. When the "doctors' plot" was announced in January 1953, this Ministry was already controlled by these two men who accused Beria in connection with the doctors' plot of lack of vigilance.

Beria who may have had a hand in sending a Jewish delegation— Mikhoels and Feffer—to the U. S. during the war was rumored to have been partly of Jewish extraction, and allegedly to have shown favoritism to Jews; he was also accused of encouraging Jewish nationalism. It is almost impossible to establish the truth, if any, in these charges, since Politburo members, increasingly afraid of Beria amassing much power in his hands, were prepared to use all means, including anti–Semitism, to diminish his stature. As one close student of the domestic in–fighting under Stalin concluded:

> The doctors' libel also aroused the opposition of persons [members of Stalin's Old Guard] who had previously contributed to his anti–Semitic hysteria and had participated in the anti–Semitic operations of the "black years."

The article in *Pravda*, dated April 6, 1953, laid, as said, primary responsibility for the false accusation on Ryumin, the director of the department of investigation, and Ignatiev, Minister for State Security, denouncing the first–named as a "criminal adventurist" and for "arousing national antogonism," and the latter for "political blindness and heedlessness" and for "slandering . . . an honest figure" like the late artist Mikhoels.[77] Since Mikhoels a few weeks before had been pictured as the chief contact between the Joint and the "terrorist" doctors, both were thus exonerated, implicitly at least. Ryumin and Ignatiev were "people who have lost their Soviet character and human dignity" going so far "as to unlawfully arrest Soviet citizens, outstanding figures of Soviet medicine" and have stooped to directly falsifying the investigation and criminally violating their duty as citizens." According to *Pravda*, the Soviet government, "bravely disclosing shortcomings in state departments, testified thus to the great strength of the Socialist order."

Could Stalin by himself have invented the gigantic hoax or did he fall victim to the fabrications on the part of powerful anti–Semitic circles within the government? *Pravda* itself hinted that political anti-Semitism was at the root of this grotesque falsification and that some groups and concocted this absurd scheme. It castigated "despicable creatures in the Ministry of Security . . . who have tried to arouse in Soviet society feelings of national enmity that are completely alien to socialist ideology" and denounced the "shameless slander of reputable Soviet men."[78] But the truth of the matter was that throughout the Soviet period attacks by such disreputable men have become a steady fare, a perennial feature of Soviet politics, often with Stalin's encouragement and at his instigation.

Of those primarily involved in the plot, Ryumin was shot after a secret trial in July 1954, being accused of having "falsified evidence."[79] Ignatiev, who seemed to have objected to Stalin's suggestion of applying torture to the accused doctors, escaped with his life, but was forced to accept an inferior provincial post. Stalin himself, ready to start a new wave of official terror, following the pattern of the terror of the late 1930s, appears in his last days to have believed that he faced two different conspiracies,[80] next to Zionist–American–Titoist ploters who had infiltrated the Communist movement, another group which involved his senior colleagues in the Politburo.

An Israeli communiqué of April 4, 1953 welcomed the announcement that the libel against the Jewish doctors had been "proved false." It reminded the world that at the same time false charges had been levelled against Jewish organizations throughout the world such as the Joint and the Zionist organizations and that they were part of a comprehensive plan. Notwithstanding the cessation of outright anti–Semitic domestic manifestations, the Soviet policy toward Israel underwent no major changes, though the Soviets renewed diplomatic relations with it. In accordance, however, with its desire to move closer to the Third World, Moscow also decided to lend support to the Arab states. Touching all bases, it aimed at playing the role of a world power in the Mideast.

Disavowal of the Plot—Its Significance and Repercussions

On April 7, 1953, *Pravda*, rather than voicing its shame over the false Soviet accusation, proclaimed that Soviet ideology, the "most progressive ideology," was an "ideology of equality of all races and nations, an ideology of the friendship of peoples." At the same time imperialist ideology was painted as one of "nationalism and race hatred."[81] In Soviet society there was no class basis for the ascendancy of bourgeois ideology or for the dissemination of reactionary ideas such as nationalism and "cosmopolitanism."

For a good number of years, internationalism, part and parcel of the Communist creed, was strong enough to restrain the anti–Semitic legacy and instincts of the Vozhd and of the Soviet elite. In the end, however, Russia's traditional Jew–hatred and Stalin's paranoia gained the upper hand over internationalism and proletarian brotherhood. Unrestrained power concentrated in the hands of one man and the cult of the individual did the rest, removing any obstacles to the deepening and spreading anti–Semitic poison. The early animosity toward Jews and Zionists, already evident in Stalin's 1913 essay on the nationality question, had grown to uncontrollable proportions. Adam Ulam judged thus: "He [Stalin] was not a simple anti–Semite any more than he had been anti–peasant, anti–Old Bolshevik, or anti–military."[82] It is of course true that he had waged fanatic campaigns against all these classes and groups. His inborn suspicion had turned all who in his perception opposed and criticized him at one or the other time into deadly enemies and traitors who had to be disarmed and made innocuous.

Yet there was one substantial difference between Jew–hatred and the persecution of other classes and groups. Russian anti–Semitism was endemic, while the hatred of other groups was not a perennial phenomenon in Russian history. The Old Bolsheviks, the peasants, and the military were the targets only of transitory persecution.

V.   UNDER KRUSHCHEV—Malenkov and Krushchev

In the post–Stalinist era some liberalizing measures raised the hopes of many Soviet Jews. Still, they doubted that Malenkov was their friend. Closely associated with Stalin who tried to make him his political heir, he had in 1948 succeeded A. Zhdanov in the Secretariat of the CPSU. He was known as a nationalist and an anti–Semite. *Pravda* and other Soviet dailies were soon to unleash an anti–Jewish campaign. In his address at the Nineteenth Party Congress in 1952, the last which Stalin attended, Malenkov was Stalin's apparent personal choice as successor. He denounced on that occasion Israel as a "puppet" of American imperialism, the first time that a Soviet leader made such a startling accusation. Here was an example of the striking reversal of Soviet policy since Moscow had extended diplomatic recognition to the new state of Israel. Years later, after Stalin's death, the government proclaimed an amnesty for prisoners and inmates of concentration camps—the existence of which they had steadily denied. Among the beneficiaries of the amnesty were thousands of Jews. In Moscow alone about 70,000 of them were freed.

In the last days of Stalin, on occasion of a bomb explosion in the Soviet Legation in Tel–Aviv, Moscow had broken off all diplomatic relations with Israel. But under Malenkov, relations were restored and the Legation even raised to the status of an Embassy. An Ambassador soon returned to Tel–Aviv to resume his duties. Russian Jews also hoped to obtain cultural rights—the reopening of schools, of theaters, and the publication of newspapers in the USSR—which other Soviet minorities enjoyed, notwithstanding their second–class status. But once again Russian Jews' hopes were shattered.

The dualism of Krushchev and Malenkov from early 1953 to 1955 was replaced by that of Krushchev and Bulganin.[1] For all practical purposes, however, it was Krushchev alone who was in the driver's seat. It was under his leadership that a "thaw" set in and that Stalin's rigid policy was sharply altered. But the policy toward the Jews showed no liberalization, it even worsened in some respects. Political inequality, cultural repression, and national assimilation continued as the basic features of Krushchev's policy toward the Jews.

Krushchev's Prejudices

It is doubtful that Krushchev was ever thoroughly acquainted with either Marx's, Lenin's or Stalin's teachings about the Jews. But he unquestionably knew the practical goals which the Soviets wanted to achieve. As Party leader in the Ukraine, where Jews were still rather numerous, he was up–to–date regarding Soviet policy to- ward all minorities. He himself disseminated the story that back in 1913, six years before he joined the Party, he had defended Jews in a pogromist attack in Mariupol, a small Ukrainian port.[2] For many years Krushchev was the protegé of a prominent Communist, Lazar Kaganovich, a Jew. Krushchev's own son was married to a Jewish girl, the daughter of a Kievan doctor. He frequently talked of his daughter–in–law and of his grandchild as a sort of alibi which was to prove that he was never anti–Semitic.

But Krushchev did not extend help to Kievan Jews when the city was liberated from German occupation. When Jews returned to Kiev to retrieve their property, several anti–Jewish riots broke out in Ukrainian localities. As head of the Ukrainian and Byelorussian par- tisan units Krushchev listed the many nationalities who composed them, "Ukrainians, Byelorussians, Poles, Czecho–Slovaks, and So- vaks," but ignored the Jews.[3] In 1956, when visiting London and the U. S., he refused on both occasions to meet with members of the British Board of Deputies who were anxious to discuss with him the situation of Soviet Jewry, and to meet with representatives of two ma- jor American Jewish organizations in the U. S., despite the personal request of President Eisenhower. On occasion of the publication of Y. Yevtushenko's poem "Babi Yar"—the name of the ravine near Kiev where the Nazis had mass-murdered the city's Jews—Krushchev cas- tigated the young poet who in his criticism had included the Soviet failure to erect a monument for the commemoration of the primarily Jewish victims of Babi Yar. Soviet officials had retaliated angrily. It was widely assumed that their criticism originated with the Secre- tary General. Jews abroad had expected a different reaction recall- ing Krushchev's familiarity with Babi Yar, since details of the Nazi massacre had been submitted at the Nuremberg trial by a Russian commission headed by Krushchev himself.

It was after World War II when Krushchev was head of the Ukrainian Party that numerous anti–Jewish measures saw the light of day. Among them was the willful arrest of a group of Jewish writers in Kiev and their subsequent brutal murder. Following Krushchev's revelation in his anti–Stalin oration at the Twentieth Party Congress in 1956, more attention was focussed on the shocking fate of these authors. First, Soviet officials had denied outright that they had become victims of foul play. But the truth became known when the Warsaw Yiddish Communist daily, the *Folksztyme* [Voice of the People], confirmed the Soviets' involvement in the bloody crimes.

When Krushchev in 1956 sharply rebuked Stalin's policies, he characteristically confined his condemnation to his misdeeds against fellow–Communists rather than against the Russian people in its entirety. Though he denounced the "doctors' plot," he fell short of admitting that it was primarily an anti–Jewish scheme. He had neither the inclination nor the political courage to weather the anti–Semitic waves which had inundated the Soviet plain under Stalin and still flooded it. He criticized Stalin and fellow conspirators and plotters, while himself continuing in a conspiracy of silence about Soviet anti–Semitism. The latter was admittedly a delicate subject in view of Tsarist Russia's anti–Semitic record, the forcible Russification and the maltreatment of many national minorities and especially of Russian Jews. Besides, anti–Semitism, Hitlerism's primary propaganda weapon, recalled National Socialism. This would have raised the question of what distinguished Stalinism from Nazism and what united them. Furthermore, Krushchev, the recipient of numerous Stalinist recognitions and distinctions, would have had difficulties distancing himself from Stalin.

Krushchev disclosed some of his prejudices, apparently shared by many high–placed Soviet officials, also in several interviews. In August 1956 he revealed to a leftist delegation from Canada that among the "negative qualities" of Jews was a determination to avoid manual labor; he adduced a questionable example of an incident in Chernovtsy after his capture from the Romanians and the Jews' predisposition, whenever he "settles in a place," to "immediately begin building a synagogue." In an interview with a French Socialist delegation in May 1956, he had pointed to another "negative" trait of the Jews, "clannishness," and in April 1958 he disclosed to the editor of *Le Figaro*, George Groussard, the Jews' cardinal sin, their "individualism" (this despite the alleged "clannishness"): "They do not like collective work or group discipline."[4] These dubious stereotypes were apparently widely current in Soviet life. Such biases contributed to the judgment of the Jew as a "cosmopolitan" and an "alien." These chauvinist traits and totalitarian leanings of Soviet people, which molded its attitude toward the Jews, were only deepened during the period of the Cold War.

Krushchev Visits Poland

Voices from the liberal intelligentsia raised against anti–Jewish discrimination had no immediate impact upon the Soviet leadership and its policy. After the revelations of Krushchev's anti–Stalin address in February 1956 and the denunciation of the "cult of the individual"—though abstaining from criticism of his anti–Semitism—the Soviet policy toward Jews was affected only little. Then came the spectacular growth of hostile anti–Jewish feuilletons in the Soviet press, which were encouraged by the authorities in Party and State. Krushchev had been a figure of rising importance ever since 1938 when he had been made Secretary of the Ukrainian Communist Party. But even after Stalin's death, voluble though he was, he had made no major pronouncement on the Jewish question.

When he journeyed to Poland in March 1956 for the funeral of Boleslav Bierut, he pointedly reminded the C.C. of the Polish United Workers' Party that the "percentage" of Jewish high officials among Poland's communists, differently from their Soviet brother party where it was "now nil," was high and added: "You have too many Abramoviches in your leading cadres."[5] Krushchev returned to Poland after the outbreak of the Polish revolt in October 1956 when, attempting to prevent Gomulka from coming to power, he exclaimed while emerging from the airplane: "Are you going to help the Yids?" —(a deprecatory term for Jews). A few hours later he recalled the sacrifices of the Red Army in the liberation of Poland and warned the Polish Communists not to deliver their country into "the hands of capitalists who are in league with Zionists and the Americans."

In several interviews in meetings with foreign delegates Krushchev bared his prejudices, resorted to using anti–Jewish stereotypes, and tried to revive the notion of "rootless cosmopolitanism" which had made so strong an impact during the late Stalinist period. According to Ilya Ehrenburg, Krushchev had simply lived too long in the Ukraine, a hotbed of Jew–hatred, not to absorb its indigenous prejudices. Like other Soviet leaders, who owed their career to Stalin, Krushchev for many years had been subject to his influences, had embraced his prejudices, and was unwilling to shed the boss's idiosyncracies and policies. Like Stalin, he—and later Brezhnev and successors—were unable to break away from the master's rigid totalitarianism, biassed nationalism, and deep-rooted anti-Semitism.

Even after Krushchev the Soviets vacillated between solemn assertions that anti-Semitism in Russia was dead and admission that it was still alive among some segments of the population. On December 28, 1965, Kosygin—who only a few years earlier had spouted anti-Semitism from the rostrum of the U. N.—proclaimed that Jew-hatred, like all other forms of nationalism and racialism, "was alien to the Communist world view."[6] According to Krushchev, anti-Semitism "did not, and what is more, could not exist in the Soviet Union." But a few months later, Aron Vergelis, a Jew, a "quasi-official" spokesman of the Soviet government on the Jewish question, admitted while visiting London that anti-Semitism was "still common in certain strata of the population and that it would be necessary to combat it for a long time."

Queries and Answers

On April 13, 1953, only a few weeks after Stalin's demise, Vyshinsky in the U. N. had rejected Israeli charges relating to anti-Jewish discrimination in the Soviet Union.[7] In his "secret" speech in February 1956 in the Kremlin Krushchev denounced Stalin. Though mentioning the "doctors' plot," he characteristically managed to suppress its most striking aspect, its anti-Semitic character. Revealingly, in meeting with representatives of the French Socialist Party, the Russian side being represented by Krushchev, Mikoyan, Shepilov, and Kaganovich, Mikoyan admitted that a certain amount of anti-Semitism still existed among Soviet people, but dismissed it, like Krushchev himself on the same occasion, as mere "survivals from the capitalist era."[8] He also denied that there were "anti-Zionist trials" in the Soviet Union for "Zionism alone." As far as Israel was concerned, it was "under the thumb of the American reactionaries." "But we [the Soviets]," he tried to assure the French delegation, "are not anti-Semites." On another occasion soon thereafter Russian spokesmen pointed to the Soviet constitution which condemned any national discrimination as "criminal;" it "was also condemned by public opinion." Ilyichev, another participant in the discussion, conceded, however, that "perhaps at certain offices and enterprises certain directors had followed a policy contrary to our governmental policy."[9]

Some of the most important Soviet policy statements were made as a result of foreign inquiries in response to journalists or politicians to disavow charges of discrimination and blunt criticism by the foreign press and media. Generally, however, such official replies to foreigners were not reported in the Soviet press and became not known to the Soviet public. On April 9, 1958, *Le Figaro* dealt primarily with Birobidzhan. Krushchev had to admit Soviet disappointment with the failure of the Far Eastern colonization project, but tried to shift the blame on Soviet Jews, their individualism and lack of "group discipline." The Jews were essentially intellectuals.[10] They "never consider themselves sufficiently educated." When Groussard interjected that the Israeli experiment was a "success," Krushchev asserted that he felt "very sorry for Jews who emigrated to Israel." While the USSR had voted in the U. N. for Israel, the latter had shown herself ungrateful and unfortunate in her foreign policy choices. "This nation plays the game of the imperialists and of the enemies of socialist countries." No hint was given that Soviet anti–Semitism and anti–Zionism might have driven Israel into this "anti–Soviet" position. On another occasion Krushchev also made reference to "most prominent" Soviet leaders who had married Jewish girls, thus discounting any anti–Semitic bias by them. He expressed his dislike both for the infamous Black Hundreds of tsarism as well as for Zionists and Bundists on account of their nationalism. Notorious anti–Semitic hooligans and adherents of a national liberation movement were thus placed on the same level!

Individual and National Rights of the Jews—from the Tsars to Krushchev

In the fields of individual rights as well as Jewish national rights there is a vast gap between Soviet claim and reality. Under the tsars the civil rights of Jews relative to residence, military service, education, and participation in government were severely restricted. But after the February Revolution and the demise of tsarism the Provisional Government abolished all limitations which curtailed the individual and perpetuated social, ethnic, or religious discrimination. There followed the removal of discriminatory restrictions against Jews in the army—in which they had been unable to serve as officers—and in the navy—in which they had been unable to serve at all. On April 5, 1917, restrictions on grounds of race or creed which had limited Jews in regard to residence, free movement, employment, ownership of property, and schooling were completely removed. After the Bolshevik seizure of power, these civil rights were reasserted on

November 14, 1917, when the Communist regime proclaimed a Declaration of Rights, once again asserting the abolishment of "all national and national–religious privileges and restrictions." This decree was signed by Lenin and Stalin, by the latter in capacity as Commissar for Nationalities. The foregoing Declaration, including the provision concerning non–discrimination on national grounds, was reaffirmed. In view, however, of the anti–religious campaign unleashed by the Soviets, non–discrimination on religious grounds seemed out of place: obviously all religions were now discriminated against. Civil rights provisions were also inserted in the various constitutions of the individual Soviet republics.

The 1925 constitution of the RSFSR reasserted the equality of the rights of its citizens in all spheres of activity as "indefeasible law." Article 135 confirmed that Soviet citizens "irrespective of race or nationality" were eligible to vote and to be elected. For decades, however, reality of Soviet life has been quite different from written constitutions and laws. Only in some areas does reality approach closely these claims. There are no restrictions in the USSR in regard to residence and participation in some fields of social life, in the army, in trade unions, social services, and clubs. Jews are still widely represented in science, arts, medicine, and law. But over the last decades their number has dropped in these fields at an alarming rate. In 1967–68 Jews were still represented at a high percentage, about half a million, as technical specialists. Among "scientific and academic workers" they still rank high, both in relative numbers and also in regard to occupants of advanced posts. As "specialists" they outnumber all nationalities except Russians and Ukrainians. In the prestigious Academy of Sciences the percentage of Jews is even higher than among "scientific and academic workers," about 10 percent as compared to their being about only 1 percent of the entire Soviet population. According to the Soviet Press agency Novosti, Jews in 1963 constituted 14.1 percent of all physicians, 10.4 percent of Soviet lawyers, 8 percent of the writers and journalists and 7 percent of actors, musicians, sculptors, and other artists of the USSR. But again, between 1958 and 1963 the percentages of Jewish doctors in the Russian Republic alone dropped radically from 14.3 percent to 10.3 percent. Discrimination against Jews still exists in many fields and it is growing. No criminal codes have been applied against anyone who has discriminated against Jews on national, racial, or other grounds.

In the early 1920s, the Soviets had no quotas in governmental employment. In Moscow, and especially in the Ukraine and Byelorussia, Jews held civil service jobs far in excess of their population. According to figures given in December 1927 at the Fifteenth Congress of the Party, Jews occupied 22.6 percent of all posts in the Ukraine, more than four times the percentage of their people in the entire republic, about the same percentage as in Byelorussia. This high proportion was due partly to the dismissal of the tsarist bureaucrats and of the lack of education of the native population. In 1957 Krushchev admitted that, "formerly backward and illiterate," the peoples of the border republics had now their "own [!] intelligentsia."[10] He spoke of the "anti–Semitic sentiments" which still existed in those regions, but at the same time asserted that these were only "remnants of a reactionary past." Krushchev actually defended the willful discrimination against Jews in the border republics, if not in Russia proper, claiming that Jews surrounded themselves frequently with "Jewish collaborators," a practice creating only "jealousy and hostility toward Jews." By dislodging Jews from civil service positions, the government and the Party removed only causes of hostility from the Soviet nationality scene, acting in accordance with the true interests of all Soviet nationalities!

On December 17, 1966, in a speech to artists, elaborating about this very matter, Krushchev pursued the same line.[11] These interviews were not published in the Soviet press. But the reality of discrimination against Jews was and is an open secret in the USSR. The Party's theoretical journal *Kommunist* defended in June 1963 anti–Jewish discrimination: quotas were an important step in the education of new cadres among less developed Soviet nationalities and republics, contributing to the "actual equality of nations."[12] "Equality"—at the expense of Soviet Jews, in disregard of the demands of justice and of Jewish past services to the Soviet Union and likely future ones. "Equality" has actually resulted in the most glaring underrepresentation of Soviet Jews in all higher Party and State posts.

In the December 1937 elections to the Supreme Soviet out of 1,143 members 47 Jews were chosen to take their seats, 4.1 percent of the total membership. In the Soviet of Nationalities, Jews numbered 32 out of 569 members or 5.6 percent. In the first election of a Supreme Soviet after the war, in January 1946, there were only five Jewish names among 601 members of the Soviet Union, less than 1 percent.[13] In the Soviet of Nationalities, Jews in 1946 ranked 26th among national group deputies, in contrast to the 11th rank they had occupied in 1937. There followed a further decline of the number of Jews in the legislative bodies of the Soviet Republics of the USSR. In 1966, Jews constituted 1.08 percent of the total Soviet population. But their percentage in the Council of Nationalities was 0.31 percent, the Jewish representation being 5 among 1,517 members. Not a single Jewish deputy represented Moscow or Leningrad, though both cities had a large Jewish population. Nor was there a single Jewish deputy from the Ukraine, Byelorussia, Lithuania, and Moldavia, all areas with still large numbers of Jews. Of even greater importance was the catastrophic drop in membership of Jews in the Central Committee of the CPSU, especially if one contrasts the number of people of Jewish descent in the CC in the early 1920s, when they constituted about one-fourth of the entire membership.

In 1961 the percentage of Jews in the Central Committee had dropped to a mere 0.3 percent. As one authority judged it: "The Jews are the only nationality whose relative weight and absolute numbers in elite representation declined constantly in both the Stalinist and post–Stalin era."[14] There are no longer Jews in the leading Party organ, the Politburo. Nor can Jews be found among top figures in the central Party apparatus and personnel and district organizations. They are, however, still strongly represented in the lower echelons of the Party. Needless to point out that these Jews who were or are Party activists have hardly ever felt genuine attachment to their people and ancestral culture and have largely espoused the anti–religious, anti–national and assimilatory views of the ruling clique. In the civil service of any department with foreign dealings such as the Ministry of Foreign Affairs, of Defense, and Foreign Trade and in the diplomatic service, there are virtually no Jews any more. As Andrei Sakharov has pointed out in 1968, after the 1930s the appointments policy pursued by the "highest bureaucratic elite of our government was consistently affected by anti–Semitic considerations."[15]

Another prominent dissident, Roy Medvedev, has confirmed this conclusion.[16] A petition of 26 Lithuanian Jewish intellectuals sent to a top Lithuanian Party official—a copy of which reached the West—complained that, though Jews were 10 percent of the population of Vilnius, the capital of Lithuania, "not a single Jew" was either chairman, deputy chairman, Secretary of the Party, of the City committee or of the regional committee, or had been appointed head of any department. Nor were they elected judges of the peoples' courts, or chosen to leading posts in the trade unions.

In 1963 the important theoretical journal *Kommunist* admitted the existence of preferential admission quotas in higher education, quotas which are annually planned. N. de Witt, an American specialist on Soviet education, has shown that the Soviet quota system is based on the principle of "equivalent balance.," which demands that the number of representatives of any national group in higher education enrollment should be proportionate to the relative sizes of the ethnic unit within the total population.[17] According to De Witt, the index of representation rose in the quarter of century after 1935 for most nationalities, but fell for Georgians and a few other national minorities, with a "drastic decline for Jews." The University of Moscow has especially rigid restrictions for Jewish applicants. While according to Roy Medvedev the quota system has varied for Jewish students in Soviet universities, military academies and diplomatic schools practically exclude Jewish youths in their entirety.

Though Jewish enrollment at the University level has been drastically reduced, the enrollment of Jews still ranked highest among all nationality groups. The percentage of Jews in the total enrollment of Soviet students at higher education is 2.55 percent. This, however, represents a radical drop compared to Jewish enrollment in 1935, when it was 13 percent. While the quota hurts the Jewish population, it has also an adverse effect upon the training of skilled professional manpower in the USSR in its entirety. Such growth, however, is vital for any state aiming at making rapid economic and technological progress.

This has dawned upon the Soviets themselves. In a rare editorial on September 5, 1965, *Pravda*[18] recalled for its readers that Lenin had demanded an unceasing "struggle against anti–Semitism, that malicious exaggeration of racial separatism and national enmity." This very editorial was reprinted in the provincial press, an indication of the importance which the ruling circles attached to it at that moment. Its major purpose appears to have been a reduction of the growing anti–Semitism and of rising discrimination against Jews.

As *Pravda* wrote in 1965, "the growing scale of Communist construction requires a constant exchange of cadres among the peoples." The author strongly criticized "manifestations of national separateness in the training and employment of various nationalities in the Soviet Republics" as "intolerable." The central authorities were simply concerned that the anti–Semitic drive in the Soviet border republics would jeopardize economic growth in the USSR. Though the local bureaucracy apparently shares the anti–Jewish bias and responds willingly to local prejudices and pressures against Jews, it finds itself also between hammer and anvil, facing opprobrium from above if it exceeds acceptable norms of anti–Jewish discrimination. Another article in *Pravda*,[19] criticized national discrimination in hiring practices in general rather than anti–Semitism in particular. Similarly, a memorandum, dated March 19, 1971, addressed by two physicists, A Sakharov and V. F. Turchin, and the historian Roy Medvedev to L. Brezhnev,[20] A. Kosygin, and President M. Podgorny, called for the abolition of the registration of nationality in passports and in questionnaires, stressing the need for catching up with the West's labor productivity and its scientific and technological progress. But Soviet-institutionalized anti–Semitism still works at cross purposes with the economic needs of the USSR.

"Parasitism" and the non–Russian Nationalities

Though after Stalin there was a noticeable decline of government terror at home and amnesty was extended to numerous prisoners, including Jews, new charges were soon levelled against them. Jews were increasingly accused of "parasitism" and of bribery. New Soviet laws provided the death penalty for some economic crimes. In a trial stages in 1961, eleven individuals were sentenced to death, about half of them Jews. In many similar cases, authorities and editors deliberately singled out the "Jewish cases" for adverse publicity. Some observers have attempted to "explain" the hostile anti–Jewish thrust of such remarks as being part of a mere ritual. Yet such apologies are hardly persuasive. To the contrary, singling out Jews as the perennial scapegoat has always been the indisputable symptom of anti–Jewish animosity.

Soviet leaders at home and abroad have denied the existence of anti–Semitic sentiments in the USSR. But there is ample evidence of manifestations of Jew–hatred in Soviet life and society. An editorial in *Pravda* on September 5, 1965[21] warned the Communist Party not to follow "mistakes of the masses such as chauvinism and anti–Semitism." Another observer of the Soviet scene admitted: "Contrary to expectations, racial and ethnic biases have not entirely disappeared . . . quite the contrary." When particular difficulties arise, they again make themselves felt, "influencing backward sections of the population." He concluded: "Whether or not the existence of anti–Semitism is officially acknowledged, it does exist in the USSR as a popular strain,"[22] finding an "outlet in crucial areas" and at critical times.

The anti–Semitism of the Krushchev era, others have held, has been marked by growing contradictions in Soviet society, by the struggle also of the various Soviet nationalities for larger representation in the Soviet apparatus in party, government, and bureaucracy in general. When Jews were expelled from leading positions, opportunities were created for greater participation in Soviet life both for Great Russians and other less developed nationalities. Soviet anti–Semitism was clearly linked with greater material and national satisfaction for new segments of Soviet society. Many of the Soviet anti–Semitic writings have been linked to unfulfilled desires of Soviet nationalities and to alleged Jewish ambitions to "dominate" the Soviet peoples and the world at large. It is almost unbelievable that this sort of propaganda could have taken root in the Soviet Union whose population, next to the Jews, had suffered most from Nazi atrocities and Nazi contempt for Slavs and from the killings of individuals of other East European nationalities and Communist Party members.

Most bizarre and puzzling were the accusations, levelled against the Jews under Stalin and Krushchev, of being cosmopolitans and nationalists at the same time! The former accusation was designed to focus on the allegedly rootless character of the Jews, making their homelessness their major fault—a centuries–old charge—and carrying in the multinational Soviet empire the specific accusation of lack of Soviet patriotism. The accusation of nationalism was directed against Jewish "separatism," and opposition to assimilation and to the extinction of their national and cultural identity. Both cosmpolitanism and Jewish nationalism were denounced and the alien character of the Jews emphasized. These contrary charges reveal a great deal about the psychological insecurity of both the Great Russians and the minorities. The shrinking percentage of Great Russians in the USSR is a demographic reality. The Great Russians fear to lose, perhaps of having lost already, the status of the major nationality in the Soviet Union. Assimilation of Jews, linguistically and culturally one of the most Russified, though ethnically still conscious elements in the USSR, while a Soviet goal, is also objected to and disliked by broad sections of the Soviet people. Whatever course Jews pursue, whether "separatism" or assimilation, they displease some political leaders of the USSR!

Bent on developing their individual talents and occupational capacities as well as their national identity, Soviet Jews were bound to clash with the egalitarian, levelling pressures of Soviet society and peoples envious of the niche Jews have carved out for themselves since the October Revolution. For some time they have succeeded due to their dedication to revolutionary change and their appreciation of education. But anti–Semitism has returned quickly, donning a new garb. It became the weapon against a historically, religiously, and nationally distinct and discriminated minority which had rapidly risen from the bottom to the top. Anti–Semites, opposing Revolution and Jewry, wanted to discredit both and to deprive the Jews of their seemingly privileged position in Soviet life. In the struggle against popular prejudices and discrimination, the Communist ideology of national equality had first gained ground. But in the interwar era already it was gradually replaced by the new ideology of Soviet "patriotism," later by innate chauvinism and rejection of "cosmopolitanism." All this prepared the ground for the new anti–Semitism luxuriating in the USSR. It was deepened by the emergence of the latest enemy, of "Zionism."

Nazi Atrocities, Babi Yar, and Soviet Memory

Information about genocidal extermination of Jews by the Nazis during World War II had been largely suppressed by the Soviets. Before 1948, the authorities had permitted the publication of only two studies dealing with aspects of the Holocaust. The Jewish Anti–Fascist Committee, formed during the war, had planned to publish in 1948 one of these, the *Black Book*, elaborating on the mass murder of Jews. But the type, already set up, was deliberately smashed when the Committee was liquidated in 1951. On the twentieth anniversary in commemoration of the Warsaw Ghetto uprising, a single article appeared in the Soviet press,[23] marked by an attack on the rulers of the German Federal Republic! There was a similar diversion, a sharp criticism of the West German government and especially of Konrad Adenauer in connection with the Eichmann trial when the Soviet press accused Israel of having concluded a "deal" with Germany to suppress revelations allegedly embarrassing for the German Federal Republic. At the time of the Eichmann trial *Vechernaia Moskva* made no mention of six million Jews having been murdered, but transformed them into six million "people" of unknown nationality and religion having been burned in gas chambers.[24] The Soviet stance has always been to play down Jewish martyrdom which, it feared, would only result in strengthening Jewish consciousness and solidarity and somehow embitter the Great Russians and other Soviet nationalities which, though experiencing no holocaust, had also suffered from Nazi brutalities. Actually, the deliberate Soviet silence on the Holocaust had probably the effect of deepening Jewish solidarity.

When the Eichmann trial began in Israel, the Soviets wavered between outright falsification and suppression of news. The lies concocted and propagated in the USSR in this context were worthy of the worst Nazi practices of earlier years. In the last weeks of the Eichmann trial two major Soviet dailies, *Pravda* and *Izvestia* made each only a single reference to it.[25] During the same period the Polish and the Hungarian press, however, despite their Communist biases and their dependence on the USSR, emphasized Jewish martyrdom.

With the German troops in Kiev, the Nazis had unleashed atrocities against the Jews of the city in the nearby ravine of Babi Yar which have been unmatched in history. Since young Jews had fled Kiev when the German troops approached the city, the Nazi killings affected especially Jewish mothers, children, the sick and the elderly. The Nazi mass murders have later been described by Ilya Ehrenburg, the Soviet novelist Anatoly Kuznetsov in his novel *Babi Yar*, and long after the war, far from Soviet territory, in the district court of the city of Darmstadt in Hesse.[26] According to Kuznetsov the Ukrainians, many of them ill-disposed toward Jews for centuries, considered them agents of the NKVD. The Ukrainian people looked at best with callous indifference upon the cruel fate of their Jewish neighbors.

A single known survivor of the Babi Yar mass murder. Dina Mironovna Pronicheva, travelling in 1967 from the Soviet Union to the Darmstadt court, testified at its proceedings, giving gruesome details of the Nazi atrocities. After thirty–six hours of shooting, the Germans had calculated that 33,771 Jews had been shot dead. The total pre-war Jewish inhabitants of the city had numbered about 180,000 out of a total population of 846,000. Some students of the mass murder however, have concluded that at least half of the Jewish population of Kiev was killed by the Nazis within two days. Kuznetsov, relying on Soviet figures, estimated that the number of Jews shot on September 29–30 was 70,000. Nikita Krushchev himself, who chaired the report of the postwar special Commission to investigate the Babi Yar murder, estimated that more than 100,000 men, women, and children were liquidated at Babi Yar.

From the beginning Soviet leaders understood that Babi Yar constituted "the most poignant example of Jewish martyrdom on Soviet soil." Did they feel any responsibility for the Nazi holocaust? Following the signing of the Nazi–Soviet pact in August 1939, the Soviets had blotted out any mention of Nazi hostility toward the Jews and thereafter of Nazi atrocities against them in neighboring occupied

Poland. Nor had they given timely warning to Soviet Jews in the border regions, which might have saved tens of thousands.

The official Soviet report of the Babi Yar massacre, half a year after Kiev's liberation, totally suppressed the massacre against the Jews. The Soviet press, even kept its silence when later Colonel Blobel, a major Nazi criminal responsible for the mass killings, was tried and executed in Germany in 1951 for his crimes. But the massacres of Jews became known to Soviet Jews through Ilya Ehrenburg's novel *The Storm*, the publications of a poem by a Ukrainian Jewish writer Savvia Golovanisky, and through the record songs of the Yiddish singer Nakhama Lifschitz. Before the anti–Semitic campaign in the USSR was unleashed in 1948, there had existed official plans for a public monument at Babi Yar. For a while, however, Kievan authorities, with some support from Krushchev, anxious to extirpate all memories of Babi Yar and its implications, planned to build a modern market or a stadium on the very site of the mass murder! It was then that the noted Soviet writer Viktor Nekrasov wrote a letter to *Literaturnaya gazeta*, which appeared on October 10, 1959, giving expression to his rage: "Is this possible? Who could have thought of such a thing? To fill a deep ravine and on the site of such a colossal tragedy to make merry and play football?"[27] He demanded "tributes of respect" for the Kievan citizens who had been murdered at Babi Yar.

A much broader audience, far beyond Soviet borders, was reached when Yevgeny Yevtushenko, almost twenty years after the Babi Yar killings, published autobiographical observations in the Parisian *L'Express* in September 1961. He identified himself in the poem with every man, woman, and "every child shot there."[28] When he read the poem to twelve hundred students in Moscow, he was greeted with enthusiastic applause which lasted "for a good ten minutes." The poem was not only a reminder of tragedy but a denunciation of historic anti–Semitism in Russia. Yevtushenko's thought challenged in several respects the accepted Soviet doctrine on Jews and Jew–hatred. His poem was promptly met by a storm of criticism including the Soviet critic Dmitry Starykov who denied the thesis of the existence of anti–Semitism in Russia, considered such a view a "provocation" and warned Yevtushenko against making further steps into this "foul swampy quagmire." In a threatening fashion he even extended his criticism to the editors of *Literaturnaya gazeta*.[29] Krushchev later disclosed that the Party's Central Committee had received numerous complaints about Yevtushenko. The Party's position was that not

Jews alone but also "not a few Russians, Ukrainians" and individuals of other Soviet nationalities had been killed by the "Hitlerite butchers."

Yevtushenko had stirred up a hornet's nest, and a reply by none else than Krushchev himself seemed imperative. That answer came at a Kremlin conference of writers and artists on March 7–8, 1962, when the Chairman flayed Yevtushenko for lack of "political maturity" and for displaying "ignorance of the historical facts."[30] He repeated the pet phrases that anti–Semitism was typical only of "capitalist society" and that it had to be judged not from a national but from a class point of view. By citing the alleged case of a Jew who had served at Field Marshal Paulus's headquarters in Russia—an outright fabrication, as was later revealed—Krushchev wanted to draw attention to the circumstance that Jews had not only been victims but allegedly also aids of the Nazis!

In the meantime, the pressures upon Yevtushenko's "Babi Yar" grew steadily especially after Dmitry Shostakovich had completed his Thirteenth Symphony, which was based upon Yevtushenko's poem. the official reaction, as expected, was a criticism of Shostakovich by the Party's ideological spokesman, Leonid Ilyichev, for having chosen "an undesirable theme for his symphony." Though the fight over Babi Yar vanished for a time from the discussion between the government and the intelligentsia, in August 1966 a literary monthly, *Yunost*, began the printing of a documentary novel, *Babi Yar*, Antoly Kuznetsov[31] who had accompanied Yevtushenko in 1961 on his visit to the site of the mass murder. For the first time the novel brought home to the Soviet public a detailed account of the Nazi massacre and the continuing murder of Jews during the 778 days of Nazi rule in Kiev. He showed that some Ukrainians received the German conquerors with open arms, that others collaborated in the killings, and that many accepted German rule without offering resistance. Kuznetsov, contrary to obvious wishes of the Kremlin, underlined that Babi Yar had been primarily a Russian Jewish cemetery rather than a general Soviet tragedy. No wonder that Soviet soldiers, exposed to extremist nationalist propaganda, were forbidden by their superiors to subscribe to *Yunost* and to *Novyi mir*, another "liberal" Soviet journal.

But the literary dispute over Kuznetsov's book did not abate. The battle over a memorial and an inscription, listing also the overwhelming by Jewish victims, persisted. The trial in the German Federal Republic in 1967 of those Germans involved in a major capacity in the Babi Yar killings was, characteristically, completely ignored in the Soviet press as a non–event which had never occurred on Soviet soil! On May 13, 1969, began judicial proceedings against Boris Kobuchibigevsky, a young Jewish radio engineer, who in 1970–71 was sentenced for slander to three years in a corrective labor camp.[32] Next to having criticized in a factory meeting the Soviet poster that Israel had waged a war of aggression in June 1967, he previously, at a Babi Yar memorial service, had added the words: "Here lies buried part of the Jewish people." Yet the historic truth was irrepressible. As Yevtushenko had said about Babi Yar: "Everything here cries in silence."

The Soviet Curriculum and Jewish History

Anti–Semitic and anti–Zionist propaganda required persistent and prolonged vicious attacks along numerous fronts. An anti–Jewish attitude had to be carefully nurtured and facts and positive statements about Jews in world history and civilization had to be suppressed. Such a policy had been pursued since Stalin and has been continued by his successors. In the article "The Position of the Jews in the Soviet School Syllabus of World and Russian History" Ruth Okuneva has come to grips with the question of what Russian school children read or did not read about the history of the Jewish people.[33] She has focussed upon the importance of teaching Jewish history and the growth of anti–Semitism in nineteenth and twentieth century multinational Russia. She stressed the need to eradicate racial prejudices to avoid degrading pupils who are not members of the national majority, and to inculcate among minority children a spirit of national self–respect. But the purpose of education in the USSR was the "arming" of pupils with knowledge that was essential for the education of what Lenin and his successors considered "active, aware builders" of communism.

Okuneva concluded that between the 1930s and 1950s there was "still an attempt, if not to create esteem for the Jewish people as possessors of an ancient culture, at least to neutralize the appearance of anti–Semitism in the prewar and particularly postwar years."[34] But in the mid–1950s there occurred a sharp turn–about. In the prescribed, generally used ancient and medieval history books for secondary–type schools no mention whatsoever was made that Jesus was born a Jew in Palestine. Only in a list of first Christians did the student encounter for the first time the word Jew. By 1954 Jews were virtually eliminated from the texts in ancient and medieval history.

In the late nineteenth century the Dreyfus affair was viewed not as a climactic anti–Semitic event in France, but as a "class struggle" of special intensity.

In the middle of the 1960s there began, according to the author, a tendency towards "absence" of Jews in Russian history. Thereafter, the author detected next to a "continuing tendency towards silence" another trend, namely that of negative information about the Jews and a total absence of any positive statements about them. Completely surprising for Okuneva was the silence about "the birth and growth of Nazism" and about the ideology and roots of fascism, including anti–Semitism. What was the motivating factor in these impardonable omissions and falsifications except the fear that the reader would begin to wonder about the ugly anti–Semitic stereotypes common to both of them, to Nazism and Bolshevism. As far as the last decades are concerned, Soviet history books are full of malice, ill will, and outright hostility directed against Israel. All this corresponds closely to the usual negative propaganda about Judaism and Israel in the press, on television, and in other media.

History texts in the USSR hardly touch Jewish history and Jewish accomplishments. Such matters have been deliberately excised. One must take into full account that such texts are prescribed and used in all fifteen Soviet republics. Thus the students graduating from Soviet schools know virtually nothing about Jewish contributions to world civilization. The names and achievements of Jews are either not listed at all or no hint given that they are Jews or of Jewish descent. Nor does the average student have a grasp of the significant role of anti–Semitism in the world, and in the twentieth century and Russian history in particular. Even Nazi anti–Semitism, when practiced on Russian soil, is virtually glossed over to avoid arousing undue sympathy for the Jewish victims or survivors. A two–part general history text for the Russian Republic, the first authored by A. V. Yefimov, the second by V. M. Khvistov, lists the names of Karl Marx, Heinrich Heine, and Benjamin Disraeli without mentioning their Jewish origin. Another textbook for secondary schools, written by I. M. Krivoguz, D. F. Prtiskei and S. M. Stetskovich briefly refers to the Nazi hostility against numerous ethnic groups including the Jews, without, however, mentioning the genocide to which only the latter were subject. The Jews and Jewish culture in the Soviet Union, as one author concluded, were simply "invisible."

The attempt to blot out Jewish history and with it even the mere memory of the Jewish people is demonstrated with clarity by an episode recounted by the American playwright Arthur Miller after a trip to the USSR in 1967. As he reported, prominent Russians had authored a children's book called *The Story of the Bible*. When the Soviet editors objected to certain concepts such as "God" and "Jewish People," the title was changed to "Myths of the People." The Jews totally disappeared as a definite historic entity in this work [35]

Little surprise that the Soviet pupil emerged from Soviet schooling as an illiterate in Jewish history, totally ignorant of the role of Jewish culture and civilization in the world. Yet in case of other peoples, the Arabs for instance, this role is not only not suppressed, but glorified. Next to the actual physical destruction of much of European Jewry in Nazi extermination camps, the Soviet maltreatment of Jews in past and present and Soviet suppression of Jewish history and of the tragedy of the Holocaust attains the goal of wiping out twentieth-century Jewish history. This serves not only to whitewash the Nazis but also to cleanse the dubious Russian record during this time of agony. It has the effect of turning the Holocaust into a mass murder of unspecified "Soviet people." Jews of course were not the only victims of the Nazi slaughter on Russian soil. But killings of individuals of other nationalities were not genocidal in character. Soviet Jews alone were mass-murdered by the Nazis, and only because they were Jews.

Soviet Communists have been persistent in disavowing obvious truths. In his notable "secret" address at the Twentieth Party Congress, Krushchev simply denied that any policy of anti-Semitism existed or was possible in the Soviet Union. Such continuing denials of its existence and actually of the escalation of Jew-hatred in the USSR are of course to be expected from Soviet authorities. Yet anti-Semitism has been Soviet state policy for decades. At various times a flood of anti-Jewish and anti-Zionist propaganda has been let loose either against Zionism in Israel or in the West and against its allegedly clandestine and anti-Soviet activities in the USSR itself! All this has been done to enhance popular "vigilance" against a "potential enemy" within. Soviet Jewry has been treated as a captive and held responsible for the alleged misdeeds of Zionism, for its collusion with reactionary, imperialist, and capitalist circles in the West! Soviet persistent threats against Jews and Zionists approach the dimensions of the Nazis' early discrimination of Jews and their propagandistic hype. This anti-Semitic propaganda aims at diverting popular wrath from the government toward a national-religious group which has been the notorious scapegoat in European and world history for centuries. The old hatred has donned a "Marxist" garb!

In more recent times the Soviet government has permitted its propagandists to disseminate anti–Semitic poison all over the globe. They have warned Third World countries of the suspect goals of the "Zionist entity," a designation used to avoid extending to Israel the honor of calling it a state. In an update of the anti–Jewish campaign, they have, following Arab practices, proclaimed Zionism the enemy of the national liberation movement. Jews and Zionists have been pictured as the "main enemy" not only of the Soviet peoples but also of the "socialist" satellites and of the Third World.[36]

In the 1961–64 period the Soviets, beset by economic problems, have unleashed a stream of propaganda against "economic crimes." The Soviet government was plainly worried about the extension of the scope of black market activities, of currency speculation, of the stealing of public property, and of bribery. The actual causes of these widespread practices was a shortage of goods which in turn was rooted in Soviet economic inefficiency, poor planning, and the policy of investing in heavy industry instead of satisfying consumer needs. Beginning in May 1961 the Soviet government extended numerous laws to prevent "economic offenses." In the judgment of the reputable International Commission of Jurists, this economic campaign was closely tied up with anti–Semitism.[37] The Commission criticized that of nearly 250 persons known to have been executed for "economic crimes" 50 percent were Jews, in the Ukraine even 80 percent, though in the latter republic Jews were only 2 percent of the entire population.

Nikita Krushchev and Bertrand Russell

In an exchange with Krushchev, Bertrand Russell, noted British philosopher and friend of left–wing causes and of the USSR in particular, wrote to the Soviet Premier that he was deeply perturbed over the death sentence on Jews for alleged "economic crimes" committed in the Soviet Union and the apparent official encouragement of anti–Semitism. "You know of course that I am a friend of your country and that I have a friendly attitude towards your personal efforts directed to peaceful coexistence, efforts which I have publicly supported." He appealed to him for an amnesty "proceeding from human considerations and out of joint interests, which consist in peaceful relations between East and West."[38]

In his reply, Krushchev rejected the notion that the Soviet action was a "manifestation of anti–Semitism" as a "a profound illusion," "a crude concoction and vicious slander on the Soviet people, on our country." Among the people punished in the USSR for "economic crimes," he replied, were individuals of virtually all nationalities, thus disregarding the strikingly disproportionate number of Jews accused and sentenced. Krushchev ended by claiming that reactionary propaganda had also in the past imputed to the Soviets "a policy of anti-Semitism" and pointed to both Communist ideology and the Soviet constitution which allegedly precluded the possibility of such a policy. But Lord Russell, dissatisfied with Krushchev's reply, sent on March 5 a two-page follow-up letter to the Soviet leader.

The correspondence between a renowned Western intellectual and champion of socialist causes with the Soviet leader became widely known in the USSR and compelled *Izvestia* to print four letters from among two hundred replies it had allegedly received from readers on this exchange. When Lord Russell's rejoinder to the letters to the editor was ignored by *Izvestia*, Russell released his letter in London on April 6, 1963, filled, as he wrote, "with concern for the Soviet people" and not in a spirit of condemnation. "The Jews have been subjected to long and continuous persecution in the history of Europe. I should hope therefore that the Jews would be permitted full cultural lives, religious freedom and the rights of a national group, in practice as well as in law. During the last years of Stalin's life, Soviet Jews were totally deprived of their national culture and the means of expressing it. Leading intellectuals were imprisoned and executed by extra-legal practices which have since been condemned." [39]

While Lord Russell declared himself a "lifelong non-believer" in religion and recalled that he had written and campaigned against superstition, he was convinced, nevertheless, "that the freedom to practice religious views should be allowed to the Jews of the Soviet Union in the same manner that such freedom is granted to people of other religious persuasion." He was "troubled" that there should be articles printed in Soviet journals of "many republics expressing hostility to Jewish people as such." Lord Russell felt that the death penalty for citizens accused of economic crimes harmed the Soviet Union. He considered the fact that 60 percent of those executed "are Jews to be gravely disturbing."

> I cannot too strongly appeal for understanding of the difficulty experienced by those in the West who are working dedicatedly to ease tension, promote peaceful coexistence, and to end the cold war. These objects are harmed by events which those who desire the cold war can exploit and which

trouble us who wish peace and good relations. I write as a friend, but one whose friendship requires honesty.

Krushchev "Remembers"

Krushchev's endorsement of domestic discrimination against Jews and opposition to Zionism emerge convincingly in his autobiographical account *Krushchev Remembers* published in the West, though the authenticity of some of his views has been questioned. But the opinions about Jews and Zionism expressed therein fit his views voiced on other occasions like a glove.[40] Both Judaism and Zionism, Krushchev asserted,

> are reactionary and inimical to the interests of the working class. It sometimes happens that people of non–Jewish nationality trip up on its slippery ground and slide either toward favoring Zionism . . . or toward becoming anti–Semites who are equally reactionary.

Obviously, such an identification is seen only through a distorting prism.

That Zionism and anti–Semitism have a common denominator, reaction, was part and parcel of Communist thought and Soviet vocabulary since the earliest ideological clash between Communism and, on the other side, Zionism and/or the Bundist national ideology in early twentieth–century Russia. Since then Communist hostility to Zionism has grown by leaps and bounds and its stance toward anti–Semitism has become more tolerant and marked by appeasement. Krushchev admitted that in Russia and Poland Zionism has sometimes been denounced "without just cause," meaning that the discrimination against Jews was characterized by false charges, that "Zionism" was often an invention of anti–Semites. But he sharply criticized the alleged promotion of Jews over Russians, other Soviet citizens, and Poles respectively. Such practice was a "crucial error and an absolutely unacceptable case of political myopia on the part of Polish [and Soviet Communist] leadership."[41] Irrespective of merit and past services, Jews, obviously for purely national reasons, should be replaced in Russia and the border republics by members of the indigenous population!

In his "last testament"—the subtitle of the foregoing work— Krushechev made repeatedly special mention of the nationality or descent of numerous Communist leaders in Russia and Eastern Europe, including those of Jewish background. He listed for Romania

Ana Pauker who among the Romanian Party members was consid-
ered to have the most thorough grounding in Leninist theory, and for
Poland, Berman, Minc, and others.[42] In connection with the Six–Day
War and Soviet policy, he claimed having warned Nasser categorically
against going to war with Israel. "It was too tough a nut to crack."
The Israelis were more advanced and had a better army, than the
Egyptians and more modernized weapons. If he were to start a war,
Nasser would also place the Soviet Union "in the most awkward position," since the USSR had voted for the creation of the state of Israel
in the U.N. Of course, the CPSU had never sympathized with Zionism. It had always regarded it as a reactionary bourgeois movement.
But "the state of Israel exists" and "everybody must accept this." He
understood that the Egyptians had to arm themselves, but, in view of
Nasser's assurances, Krushchev was persuaded to believe that "certain [warlike] speeches" made by Nasser were merely his "tribute to
the mood" of his country.[43]

VI.   AFTER THE SIX–DAY WAR. DOMESTIC AND GLOBAL ANTI–ANTISEMITIC PROPAGANDA UNDER BREZHNEV

Changing Postwar Soviet–Zionist Relations

After World War II the USSR made a striking turnabout in regard to Zionism. Ever since the Anglo–Zionist confrontation and clashes in Palestine Moscow had expected that it had a good chance of winning over Palestine's Jews to the cause of Communism and Soviet expansionism in the Mideast. While the Soviet leaders underestimated the strong ties between Russian Jews and their kinsfolk in Palestine and the U. S., they overestimated the Soviet Jews' identification with the Soviet Union, which after all had long practiced anti–Semitism at home and propagated anti–Zionism. But in the critical months of 1948 when Israeli troops staved off the Arab armies and the Arab Legion, Andrei Gromyko at the U. N. directed the struggle for numerous U. N. cease fires, which helped the Yishuv.[1] The climax of the pro–Zionist attitude had been the Soviet vote on the partitioning of Palestine in 1947 and Gromyko's pro–Zionist addresses in the U. N. Later the USSR and its Czechoslovakian satellite dispatched machine guns, rifles, and airplanes to Israel, and Russians helped Israelis to learn to fly the new Czech planes.

But there were ominous signs of a change in the Soviets' positive attitude toward Israel. Following especially the arrival of Golda Meir (Meyerson) as first Israeli envoy in Moscow in July 1948 and the enthusiasm for Israel displayed on this occasion by Soviet Jews, the Soviet leaders developed second thoughts. This was demonstrated in an article in *Pravda* by the Soviet journalist Ilya Ehrenburg.[2] Within a short period the Soviets had performed another political somersault, returning to the earlier hostile stance. The reconciliation between the USSR and Israel had proved shortlived. The intensification of the Cold War between East and West played a major role in the new turnabout and in the denunciation of Israel. The army paper *Kras-*

naya zvezda attacked the U. S. on account of a planned loan of one hundred million dollars to Israel, detecting therein an allegedly anti–Russian motivation. It claimed that Washington "aimed at converting the Middle East into a military base for Anglo–American imperialism and a springboard to attack the USSR."[3] Stalin was eager to justify severing diplomatic relations with Tel–Aviv on February 12, 1953, pointing to the bombing of the Soviet legation in Tel–Aviv.

Though under Georgi Malenkov on July 20, 1953, diplomatic relations were resumed, Soviet Mideast policy was substantially altered in favor of the Arabs. A steady feature of Soviet anti–Israeli propaganda was picturing Israel's daily life as bleak and hopeless to discourage emigration from the USSR to the Jewish homeland. On July 17, 1960, *Trud* accused Israeli diplomats and tourists of "infiltrating anti–Soviet and Zionist propaganda" into the Soviet Union. At the same time the authors of some articles in the Soviet press accused Zionists as "betrayers of the Fatherland" and rude, arrogant, unclean idlers."[4-5]

The Six–Day War

The outbreak of the Six–Day War revived Soviet anti–Zionism and anti–Semitism neither of which was ever far below the surface. The USSR once again became the advisor of Arab armies and suppliers of their military hardware. But it backed the wrong horse. Like the Arabs, the Soviet Union felt humiliated by the Arab debacle and voiced its wrath against Zionism and the Jews. Soviet Jews, on the other hand, remembering the Holocaust and their traumatic wartime experiences, took the strident Arab warnings and threats against their co–religionists seriously. Within a few days they ran the gamut from deep concern for Israel to extolling pride in its military victory. As far as the Soviet public at large was concerned, it did not share the official Soviet line of voicing solidarity with the Arab states.

According to numerous reports by Moscow correspondents and tourists in the USSR, the non–Jewish population of Russia was favorably impressed by the Israeli military victory and disclosed its disillusionment with the Arabs and with Soviet diplomacy. On the other hand, the Soviet authorities, when learning that Jewish students in Moscow were secretly celebrating the Israeli victory, clamped down on them, accused students and other citizens of "Zionism" and arrested them.[6] They tried to coax leading Jewish personalities to denounce Jewish national aspirations.[7] The Soviet propagandistic activities against Israel, Zionism, and Russian Jewry were

largely due to Soviet embarrassment over its Arab and Moslem allies and due to its own loss of prestige. Much of Soviet extremism
received a helping hand from traditional Russian Jew–hatred. That
Moscow, however, stooped down to Nazi tactics was perhaps unexpected. The Soviets followed Hitler's tactics, reversing truth and
falsehood and resorting to outright fabrications. On June 6, 1967,
Pravda and *Izvestia* reported that Israel had commenced military op-
erations against the United Arab Republic (U.A.R.) and had thus
committed "aggression."[8] While the rulers of Israel had constantly
claimed that they were waging a struggle "for the existence of Israel
as a state," according to Moscow it was precisely a "course of reck-
lessness and adventurism" which they had chosen. By unleashing aggression against the neighboring Arab states, the Israeli government
had trampled under foot the U.N. Charter and elementary norms of
international behavior. The Soviet government prophesized that the
war would "turn first and foremost against Israel itself" and pledged
its "resolute support for the governments and peoples of the UAR,
Syria, Iraq, Algeria, Jordan, and other Arab states." In another statement Israel was warned that if it should not heed the joint demand of
the Security Council for an immediate cease–fire, the Soviets would
alter their attitude toward it.[9] *Izvestia* hinted at a possible break in
diplomatic relations.

Soon after the outbreak of hostilities in the Mideast, the leading
organs of the Soviet press in their analysis and commentary on world
affairs blamed not only Israel, a "tool" of the Western Powers, but
also the latter. In an article "Self–Exposure for the Restorers of Colo-
nialism" Yury Zhukov in *Pravda* on June 12 blasted both Israel and
the West, especially U. S. imperialism. He was particularly aroused
at the *New York Times* columnist Sulzberger, who only days before
the outbreak of hostilities in the Mideast had drawn attention to
the "machinations" and "devilish plan" of the Soviet Union and had
written: "Why should Moscow not choke Europe as Egypt threatened
to choke Israel?"[10] The Anglo–American press distorted the socialist
countries' position and aims in the Middle East and played into the
hands of the hostile Peking propagandists by asserting that Moscow
gave allegedly aid to the Arab states.

But the Soviet Union was going to defend the Arabs' national independence and territorial integrity and defending the Arab peoples'
social gains achieved in the long hard struggle against the imperialists. Israel, according to *Izvestia*,[11] engaged in "brazen aggression"
and "arrogant disregard" of the U.N. Security Council's resolutions

and "gloated" in "anticipation of profits." This aggression was "not simply Tel-Aviv's aggression," but the result of criminal collusion between it and the American and British imperialists. Israel was only "the point of spear imperialism hurled into the heart of the liberated Arab world. It has inflicted a deep wound on the giant's chest, but has not felled him." Israel vainly expected "setting the yoke of new colonial exploitation on the proud brow of the Arab nation," which has made an enormous contribution to the development of world civilization. Israel's aggression and the imperialist international plot are aimed at stifling the freedom and independence of the Arab countries and people which are "in the first ranks of the national-liberation struggle." They are "an assault on other progressive, anti-imperialist, and anticolonialist forces of the present day."

The clouds of imperialist aggression were inseparable from U. S. aggression in Vietnam and "threaten other independent states in Asia, Africa, and Latin America." Due to the Israeli surprise attack the Arab armies have suffered "bitter setbacks." Clouding the true origins of the war *Izvestia* referred to the "heavy concentration" of Arab troops on the Sinai peninsula as being occasioned only "by the noble wish of Syria against which the invader's fist was raised. The national and international obligations of revolutionaries and of all honest and peace-loving people in connection with the crisis that has flared up in the Near East" were clear. "They must, regardless of their nationalities—be they Russian, Chinese, Germans, Indians, French, Poles, Czechs or Jews—be on the Arab side against the imperialistic aggressors and Israeli invaders." The threat to the freedom of the Arabs was a threat to the freedom of all mankind. The writer concluded with the assurance that in the end the Arab peoples will "triumph."

The closest partners of the Tel-Aviv "extremists" were, according to *Izvestia*, the former Nazis of the Third Reich who had committed "racial crimes."[12] An editorial "The Aggressor will answer for his crimes" proceeded to list these "crimes" which had subjected the residents of the occupied areas

> to humiliation, indignation, violence, and looting. The Israeli invaders are killing prisoners and peaceful peasants; they are holding public executions, including women and children; and they are driving residents from their homes.

The Zionist aggressors hoped to intimidate the Arab countries through their "atrocities." The Soviet press called upon the Arabs to establish unity against Israel and its imperialist allies.

Israel's claim of having fought a war of survival against Arab neighbors attempting to extinguish the new state was never taken seriously and the Arabs' deadly hostility toward Israel was virtually ignored. On the other hand, the theme of conspiracy between Israel and the Western Powers, especially the U. S. and Great Britain, was persistently emphasized. The stress on the Blitzkrieg character of the war and its allegedly "seamy side" recalled of course Nazi military strategy[13] and, in the Soviet mind, sufficed to make a valid comparison between Israelis and Nazis. Konrad Adenauer was compared to Wilhelm II, and an article in *Der Spiegel* offered proof of the forging of an alliance between Zionists and Nazis.[14] Israeli occupationists who had allegedly inflicted reprisals and humiliations upon the Arab population were guilty of "genocide, one of the greatest crimes." New York–based Jewish bankers and the Rockefellers had created Israel's military machine. The economic situation in Israel was depicted in very pessimistic colors. Unemployment, disturbances, demonstrations, and crimes were mounting, all this allegedly in contrast to the situation in the progressive Arab world.

More far–reaching than anything else Moscow did after the start of Mideast hostilities was breaking off relations with Israel, which has continued to this day. Actually, the Soviets had pursued this course once before, in February 1953 under Stalin, when they had severed relations with Tel–Aviv. From the Russian point of view, this was an extreme move. Despite earlier sharp differences of the Soviet Union with Pilsudsky's Poland, with fascist Italy and Nazi Germany in the 1930s and in the post–war period when disputes surfaced with the U. S. and with communist China, the Soviets have consistently avoided complete rupture of diplomatic relations. Only with communist Albania, which had dared challenging the USSR, had the latter broken relations.

The Soviets in the U. N., 1967. Reactions to the War in Eastern Europe and by other Communists

In the summer of 1967 the U. N. General Assembly became the arena of a vicious campaign unleashed by the Arabs in conjunction with Moscow. It was apparently initiated by the Soviet chief delegate in the U. N., Nikolai Fedorenko, on June 9, 1967.[15] He accused Israel, whose troops had advanced into Syria, of following "in the bloody footsteps of Hitler's executioners." Actually, it was Hitler's own recipe of the big lie—which the Führer thought to be popularly more believable than little lies—which Moscow itself had then adopted. Premier Aleksei N. Kosygin, arriving in New York on the fifth day of the debate, accused Israel of "heinous crimes," of burning villages and destroying hospitals and schools and ignominiously identified Israeli policy with Nazism, thus inciting fresh Jew-hatred. He also claimed that the German Federal Republic in which revanchism was reawakening, was in collusion with Israel. That the Soviets were skating on thin ice could be seen by the negative response of even the East European Communist satellites to Kosygin's harangue. Virtually no other communist-ruled countries in the U. N. debate followed in Kosygin's footsteps.

Though the communist satellites, yielding to apparent Soviet pressure, castigated Israel's military action, all of them shrank back from comparing Israeli troops with Hitler's murdering soldiers. Having experienced Nazi occupation and killings first-hand, many people in Eastern Europe even sympathized with tiny Israel which clearly was waging a war of defense against Arab encirclement that threatened to extinguish their state and exterminate their people. Bulgaria's Premier Zhivkov[16] assured the General Assembly that the Bulgarian people "have never been and will never be against the Jewish people." The chairman of Poland's Council of Ministers, Jozef Cyrankiewicz, acknowledged the "solidarity and compassion of world public opinion "for the Jewish martyrology," though he disapproved of the Israeli "Blitzkrieg." Ion Georghe Maurer, chairman of the Romanian Council of Ministers, not only refrained from criticizing Israel but openly advocated direct Arab-Israeli negotiations to establish permanent peace in the Middle East. Only Yugoslavia, though the most independent of Communist states in the Balkan, apparently stung by the defeat of Tito's ally, the "non-aligned" ruler of Egypt Abdel Nasser, went overboard by accusing Israel of violence "having the character of genocide."

Needless to say that in the General Assembly the voices heard from the Premier of Byelorussia, Tikhon Kiselev and of the Ukrainian Premier Vladimir Shcherbitsky members of the Soviet "family" of nations, spoke in as strident a tone as the USSR itself.[17] They repeated the theme song that Israeli military action reminded them of Hitler's aggression. This very comparison was eagerly seized upon by Arab and other Moslem countries. Some of the most ludicrous oratorical excesses were committed by Saudi Arabia's representative in the U. N. General Assembly, Jamil Barrody. Though Moscow tried to apply

Leninist terminology to the Arab–Israeli war and continuing dispute and condemned Israel on "scientific," on Marxist grounds, the war obviously divided communists of different countries.

On June 9, Bukharest, though pressured by Moscow, simply refused to sign a joint declaration of the European Communist countries which branded Israel as aggressor; it also rejected to break relations with it. On June 23 the Romanian Premier Maurer declared in the U. N. Assembly that the Arabs' refusal to recognize Israel prevented the peaceful settlement of the Mideastern dispute.[18] Another Communist–ruled state which opposed the Soviets' breaking off relations with Israel was Cuba, though Fidel Castro's media carried on a vituperative campaign against Israel. Still, in an interview with a reporter of the *New Statesman*, Castro expressed "shock" over the lack of Soviet revolutionary principles: "After all, true revolutionaries never threaten an entire country with destruction."[19] One could not deny Israel's right to exist.

Warsaw was torn by internal contradictions. Władysław Gomulka warned "Polish citizens of Jewish nationality" not to express enthusiasm over the victory of Israel, an "aggressor." But in the U. N. the Polish position was one of restraint. According to the report of a *New York Times* correspondent from Warsaw "a number of leading Polish intellectuals resigned from the C.P., obviously angered by the official Soviet attitude and policy in the Mideast."[20] Hungarian Communist leadership was even less critical toward Israel than Polish official opinion. Unlike Gomulka, the Hungarian leaders castigated anti–Semitic incitement and like the Romanian Communists urged Arab–Israeli negotiations. Though Czechoslovak Party leaders parrotted the official Soviet line, the noted Czech novelist Ladislav Mniachko, a Communist Party member, claimed that the general mood in Czechoslovakia was in favor of Israel, denounced the policy which aimed at the extermination of an entire people and the liquidation of its state! The official Party organ *Rude Pravo* made clear that the sympathy of Czecholsovakia, "a small country," was with "small" Israel![21] Though Yugoslavia was denouncing Israel, some Central Committee members raised dissenting voices, criticizing the Arabs' "Holy War" against the Jews and their being led by feudal rulers. So did also the Yugoslav journal *Ekonomika Politika*[22] when it recalled that "progressive circles" in the Arab world had "never" opposed Arab warmongering.

With less dependence on the Soviets, Western Communist parties were even more critical of Soviet policy concerning the Mideast conflict than the USSR's immediate neighbors. The leading organ of the Dutch Communist Party questioned outright the identification of the Arab movement as a "progressive" national liberation struggle, pointing out that the Arab countries were partly capitalist, partly feudal. Egypt's and Syria's appeal for the "extermination of Israel" had not stopped the dispatch of material help from the Soviet Union. The Dutch Communist Party condemned the Soviet "white-washing" of the Arabs, while Israel was condemned as a capitalist state. "Could the fact that Holland being a capitalist state justify a declaration about exterminating Holland?"[23]

The C.C. of Maki, the wing of the Israeli C.P. headed by Shmuel Mikunis and Moshe Sneh (Rakakh, largely composed of Arabs, following the Soviet line) sharply criticized Moscow. Sneh called the Soviet press campaign against Israel an "atrocity." Disputing the Soviets, he insisted that the recent war was on the part of Israel a defensive war, a war waged for Israel's "physical existence against a scheme of liquidation and extermination."

Each of the three Scandinavian Communist parties endorsed the Maki analysis of the Mideast hostilities. Austria's Communist Party likewise came out in its support.[24] Though the Italian and French Communist Parties supported the Soviet stance, each encountered considerable opposition in its respective Party. The chairman of the Party fraction in the Italian Senate, Umberto Terracini, reaffirmed Israel's right to independent and sovereign existence. The prominent Party leader Luigi Longo not only avoided repeating Soviet accusations of alleged Israeli atrocities, but also insisted upon Israel's right to independence. Another Italian communist, Dr. Fausto Coen, was even more sympathetic to Israel (*Paese Sera*),[25] and other leading Italian communist journals appealed for direct Arab–Israeli negotiations. The French Communist Party, known for its subservience to Moscow, was on the other hand well aware that most of its own members were friendly toward Israel, as numerous letters published in its journals testified to. On May 30 about fifty leading intellectuals, among them Jean-Paul Sartre, Simone de Beauvoir, Pablo Picasso, and others came out in support of calling upon France to back Israel's right to exist.[26]

The smaller communist parties in the United Kingdom and the U. S. followed the Soviet line, though without Soviet expression of ill will. Again, letters to the editor showed the extent of the dissent from the official position. Among leftist organs in the U. S. *Jewish Currents* and the Yiddish *Morning Freiheit* took Moscow to task for its strident criticism of Israel. To repeat, it was revealing that not a single Communist Party outside the USSR showed Moscow's hostility by going so far as to compare Israel with Nazism! Not even the domineering USSR could persuade them that tiny Israel which was waging a defensive war for its very existence against seemingly overwhelming enemies was a threat to them.

Russian voices other than the official soundings were of course muzzled. In 1968 Andrei Sakharov in *Progress, Coexistence, Intellectual Freedom* blamed the Soviet Union for bearing "direct responsibility" for the Mideastern war, since it had engaged in "irresponsible encouragement" of the Arab powers. The latter were in no way "socialist" but "purely nationalist" and "anti–Israel." He also faulted the Soviets' breaking off relations with Israel.[27] Roy Medvedev, taking a similar position noted that the Israelis tried only to prevent their planned annihilation[28] and pointed out that the Israeli action was supported by the majority of European public opinion, including all Socialist parties. As noticed, even foreign communist parties reminded the Soviets that they did not agree with the Soviet appraisal of the events in the Near East. As an unsigned letter of Soviet dissidents to the *New York Times* stated, a significant section of the Soviet population, especially the intelligentsia, had taken a position quite different from the official view."[29]

New Soviet Mythology: "International Zionism "

Following the 1967 war, Soviet official reaction was plainly anti–Zionist and anti–Semitic. The Soviets attempted to intimidate Israel by declaring that the Israeli ruling circles "jeopardized the very existence of Israel as a state." This threat far surpassed any threat ever uttered by the Soviets against any other "bourgeois" and "capitalist community."

Before the Six–Day War Jewish and Israeli leaders were pictured as bent on creating an empire "from the Nile to the Euphrates" and Israelis were compared to Nazis and "allies of neo–Nazis." The Soviets thus borrowed heavily from the arsenal of extremist Arab propaganda against Zionism and Israel. Moscow even accused Zionists of establishing a Fifth Column inside socialist countries, which stamped them as enemies of communism and as an ally of world imperialism. If there had been any difference in the degree of anti–Semitism between Nazism and Soviet Communism prior to the war, it was virtually wiped out thereafter by the poisonous and ever mounting hostile Soviet propaganda. The Soviets now permitted the denunciation of

Judaism as a "reactionary religion," one which called for "genocide and enslavement of all other peoples by the Jews!"

The military defeat of the Arabs in the Six–Day War had infuriated them as well as their protector and fellow–propagandist, the Soviet Union, and had whipped up Jew–hatred among them. The Soviet press, radio, television and international broadcasts became unashamedly hostile and vituperative. The Soviets used an international forum such as the U.N. to blow the anti–Jewish trumpet louder than the Nazis had ever done in the 1930s. As one foreign diplomat to the USSR noted in August 1957: "It's going to be hard to convince some latent anti–Semite in the Ukraine and Byelorussia that this isn't the signal to let himself go." The impassioned demagogy of anti–Zionism had a devastating impact upon the Soviet population, which was already conditioned to strident anti–Semitism under Stalin, the alleged postwar "economic crimes" committed by Russian Jews, and by the threats which hung over them ever since the mass annihilation of Jews by the Nazis.

Soon after the outbreak of the Six–Day War, there appeared in August 1967 an article "What is Zionism?"[30–31] which was published simultaneously in many Republics of the Soviet Union. It was as if the Soviet leaders wanted to test the waters first in the less developed outlying Republics before embarking on a full–blast anti–Zionist and anti–Semitic campaign in the interior of the USSR. The Soviets clearly felt the need for diverting public attention from its foreign–policy debacles, from the defeat of the Arab client states, the poor performance of Soviet weaponry dispatched to them, and, last but not least, from the diplomatic defeat suffered in the U.N. to force Israel to withdraw from the occupied territories. The circumstance that tiny Israel would inflict a military debacle on the Arabs and that the Soviet Union was revealed as a helpless giant in the Middle East, infuriated and frustrated the Soviet leaders. It made them resort to inventing myths and fables which were to "explain" to a captive audience the apparent riddle behind the stunning military success by the small Jewish state. The totalitarian propaganda machine set in operation produced the myth of an all–powerful "world–Zionist" movement, capable of overwhelming its numerous Arab foes. The more the Soviet leaders were startled by the sudden turn of events in the Mideast, the more they felt the need to distract the attention of their people from their own incitements and miscalculations. They resorted to the most ludicrous "explanations" of the latest developments in the Arab world.

In the hour of confusion and frustration they rediscovered the time–tested diversionary Jew–hatred of tsarism as a solution of their dilemma. They seemed unaware that they thus discarded "scientific" Marxist analysis. In October 1967 *Komsomolskaya Pravda*, the newspaper of the Young Communist League, the enemy was described as an "invisible [!] but huge and mighty empire of financiers and industrialists" and Zionism as its "lackey."[32] "Zionism had overwhelming economic and political power" and "effective moral and psychological [!] influence upon the sentiments and minds of people . . . in many countries." Characteristic in this description were not only the inherent exaggerations, but its infusion with mysticism and clandestineness. It had more to do with the conspiracy theories of the *Protocols of the Elders of Zion* and with Nazism than with Leninism. The U. S. in particular was declared to be subject to Zionist influence. The number of Zionists in the U. S. was claimed to be between 20 and 25 million, about four times the total number of American Jews! These data actually were first presented in an obscure pamphlet of 81 pages entitled *America—a Zionist Colony*[33] which had been published in Cairo in 1957 by one Seleh Dasuki and was the collaborative work of a German Nazi and an Egyptian anti–Zionist propagandist!

Another piece of outrageous falsification was produced by T. Kichko, the author of *Judaism without Embellishment*. At the time of its publication in 1963 it had aroused a great deal of sharp criticism within the USSR and beyond its borders and was for a while withdrawn from publication. Nevertheless, on October 4, 1967, Kichko wrote in *Komsomolskaya Pravda*, a journal of the Ukrainian Party youth organization, an article describing a plot of "international Zionist bankers," including the Rockefellers, which was to transform the Middle East into a "strategic launching pad aimed against the socialist world."[34] In January 1968, Kichko, celebrating his comeback, was awarded a "certificate of honor" by the Supreme Soviet Presidium of the Ukraine which embraced thus his type of vulgar anti–Semitism.[35] Thus encouraged, Kichko published in Kiev a new book *Judaism and Zionism* (1968) in which he denounced Judaism for teaching "thievery, betrayal, and perfidy" and striving for domination of the world! Global domination clearly required a major, an "international" effort. "International Zionism" became thus a primary Soviet target. It meant attacks against Jews everywhere, since they had rallied to the moral and material support of Israel. Attacking "international Zionism" offered a theoretical excuse for opposing Jews on a global scale.

The Soviet target was not merely Jewish solidarity, but Jewish nationalism, "separatism" on Soviet soil, and leaning toward the Western Powers in the Mideast. The Soviet Union came to oppose all "international" ties between its own Jewry and Jews elsewhere as allegedly detrimental to its own national interests. Soviet communism upholds "internationalism" as such—the "international" proletariat and the "international" communist movement—as opposed to nationalism or chauvinism. But it opposes the "internationalism" of any other real or imaginary adversary. Internationalism is praiseworthy if it helps the Soviets' own ranks, but it is to be condemned if it strengthens the enemy's camp. Thus the Soviet Union is always international-minded, while its foes are moved by national chauvinism, made more threatening by its disguise as "internationalism."

The Russian people, victimized by incessant Soviet propaganda, has long been aware of the extreme Communist opposition to Zionism as allegedly "reactionary" and anti-Soviet. To the Russian government it was just one step from "domestic" and Israeli Zionism to "international" Zionism. The struggle against imperialism and "international Zionism" is unlikely to be buried in the foreseeable future, though it could play a lesser role under more favorable international circumstances.

The Soviets have helped create a new mythology that staggers the imagination and defies all bounds of objectivity and decency. They have invented the myth of a clandestine and sinister "Jewish conspiracy" aiming at the domination of the Russian state, its peoples, and the world at large! This myth reached its climax in a Russian version of the notorious *Protocols of the Elders of Zion.* It demonstrates the bankruptcy of Soviet ideology which has stooped to the lowest level to embrace racism and anti-Semitism.

Anti-Semitism of the Nazis and Communists. The West's Response

Characteristic of Nazism was its overtness in most regards, including the Jewish question. True, even the Nazis euphemistically talked about the "Endlösung" [final solution] of the Jewish question rather than of the planned physical extermination of Jews, but on the whole it had very little of a mendacious façade in this regard. There could be no mistake of what the Nazis were after when Hitler in *Mein Kampf* called the Jews "devils," pernicious bacilli, a plague, vampires, parasites, the enemies of culture and of the human race. While aiming at German world domination, he wanted to deflect attention to the Jews and their allegedly pernicious goals.

Soviet Communism on the other hand talked only of freedom from oppression everywhere rather than preaching conquest and subjugation of other nations. When it spoke about the strengthening of the state it held out the hope, if not the certainty, that in the end it would "wither away." The Soviets promised as ultimate goals national self–determination, freedom, equality, and democracy. However it deprecated ideology as a causative factor in history. Actually, Soviet Communism, like Hitlerism, underestimated the force of it and of unrelenting propaganda in the battle for the people's mind. Though Nazism had contempt for intellectuals and intellectualism, Soviet Marxism with a tradition of respect for the mind attracted the intelligentsia.

The Nazis extolled the German superrace and the German right to "leadership" and outright domination. The Communists, hiding their nationalist great Russian ambitions, were unwilling to relinquish their multinational empire and imperialist drives. But they concealed their expansionist schemes beneath pious phrases of communist independence and liberty. While nationalism was a key element in Nazi ideology, the very concept of nationalism was proclaimed the main foe of communist ideology, though it soon reappeared under the deceptive banner of Soviet "patriotism" as a powerful force and main prop in Communist thought.

The greatest Soviet turn–about, however, came in regard to anti-Semitism. Though disclaiming, as they do to this day, that anti-Semitic doctrine and practice reign in the USSR, the Soviet Union is generally considered one of the prime sources of anti–Jewish, anti-Semitic, and anti–Zionist propaganda. Moscow acknowledges the latter, though it steadfastly denies anti–Semitism. But it is its main purveyor and virtual heir to National Socialism. Anti–Judaism—an imperative of atheistic philosophy—and anti–Zionism have both become part of official propaganda and ideology. They cover the entire spectrum of the anti–Semitic world view and are hardly different from the rabid Nazi anti–Semitism of the 1930s, the precursor of the Holocaust. If there is a single major difference between the two totalitarianisms, it is the widespread confusion even in circles of communists and extreme leftist groups, some including Jewish groups, which is produced by high–sounding universalist "democratic," "pacifist" and "humanitarian" phraseology. The latter tends superficially to hide anti–Semitism and racism. Soviet tactics consist in diverting attention from its own misdeeds and crimes. While practicing themselves anti–Semitism and racism, the Soviets accuse Israel of "racism." It was the Soviet Union which in 1975 bore major responsibility for the "Zionism is racism" resolution in the U. N., which was aimed at the delegitimization of Zionism and Israel in the world community.

For both the Nazis and the Soviets the Jewish "problem" is not merely a domestic and national issue, but has international dimensions. Nazism, and Communism during the last decades, saw in the Jews the devil incarnate. Yet there are differences between them. The Nazis were always fanatical anti–Semites, from the beginning to the end. The Soviets, however, have long disavowed the anti–Semitic component of their ideology. But for foreign policy reasons as well as domestic ones, they have come increasingly to adopt Jew–hatred. Stalin and his successors have widened the highway of anti–Semitism on which they have travelled with increasing speed and reckless abandon.

The more the Soviet Union has lost its propagandistic attraction as an economic, social, and political model, the more it has tried to replace its ideology with greater doses of racism, anti–Semitism, ultra–chauvinism, militarism, and Great Power politics—which is all reminiscent of German Hitlerism. It is no accident that the Soviets' communist rival, China, has repeatedly compared Soviet drives and ideological bent with the National Socialism of the Third Reich.[36]

What Soviet propaganda has increasingly come to practice is the perfection of Hitler's "big lie." "According to the Führer, "little lies" can be easily detected; few people, however, can be expected to resist "big lies." In accordance with this principle, it is Zionists whom Soviet propaganda has accused of virtually every imaginable misdeed and crime.

One of its "big lies" pertains to alleged Zionist interests and goals regarding the Third World. Actually, Jews and Zionists have relatively minor interests in the Third World though they want to restore and improve the good will or at least neutral relationship which had marked especially Israeli–African and much of the Israeli–Asian relationship that existed in previous times.

In the West, especially the U. S., public opinion and government spokesmen have, after the Soviet campaign against Zionists and Jews intensified, duly taken note of its malicious and dangerous utterances. James Roosevelt, the eldest son of Franklin D. Roosevelt and U. S. representative in the U. N. Economic Council, blasted thus Soviet policy on the Jews:

> The Soviet Union intends to atomize the Jewish community, to estrange it from its past, to pulverize its identity, to crush

its historical consciousness, to destroy every possibility of
Jewish group survival.[37]

Rejecting the argument that the Russian treatment of Jews was comparable to the American treatment of blacks, Roosevelt pointed out
that "here in the U. S. the Negro has the right to take the fight into his
own hands and public opinion has helped his cause." Bayard Rustin,
a prominent black leader, declared: "We who have suffered oppression for three hundred and fifty years know what it is to face the sort
of pressures exerted by the Soviet government on its Jewish citizens."
Earlier, Martin Luther King had pleaded to his audience: "You must
not relent until the religious and cultural depravation of three million Soviet Jews are completely exposed and conditions changed."[38]
Similar pronouncements were repeatedly made by leading Protestant
and Catholic clergymen and representatives.

U. S. representatives in the U. N. such as Morris Abram, chief
U. S. delegate to the U. N. Human Rights Commission, warned in
this forum against the "vicious Soviet cartooning and harpooning of
Soviet Jews," recalling the days of the anti–Semitic tsarist and Nazi
themes of conspiracy. He castigated the anomaly of Soviet condition
where laws forbid discrimination "in the most forceful terms," but
actually "deprive" the Jews of "the religious and cultural heritage
which make this group unique."[39] Such speeches and demonstrations
of U. S. spokesmen contrast, however, with the widely observed practices of other U. S. officials, including at times even ambassadors and
journalists, who have warned against outright sponsorship of Soviet
Jewish causes, likely to be interpreted as "interference" in Soviet international affairs. Such attitudes recalled the often silent treatment
accorded to the persecution of Jews in the Third Reich by representatives of some countries and the frequent overly cautious response
by some American officials.

The Soviet leadership, while brusque and offensive in what it
considered internal policy, has not been insensitive to protests from
abroad, especially if they seemed to affect adversely their national
and international interests. Its response, consisting of minor retreats,
occasionally showed some special sensitivity to criticism by left–wing,
socialist, and liberal circles, and to the apparent rejection of anti–
Semitism by Western communist parties. In 1963 a British Labor
Party delegation met Krushchev who was seeking a Soviet–British
trade agreement. He was bluntly told by its leader, Prime Minister
Harold Wilson, in no uncertain terms: "How can we recommend that
our government deal with you when you are barbarians,"[40] and he

gave the startled Soviet leader the names of seven persons separated from their families since the Nazi Holocaust. Four months later the first of the seven Jews arrived in London ending a cruel and senseless separation.

Czechoslovakia and Jewish Conspiracy

What actually caused the flame of anti-Semitism in the USSR to soar suddenly so high in 1967? It was first the Arab military debacle and closely linked with it, the military and diplomatic setback suffered by the Soviets in the Mideast. Soon thereafter, in the summer of 1968, Soviet vituperative accusations against Zionism and its alleged plots were voiced on account of developments in Czechoslovakia, where Alexander Dubcek's reforms seemed in Moscow's perspective to threaten its very own interests. Zionism, Moscow proclaimed, showed the menacing hand in central Europe itself! Israel, West German revanchism, and U. S. imperialism were all allegedly in collusion to wrest Czechoslovakia from behind the Iron Curtain. Zionists and Jews in Czechoslovakia, actually a tiny remainder of prewar Jewry, played, according to Soviet mythology, a decisive role in the plot aimed at subverting Czechoslovakia. Czechoslovakian Jews, as K. Ivanov, an old Soviet hand on Zionism, in an article in *Mezhdunarodnaia Zhizn*[41] charged, were responsible for the subversive activities of the Zionists.

In the very days before the Soviet invasion of Czechoslovakia *Krasnaya Zvezda*, the Defense Ministry's newspaper, as well as *Komsomolskaya Pravda*[42] referred to "saboteurs." bent on undermining the socialist commonwealth and, to leave no doubt about their specific national origins, attacked Judaism as justifying "crimes against gentiles." How far had the Soviets ideologically travelled since the days of Lenin! While attacking Jews, they tried to cover their own tracks in preparation for the invasion of Czechoslovakia! The Soviets had made clear that their particular targets in Czecholsovakia were Eduard Goldstucker, Frantisek Kriegel, Otto Sik, and Bohumil Lomski, all of whom they considered Jews; Sik himself denied any Jewish descent. The Soviet leaders also made spurious charges that other prominent men in the anti-Soviet camp were Jews and Zionists. Such accusations were levelled at them in the official white book *About Events in Czechoslovakia*, a documentary collection by the Soviet government published on September 10, 1968.[43] The book charged among other things that agents of international Zionism wanted Israel, which the Socialist countries had condemned for the 1967 war, to bring about political and economic changes in Czechoslovakia. The purpose of the alleged Zionist coup was "to restore diplomatic relations" with Czechoslovakia! The same anti–Zionist interpretation of the root causes of the events in that country came from the Polish and East German communist press. The last–named organs were especially vituperative. Bertrand Russell in a letter to the *Times* of September 16, 1968, reported that the Soviets were even pressing beyond the Soviet boundaries for a new show trial in Czechoslovakia for their own dubious purposes.

Soviet Constitutional Pledges and Treaties on Human, Religious, and National Rights

The All–Union constitutions of 1936 and 1977 provide a good number of "guarantees" to national minorities, extending also to Soviet Jews. But they subordinate minority rights and privileges to the interests of the working class and in particular to Party and State. Article 52 of the 1977 constitution repeats the pertinent article 129 of the Stalin constitution, pledging "freedom of religious worship for all [!] citizens."

Article 34 of the Constitution underlines "equality before the law" of all Soviet citizens, "irrespective of nationality, race, language, or the attitude toward religion." Still, other articles of the 1977 constitution stress that the rights of citizens and their freedom "must not harm the interests of society" and the state—words which lend themselves to broad interpretations likely to curtail individual rights. While the constitution does not list any demand for ultimate "fusion" of Soviet nationalities, it unquestionably strengthens centralism further in the USSR. On the whole, constitutional and legal "guarantees" of nationality rights are in the case of the Jews undermined by repeated assertions of prominent Soviet leaders that Judaism and Jewish cultural and religious practices are socially retrogressive. The Jews, frequently considered a caste rather than a nationality, are destined to disappearance, to national–cultural and linguistic death, and are in fact singled out for speedy assimilation.

On the other hand, having voluntarily subscribed to numerous U. N. covenants and conventions on human and national minority rights, the Soviets were legally and morally bound by them. Having participated in the Conference on Security and Cooperation in Europe, final Act, they became also a signatory to the Helsinki accords. These accords represent Soviet concessions to the free world and also to the Third World. Most important among the relevant U. N. agreements is the "Universal Declaration of Human Rights," adopted by the U.N. General Assembly in resolution 217 on December 10, 1948. Forty-eight states approved this declaration. Among the eight states which abstained were the USSR, other Communist states, Saudi Arabia, and South Africa. The automatic observance, however, of all the provisions of the 1948 Declaration was conceded in two subsequent agreements reached in the U. N. in 1966.

The 1948 deliberations have revealed Soviet hesitations and their qualifications of the foregoing rights. They stressed the importance of the concept of sovereignty of the member states, laid emphasis on the duties of citizens in their respective countries, and on the individuals' observation of the particular economic, social, and national conditions prevailing in each member state. They emphasized the right of emigration and of the return to one's country of origin. The Soviet Union first withheld its approval of this Declaration in the U. N. Assembly which voted for it on December 21, 1965, but ratified this document three years later. In 1966 the Soviet Union again abstained from voting on "The International Convention on Civil and Political Rights," which reiterated and in some cases enlarged also upon national minority rights. While the Helsinki Agreement of 1975 is not a treaty in the proper sense of the word, it was linked with previous U.N. agreements on human and national minority rights issues. Relating to the individual's right to travel, it is more restrictive than earlier U. N. agreements, especially those adopted in 1948. It emphasizes the right of emigration on the basis of the "unification of families," in principle already acknowledged by the USSR, and on the basis of marriages between citizens of different states. It is also related to a number of other procedures which made emigration cumbersome and expensive.

At Helsinki the Soviets were anxious to have their post-World War II European borders recognized and to gain concomitant advantages. In practice, the Soviet concessions to the West in regard to human rights and nationality issues—which they still consider "internal issues"—have been minor ones. Though Western nations also have been slow in ratifying some of the foregoing covenants, the Soviet Union has been clearly in violation of many of the foregoing rights, especially of those relating to religious training facilities, religious instruction of children, and of the "separation of church from state and schools from the church."

The CPSU on Assimilation and Russification. Politization of Nationalism

The new Party program adopted in 1961 disclosed once again the ultimate Soviet scheme of assimilation and amalgamation of its peoples and languages.[44] At the Twenty-Second Party Congress Krushchev renewed his call for speedy Russification. There was no actual let-up in this process, since many individuals of the various Soviet nationalties, especially Soviet Jews, found it to their advantage to turn more and more to the Russian language which speeded their individual assimilation to the dominant culture and nationality and also facilitated their personal career. Still, in the 1959 census about half a million Jews listed Yiddish as their mother tongue—which was considered by many contemporaries an understatement. In 1963 only sixty-six languages were listed as being in daily use among the various Soviet peoples. If one compares with it the much greater number of languages listed after the October Revolution, the decline is striking. The 1963 statistics shows the progress of linguistic assimilation to the Great Russian language. Russification, clearly the official Soviet policy has made great strides during the Soviet period, though the ruling clique is far from being satisfied with the progress made.

A powerful trend which has emerged in Soviet politics is the politization of nationalism within the CPSU. The relative decline of the birth rate of the Great Russian nationality, of all Slavs in the USSR, as compared with the birth rate of other Soviet nationalities, has given encouragement to the non-Slavic peoples and simultaneously aroused fear among the Slavic population of the USSR in regard to its future national composition. It has given rise to strong local patriotism and has led to the greater cooption of regional leaders into the Politburo. The nationalistic issue has thus penetrated into the inner sanctum of the centralist CPSU.

In the period following Stalin's demise, the fellow-Georgian Beria became a focal point of the nationality struggle in the Politburo and among the top hierarchy of the Party. In his toast to the Great Russians on May 25, 1945, Stalin had conspicuously praised the Great Russians. So did General Secretary Brezhnev. When reporting to the Twenty-Fourth Party Congress, he lauded the revolutionary energy, the diligence, and profound internationalism of the Great Russians.[45] After coming to power, Brezhnev had first hesitated between siding with the less developed nationalities or the Great Russians. Finally, he had swung to the latter, espousing the "Soviet people" concept

against those in the Party who supported the course of "separateness" of nationalities. This renewed turn toward the Great Russians
boosted the latter's nationalistic sentiments and, with it, of anti–
Semitism.

Though for decades the Soviet Union has presented itself as a
classless society, in contradistinction to the class structure of Western
countries, it is in reality socially and economically a class society.
It is torn not only by economic and social differences but also by
deep national tensions. The economic and social structure of Soviet
Jews, quite different from that of the tsarist era, has undergone major
changes. On the whole, however, it was and still is different from
that of the Russian nationality and that of other nationalities in the
USSR. Jews today are intellectuals and white collar workers. Many
other nationalities are largely part of the lower classes, are laborers
in villages and manual workers in towns and cities. The national
differences between Jews and other nationalities are still enhanced by
social and economic differentiation.

There are numerous differences between Soviet Jews and the
nationalities of the border republics in particular. The usual anti–
Semitic accusations, in many instances Moslem–Jewish dissensions,
are magnified by Soviet Mideast policy and propaganda. In many Soviet republics, Jews—partly immigrants to the area from European
Russia during World War II—are also resented as belonging to a socially and economically privileged group. They are also resented as
Russifiers. Opposing extensive Russification of the border regions,
the native population, unable to attack this policy in an overt manner, have diverted their opposition to it toward Soviet Jews. The
latter, highly assimilated, are culturally and linguistically the ally of
the Great Russians. The indigenous population has adopted anti–
Semitic slogans to register its hostility against Soviet Russian nationality policy, its disapproval of Moscow's alleged preferential treatment
of Soviet Jews, its cultural ally. Soviet retreat in the border regions
has taken the form of permitting the replacement of Jews by members of the indigenous population. But while yielding to the latter,
Moscow still insists on the continuation of the policy of Russification
of the border regions.

The Literature of Hatred. Books and Journals

Many of the anti–Semitic books published in the USSR since the
Six–Day War were printed in mass editions. One authored by Yuri

Ivanov had 70,000 copies, another edition of the same book 200,000. Two books written by V. Begun had 25,000 and 150,000 copies respectively, one by Y. Yevseev, 75,000 copies. The apparent reasons for this mass printing of hate propaganda must have been either that the anti–Semitic appeal was considered great enough to warrant the huge investment or that the "noble" cause of "enlightening" the public deserved taking publishing risks!

A few examples from these "works of literature" may be given in the following. In *Beware Zionism! Essays on the Ideology, Organization, and Practice of Zionism* (Moscow: Politizdat, 1961)[46] Yury Ivanov wrote:

> With the Israeli ruling class's June [1967] aggression against the Arab peoples, we saw emerging from the shadow the organizers of international provocation, of dirty intrigues and crime. The Zionist operators were prepared to trample on everything in their quest for profit and power.

According to Yevgeny Yevseev, *Fascism under the Blue Star. The Truth about Contemporary Zionism. Its Ideology, Practice: the System of Organizations of the Jewish Haute Bourgeoise* (Moscow: Moloday Gvardiya, 1971), fascism does not change its class character whether the flag displays "a brown swastika, the blue star of Zionism, or the stars and stripes of American imperialism." In *The Creeping Counterrevolution* (Minsk, 1972) V. Begun traced the "ideological origins of Zionist gangsterism" "way back to the Holy Thora scrolls, to the Talmud's prescriptions," while V. Skurlatov in *Zionism and Apartheid* (Kiev, Ukrain: Politzdat, 1975) pointed out that both Zionism and apartheid were related to Nazism; they were "merely present–day varieties of this myth concerning the alleged congenital inequality of peoples and races."[47]

Such utterances from these pamphleteers and like–minded Soviet authors, all operating under the watchful but benevolent eyes of Soviet censorship, could be multiplied *ad infinitum*. They give a clear picture of the vicious tone, the reckless charges, the low–type polemics and the boundless hatred of the writers. They revel the extent of vilification to which Jews and Zionists in the Soviet Union and abroad were subjected. All this was permitted by Soviet authorities, despite solemn constitutional guarantees prohibiting spreading religious, national, and racial animosity and propaganda. But the Soviets have continued to assure everybody that since their proclamations of national equality in 1917–18 the "Jewish question" had been fully revolved. While totally ignoring Jew-hatred in their own backyard and in other Communist-ruled countries, not to mention the Moslem states of the Third World and beyond it, the Soviets have dared voicing concern over anti-Semitism in the West!

In an *Izvestia* article on April 5, 1964, "Much ado about nothing," referring to the publication of J. Kichko's *Judaism Without Embellishment,* the reviewer admitted that there were "some mistakes" in this book.[48] Though the author had used "new material" in analyzing the reactionary nature of Judaism as a form of religious ideology, the booklet, "in addition to correct statements," contained "historical and factual mistakes and imprecisions which may be interpreted as contradictory to state policy on religion. Many of the pictures of the book may offend believers and be interpreted as anti-Semitic." It quoted the newspaper *Radyanska Kultura* which had criticized "certain erroneous statements made in this book." *Izvestia's* reviewer of Kichko's tract actually beat full retreat. But the anti-Semitic "study" was simply too valuable for *Izvestia* and anti-Semitism in the USSR too widespread to disavow the book completely. It had to be salvaged! According to the reviewer, the initiators of the present anti-Soviet propaganda—meaning the critics of the widely anti-Semitic tract—used it to discredit Soviet policy on the nationality question! The communist daily pointed to the constitutional guarantee of national equality and other pious declarations to prove Soviet good faith.

Yury Ivanov's *Beware Zionism!* (1961)[49] is one of the earlier Soviet expressions of virulent anti-Jewish and anti-Zionist hostility and of its repudiation of "international Zionism" in particular. "International Zionism is the enemy of all [!] peoples and of all national groups and nations." No proof whatsoever was offered for such a preposterous slogan. The author also claimed that Zionism was based on the theory of Jewish "racial superiority." This ideological hodgepodge was allegedly advocated by the anti-Soviet American scholar Walt Rostow. Ivanov's tone was the equal of the worst in Nazi rhetorics.

The flood of Soviet anti-Semitic propaganda in pamphlets and articles has not stopped in the aftermath of the 1967 and 1973 wars in the Mideast between Israel and her Arab foes. In a series of articles dripping with anti-Jewish venom, M. Donetsky, "Danger: Zionism"[50] in *Vechernaya Odessa,* in June 1975 presented a picture of complete distortion of recent Jewish history. According to it, Nazis and Jews have always worked in close collaboration, the latter being supported by international capitalism. The Zionists, having allegedly embraced Nazi theory and practice, had made "full use of the German fascist experience."

Y. Yemeleganov published in "Zionism Unmasked," *Nash Sovremennik*. 1978, a review of V. Begun's *Invasion without Arms* (Moscow, 1977). It was only slightly over a decade since the Israeli "aggression" began in June 1967, wrote the reviewer, that the word "Zionism" had made its appearance in wider circles. Israel was only a small subdivision of international Zionism without which it would not last one day. The Soviet Union did not oppose Israel, but only the politics of its Zionist government which is militaristic, anti–Soviet, and contrary to the interests of the Israeli people itself. That Zionism tried to destroy the solidarity of the Socialist community by covert methods, was exemplified by events in Poland and Czechoslovakia. The "monstrous chauvinism" of Zionists was aimed not only against Arabs, but against other nations as well! "Many apologists of [Zionist] ideas express their 'haughty disdain' of the peoples of Russia."[51]

While anti–Zionism has become a cardinal faith of Soviet Communism, the latter, in accordance with its usual tactics, claimed that not Sovietism, but Zionism was the aggressive party. This was clearly expressed in the title already of the book *Anti–Communism and Anti–Sovietism are Zionist Professions*. This claim in turn is a mere Soviet version of the Nazis' assertion that their entire Jewish policy was only a justified "defense" of the German people against the centuries–old oppression by the Jews! In Nazi and Soviet thought everything is turned upside down, lies are transformed into truth, the aggressor into a mere victim! And Zionism is painted as the enemy of the entire Socialist bloc of nations rather than as its innocent target.

The reviewer of a book by Yevgeny Yevseev, *Fascism under the Blue Star* (Moscow, 1971) in *Molodaya Gvardiya* questioned the Zionist thesis of the existence of "a single Jewish people,"[52] and the term "Jewish People in the Diaspora"—both of which ran counter to Soviet dogma. Agents of the Zionist Secret Service have often set fire to synagogues, desecrated Jewish cemeteries, and carried out "many other vile provocations." Zionists were propagandists of "racism," the reviewer declared here, only a few years before Arab and Soviet propaganda succeeded in putting the label of "racism" on Zionism in the U. N. According to *Judaism and Zionism* there were only two nations, Jews and "goyim" (non–Jews), and the latter were the Jews' enemies.[53]

Slander, insinuation, murder, theft, provocation, spying, expansionism, aggression are only part of a long list of crimes perpetrated by international Zionism, operating all over the

world as an active phalanx of anti–Communism, as a perfid-
ious enemy of national liberation movements of many peoples.

The author compared today's Zionists with yesterday's Nazis.

By every standard, the Jew–hatred springing from these pages
was comparable to that of the Nazis. Of course, without official Soviet encouragement such vilifications and propagations of boundless
hatred would never have seen the light of day. The day when Soviets
under Lenin had battled anti–Semitism—never out of philo–Semitism,
but motivated by self–interest—belonged to the irretrievable past.

A book, *The Creeping Counter-Revolution* by another prolific
Jew–hater, Vladimir Begun, which appeared in Minsk in 1972, had
the following revealing subtitles: "Hatred of the Doomed," "Under
the Flag of Culture," "Invasion without Arms," "Gangsters of the
Pen," "Legalized Crime," "Service of Espionage," "Sinister Alliance,"
etc. Zionists were accused of "artificially inciting anti–Semitism"
through destroying cultural centers, forging foreign anti–Semitic propaganda material, while "pen–pushers" invented the "next canard to
support the fallacious thesis of eternal anti–Semitism."[54] Some subdivisions and chapters of the pamphlet *Zionism and Apartheid* by
Valery Skurlatov,[55] published in Kiev by Politizdat, 1975, carry the
following titles: "Racist Myth of the 'Chosen People' as Justification
for the Exploitation of Peoples," "Zionism as a Colonial Venture,"
"Apartheid—the Logic of the 'Chosen People,'" "Counting on Terror
and Coercion," "Criminal Alliance," "Birds of a Feather," "Against
Peoples." Vladimir Begun's foregoing book had similarly endearing
chapter headings: "Signs of Arrogant Contempt!" "Biblical Prophets
and Cynical Virtues," "Crocodile Tears," "The Ideological Sources of
Terrorism," and "The Espionage News Exchange." Christian Zionists
were either "fooled by Zionists or bought" by them. "In the Zionist
leader Achad Haam" one is "able to smell the fascism of the 'sage'."

G. M. Shimanov, *Jews in the USSR* (Moscow, 1976)[56] when
asked by a correspondent of the magazine, denied the rumors that
he was Jewish and claimed that he had "purely Russian blood." Like
German anti–Semites of recent times, he embraced the "organic" theory of the nation, asserting that no people will ever assimilate Jews. A
true solution to the Jewish problem was possible "only under universal Christian theocracy whose new growth is distinctly observable" in
the Soviet Union. Clearly, here are anti–Semitic views which, though
uttered by some of the Christian opposition, were tolerated by the
Soviet authorities. A letter from three believers to the "Sovereign

Archbishop," the "Very Reverend members of the Great Synod"[57] made the attempt to show solidarity of some religious groupings in the USSR with the Communist state against the Jews! Shimanov points "to the fact that world Zionism is conducting a perficious war against our state, both from abroad and from within." Though religious-oriented, he rallied to the defense of the atheistic state against the common enemy—the Jews.

On January 10, 1971, a Russian letter–writer, the "domizdat" journal *Veche*, was dissatisfied with its first eight issues,[58] proclaiming the need for more articles rejecting attacks by Zionists against "honest Russians" and peoples of other nationalities.

> We must demand a fair distribution of apartments for the native population, including the Russians and not the Zion-izers. . . . We must demand a quota which accords with the population of a given locality and representation in in-stitutions and other places of higher education and so forth.

The journal should come out with the banner headline "Death to the Zionist aggressors!" The coarseness and vile purpose of such outbursts as well as Soviet permissiveness and willingness to disseminate this hate propaganda are unmistakable.

The crude Soviet anti–Semitic propaganda is aimed at little edu-cated and sophisticated people rather than at the Russian intelligent-sia.[59] Some elements of this propaganda are clothed in the language of "internationalism," "proletarian brotherhood," anti–Cosmopolitanism, anti–racism, and struggle against fascism—all words which actually need decoding. While many of the communist slogans are distinct from the language of the Third Reich, the substance of the anti–Semitic, pogrom–like propaganda, having escalated especially during the last three decades is virtually identical with that of Nazi Germany. The hatred unleashed by the Soviet regime is government–approved. Nazi racial hatred led directly to the holocaust. Even if the future should turn out to be brighter for Jews than decades and years of most vicious Soviet anti–Semitism give reasons for assurance, the fact re-mains that the Soviet propaganda war against Jews and Zionists has been waged ruthlessly and shamelessly. It violates the spirit of de-cency, of democracy, of socialism and of international brotherhood. It may prepare the way for racial, religious, and national explosions, of pogroms worse than any which have occurred in Tsarist Russia.

Soviet Anti-Semitism as Judged by Israeli Scholars and Soviet Emigrés

Few are better prepared to judge authoritatively the situation of Soviet Jewry than those who were born and educated in the USSR and know Soviet conditions and Jewish–gentile relations in the country first–hand. Often jailed on spurious political charges because of dedication to Zionism or interest in cultural and religious Judaism, some were finally permitted to leave and established themselves as scholars in Israel. Several of them formed a study circle in the home of the President of Israel, Chaim Herzog.

The widely known Israeli scholar Shmuel Ettinger has pointed to published Soviet articles and books as "of the most abusive nature ever recorded." In his lecture on February 21, 1984, he called the campaign unleashed against Zionism, which had started seventeen years before, the "longest of all the propaganda campaigns so characteristic of the Soviet state." Its promoters apparently wanted to make it "part of the official ideology." Since the Soviet publications, apart from Samizdat, are "all official and come under the censorship of the Glavlit, which supervises the admissibility of all publications, they are in fact directed by government authority."

Between 1926–1931 there were dozens of publications whose express purpose was the struggle against anti–Semitism. But by 1984, according to Ettinger, the possibility of resistance and opposition to anti–Semitism was in fact brought "to a complete halt" by the Government. It has become official policy that populist and governmental anti–Semitism were not to be met by resistance on the part of Jews or non–Jews.

The most outstanding among those leading the anti–Jewish campaign were "a number of journalists and persons, not very large, working in research institutions," dealing with questions of ideology, who are apparently considered experts on Zionism, "such as Begun, Yevseev, Korneiev, Bolshakov," and others. Yet the fact remained that their views are widely disseminated by some authority and that certain groups were interested in developing these views; others were "still hesitant."

Many students of Soviet and Jewish affairs take a more critical and less benign view of the official Soviet attitude which after all gives free reign to their anti–Zionist and anti–Semitic propaganda. Ettinger conceded that this group of intellectuals was "the people who create the ideologies" and that there is an "unquestionable danger of

Nazi–style anti–Semitism developing." He still held, however, that "the present regime, despite the tendency to exploit hostility towards the Jews for its own political purposes and despite the numerous difficulties faced by the Jews, still serves as a barrier against mass anti–Semitic riots."

It might be added that if any restraint has been demonstrated by Soviet authorities in regard to Jews, it was rooted in fear of any initiative taken by the "masses" which might possibly extend to other segments and policies of Soviet society. The causes of restraint in their Jewish policy do not lie in any sort of Judaeophilia or general humane considerations. Though the Soviet regime day in and day out proclaims itself as "revolutionary," it actually fears "revolution," and any populist initiative. It apparently fears that the fury of anti–Semitism, once unleashed, may turn against the Party and the government.

Who are the segments of the Soviet population most susceptible to anti–Semitic agitation? Ettinger pointed to the widespread distrust toward the Jewish community in the USSR, not only toward those anxious to leave the Soviet Union, but toward all Jews, including the many compelled to abjure Zionism and religious Judaism and protesting their loyalty to the USSR. Many Soviet officials were the first generation of peasant people leaving the countryside. They brought with them all the prejudices prevailing in village society, including those held by the Greek Orthodox Church, toward the Jews. The new Soviet anti–Semitism rested thus in centuries–old religious biases. The anti–Western and anti–imperialist Soviet propaganda, closely tied up with anti–Zionism and anti–Judaism, sharpened the image of Russian Jewry as the West's ally, as the "Fifth Column" of the enemy.

In the discussion following Ettinger's presentation, Dimitri D. Segal judged the situation of Soviet Jewry as "unprecedented even in the worst period of the tsarist regime in Russia." In the tsarist period pogroms were "followed almost immediately by a condemnation on the part of the Russian intellectuals and the general population." But this was no longer the case in the Soviet Union. Segal stressed the "gravity of this absence of any Russian reaction to anti–Semitic manifestations and anti–Israeli policy on the part of the Soviet Regime.[60] Nor was there such reaction on the part of Russian society living beyond the borders of the USSR. He especially singled out the Nobel prize laureate Alexander Solzhenitsyn who had not made any clear unambiguous statement against anti–Semitic propaganda or anti–Israel policy. The Orthodox Russian Church to this day, if compared with the practices of different branches of Protestantism, included in its official dogma "extreme anti–Semitic pronouncements." "The deletion of any reference to the Jewish people" in Soviet newspapers, schoolbooks and all literary works in the USSR was, in Segal's opinion, "even more serious than overt anti–Zionist propaganda. Not only are the Jews considered evil, but they are not even able to speak out and proclaim that they are Jews." Such a situation did not exist under the tsarist regime, despite the pogroms. He concluded by raising the question: "Where are the intellectuals and the general public, who could raise their voices against the defamatory pronouncements made by the Soviet regime against the Jews daily? Their voices are not heard . . . "

The emigré Michael Zand distinguished between the various types of anti–Semitism in Russia and the Soviet Union respectively, the Slavic type with its subdivisions, the Russian, Ukrainian, Byelorrusian, Moldavian types, and on the other hand the Christian anti–Semitism and the Moslem one. While Christian anti–Semitism depicted the Jew as demonic and evil, the Moslem type perceived the Jew as a contemptible, subhuman character. Both derided and despised the Jew, while the average Russian considered him at the same time invincible because he allegedly possessed Satanic powers. The Israeli President Chaim Herzog, recounting a conversation with the Soviet representative to the U. N. Jacob Malik, pointed to the deep-rooted religious prejudices expressed by the latter when he had raised the question: "What right has your people to claim that you are entitled to sit closer to God than we are? By what right are you the chosen people?" Others distinguished between official and populist anti–Semitism, the latter also with strong religious biases, stressing the contradiction between Judaism and Christianity. The populist anti–Semitism included many opponents of the government and saw in the Jews a negative and destructive element. There is a strong link between this anti–Semitism and the theories of reactionary and conservative Slavophilism dating back to the nineteenth century.

There was finally, according to some participants in the foregoing exchange an "intellectual anti–Semitism" which had also economic and social roots. The Russian and non–Russian intelligentsia battled the highly competitive Jewish intelligentsia in order to squeeze them out of the Soviet economy and take their place. They have concluded that Soviet Jews are vulnerable and that the ruling Communist Party was prepared to develop native cadres at the expense of the Jews. Though the anti–Semitic intellectuals are "still restricted in number," they spread their ideas far and wide," "through historic novels which are widely read in Russia or through biographies. This sort of anti-Semitism, some feared, might become "an integral part of a total ideology." The role assigned by these authors to the Jews, that of evil and opposition to all positive trends in history, constituted "a real threat to Jewish existence."

A few Soviet Russian intellectuals have taken up the honorable tradition of defending Soviet Jews. They have demanded ending their persecution and granting them the right to emigration. Those who prefer to remain in the Soviet Union should enjoy full equality. The distinguished physicist N. Chalidze, also founder of the Soviet Committee on Human Rights, addressed a letter signed also by A. D. Sakharov, co-discoverer of the hydrogen bomb, and A. N. Tverdokhlebov, another prominent physicist, to the government.[61] It showed that an important segment of the Russian intelligentsia completely rejected the official hostile Soviet popaganda against Israel and Soviet Jews. It was plainly ridiculous, they pointed out, that Zionists wished to undermine Soviet power.

> Their main principle is non-interference in [Soviet] affairs here. They observe the non-interference so painstakingly that they are sometimes reproached for egoism by those who are concerned with defense of human rights in our country.

The writers denounced the entire procedure for making applications for exit visas as "excessively cumbersome." The letter-writers called for an end to the "persecution of Jews: and for the dismissal of criminal charges against them." They forwarded this letter to the Presidium of the Supreme Soviet.

Ten days later, on May 31, 1971, Chalidze, turning again to the theme of emigration rights for Jews, sent the letter signed by two other fellow-scientists, both to Premier G. A. Kosygin and Golda Meir, and a copy to the U. N. Secretary General U. Thant. In a letter to President Podgorny, Chalidze charged that the government policy held Jews in the country "by force." In the first week of October Sakharov accused the government that the lives of would-be emigrants were "transformed into constant torture by years of expectation only to receive unjustified refusals." Their breaking the law was "prompted by extreme necessity." The courts considered them guilty of having "betrayed the motherland" and imposed the most severe punishment on them. Considered second-class citizens, their very indication of the desire to emigrate was met by prompt ouster from their positions as workers and professors at universities. A free country "cannot resemble a cage even if it is gilded."

A prominent dissenter, Roy Medvedev, urged the Soviet government to carry out "consistently" the most important instructions of Lenin and the CPSU program on the nationality question which so far had been ignored. "All manifestations of open and secret discrimination of Jews must be unconditionally abolished." Jews must be granted equal rights "to participate in political, cultural, and economic affairs. It was necessary to abolish the fifth point in questionnaires and the third point of passports [asking for the nationality of the bearer]." All these reforms should be openly proclaimed by a Party Congress and mistakes and misrepresentations of past years be openly admitted.[62] Many, if not most Soviet Jews, however, remained skeptical about the Soviets having the will and the ability to end anti-Jewish discrimination and Jew-hatred. As Zand's *Theses* pointed out: "All sections of society are infected with anti-Semitism in everyday life."[63]

Soviet Nationality Theory Since 1967. Internationalism, Patriotism, and "Bourgeois Nationalism"

Since its establishment the Soviet regime, excepting perhaps most recent developments, has not undergone radical political changes. But in Soviet economics, society, and ideology fundamental changes have taken place, including in nationality relations and nationality theory and policy. "Bourgeois nationalism," however, remains a basic foe. It often simply designates a nationalism in opposition to the ideology of Soviet "patriotism," a nationalism aiming at greater autonomy, in some cases at secession.

In a *Pravda* article "Question of Theory: The Class Content of Internationalism and Patriotism," A. Kapto, Secretary of the Ukrainian Communist Party (August 23), dealt with the problem of "combatting ideas of bourgeois nationalism."[64] Imperialist propaganda was waging "a malicious" offensive against developed socialism in many fields, especially that of nationality policy. "Right-wing and left-wing revisionism and foreign bourgeois-nationalist, Zionist, and clerical centers are uniting under anti-communist banners." It is revealing that these terms—with the exception of Zionism which is singled out as referring to a particular nationality, the Jews, and has a definite anti-Semitic point—are all general in character and not aimed against a special national or religious group. As usual, Jews are given exceptional treatment!

"Internationalism and patriotism are intrinsically inherent to the working class. By its very nature, nationalism is alien to it." The foregoing first two concepts have been raised to sainthood by Communists, the last–named, nationalism, has been condemned as an evil. Youths are especially vulnerable to nationalism and must be properly educated; their fidelity to revolutionary duty, to internationalism and patriotism, must be awakened. Both above concepts, internationalism and patriotism, have, according to Lenin, a definite class nature. The Soviets have found it useful to merge "internationalism" and "patriotism" and glorify both.

Bourgeois interpretation of patriotism is "narrow, hypocritical, and must be rejected." But it was wrong to ascribe "national nihilism" to Communists. Communists endorse nationalism in the form of national self–determination and national liberation, while imperialists and bourgeois movements allegedly oppose national self–determination. Apologists for imperialism battle the Soviets who fight Ukrainian bourgeois nationalism as well as international Zionism.

For a number of years nationalists in the Soviet Union, both of the Great Russian nationality and of the national minorities, have extolled not only Soviet "patriotism" but also increasingly their own distinct and separate naitionalism, bent on reconciling the one with the other and, of course, both with Leninist thought on national culture. Differently from the past, the Soviets now extol their new ideology of "patriotism," "fatherland," and "national pride," and castigate the "imperialist ringleaders" who portray such concepts as "hopelessly outdated."[65]

In theory and language the Soviets have made substantial concessions to nationalism, without, however, surrendering to it. In practice they are holding their own, yielding little. On February 17, 1987 in "Questions of Theory: National Processes in the USSR, Achievements and Problems"[66] the author holds that the Soviet Republics were becoming increasingly multinational. At present roughly 20 percent of the country's population is made up of people who do not belong to the indigenous nationalities of the republics in which they live. All republics have also developed a national intelligentsia. But the growth of national consciousness has both positive and negative phenomena.

> Unfortunately, in some works of belles lettres and in some scientific works one encounters attempts in the guise of national distinctiveness to idealize reactionary national and religious vestiges and to embellish the history of one people while belittling the role of others.

The free development of national languages with the simultaneous dissemination of the Russian language as the language of communication bertween nationalities was a major achievement of theParty's Leninist nationalities policy.

Though, in the 1970s, the percentage of individuals of non–Russian nationalities who were fluent in Russian has increased, the author conceded that still one third of all individuals of non–Russian nationalities was not fluent in Russian. Besides, the Russian language was making uneven progress among the Union Republics' indigenous nationalities. The qualitative improvement of the knowledge of the Russian language especially in the rural areas of Central Asia, Transcaucasia, and the Baltic Republics remained therefore an urgent task.

The internationalization of most spheres of life of Soviet society is "accompanied by an increase in national self–awareness." There is a legitimate national pride, as well as an all–Soviet pride and an all–Soviet self–awareness. But some manifestations of nationalism "forms of egoism—the desire to secure privileges for one's own nationality at the expense of others"—are not justified from the Soviet point of view. Some nationalities, on the other hand, feel that "the legitimate process of the internationalization of culture and the inter–ethnic mingling of population" is a "threat" to their national distinctiveness, culture, and language.

This leads to some sentiments of traditionalism, the underestimation of the Russian language as the means of communication among naitionalities, the temptation to shut oneself up within the narrow confines of national culture.

Nationalistic elements take advantage of these sentiments—and "sometimes not without success."

The Soviet press frequently gives expression to its concern over the rising nationalism of some of its nationalities, including those of Central Asia. For instance, the Kazakhs' share of the Republic's population, it is judged, is seen as rising to 50 percent by the year 2000, eventually to 65 percent or 70 percent. T. Yesilbayev criticized Kazakhs and Kazakhistan for "national self–admiration,"[67] "jingoistic slogans," and a press which focuses on matters Kazakh, though the Kazkh population was at present less than a majority. The Kazadhs are admonished to remember that it was their duty as part of the USSR to be "internationalist" in outlook. The magazine of the Kazakh Writers' Union, according to *Pravda*, very rarely acquainted its readers with the works of Russian writers or of writers of other nations, and was taken to task on this ground. In his address "Tackling Kazakhistan's Language Problems" G. V. Kolbin, First Secretary of Kazakhistan's CPCC, criticized at the Seventh Congress of the Republic's journalists, first, that Kazakhs were not fluent in their own native tongue, and second, they they did not adequately know Russian or Kirghiz, German, or other peoples' languages who lived in the Kazakh Republic.

Nor are Soviet leaders and the Soviet press satisfied with the nationalistic and religious biases of the Tadzhiks and of Tadzhik youth in particular.[68] In *Kommunist Tadzhikistana* on February 20, R. K. Alimov, prominent Tadzhik Party member, in an address to the Tadzhikistan YCL Central Committee in Dushanbe, singled out Tadzhik "nationalistic" and "religious vestiges" for criticism. Tadzhik youth were taken to task for its "social infantilism," and for

> showing off, eccentricity in clothing and hair styles, drunkenness, drug addiction, dissoluteness. . . . Political naiveté and an inability to withstand the influence of bourgeois ideology and religion are manifesting themselves.

In many student dormitories there were "frequent manifestations of nationalistic vestiges." "Religious vestiges and a feudal–bey attitude toward women are being overcome only at a slow pace." The struggle to eradicate Moslem and Christian ceremonies and holidays still lacked aggressiveness. Certain Young Communists were even taking part in observing such ceremonies. The First Secretary of the Tadzhikistan CPC recalled M. S. Gorbachev's admonishment to safeguard the rising generation from "the corrupting influence of nationalism" and to avoid "national narrow–mindedness and conceit." He wanted to change the separate schooling in Tadzhik, Russian, or Uzbek.

National Pride and National Arrogance

"Legitimate" ethnic pride is good, declared Professor E. Bagramov[69] in *Pravda* on December 28, 1985. The new historical community which has allegedly developed in the Soviet Union, has eliminated the barriers that capitalism has erected between nations and no longer uses national differences to kindle discord and alienation between peoples, even though the USSR included more than one hundred nations, nationalities, and national and ethnic groups. The draft of the new version of the Party Program noted that the CPSU gave comprehensive consideration to the multinational nature of society.

> During the transition to Communism . . . complete unity
> will come about on the basis of the further convergence of
> Union and national statehood. Class–based national self–
> awareness is compatible with growing convergence of Soviet
> nationalities.

This claim, according to other Soviet accounts, lacks veracity.

The Party, Bargramov continued, pays special attention to the
"Soviet people's unified culture—socialist in content, multifaceted in
national forms and international in spirit." Yet "the unprecedented
leap from backwardness to progress and the flourishing of Soviet national statehood . . . has stimulated national feelings." The Soviets therefore must see to it that the "legitimate national pride does
not take the form—as sometimes still happens—of arrogance or conceit, so that love for one's own people is always combined with love
and respect for other peoples." The warning against national arrogance or conceit is clearly directed at the less developed nationalities
of the USSR, not at the Great Russians. It simply does not occur
to Russian Communists that their dominant nationality ever shows
"arrogance or conceit" and slips into "national exclusivity" if they
spout anti–Semitism and practice it against Soviet Jews. In propa-
gating anti–Jewish sentiments they are actually denying what they
are preaching.

While the Soviets admit that there exist many "national characters" within the USSR, "at the same time," they claim, there existed
a common "Soviet character," made up of

> such features as love for the socialist homeland, collectivism,
> the friendship of peoples, implacability toward the enemies
> of socialism, and a feeling of class solidarity with the working
> people of the fraternal countries and with all those who are
> struggling against imperialism and for social progress and
> peace.

But these undeniability noble sentiments are not voiced toward Soviet
Jews. To the contrary, it is not friendship, but ill will and hatred that
have been expressed toward them.

Persecution of Russian Zionists. Suppression of Judaism

Parelleling this Soviet attitude has been the unprecedented persecution of Jews, Judaism, and Zionists throughout the Soviet period,
the policy of forcible assimilation and amalgamation of Soviet Jewry
with the Soviet people especially as distinguished from Soviet policy

toward other national minorities and, last but not least, the virtual prohibition over many decades of Jewish emigration from the USSR. This prohibition has been slightly relaxed during the last two decades.

Lenin recognized that anti–Semitism was not only an enemy of the Jews but also of Bolshevism and battled it vigorously. But with the end of the Civil War the threat of an overthrow of Soviet Communism receded. Stalin's persecution of Russian Zionists already in the 1920s and 1930s was motivated by domestic considerations, primarily by the desire to speed the Russification and assimilation of Jews and to terminate their separate cultural, national, and linguistic existence. Thousands of Zionists all across Russia were arrested and sent to concentration camps where many spent years of their life and others perished.

Atheistic propaganda instigated by the authorities took many forms, including "show trials" against religious establishments, synagogues, cheders (schools) and Yeshivas (training institutes for rabbis). In some of these "trials" the defendants, yielding to brute force, openly "admitted" their intention of keeping the congregants in ignorance and of preserving their prejudices to keep the Jewish masses in slavery! Occasionally rabbis and other congregants were even accused of bizarre crimes, of "Trotskyism" and of polemicizing against the Birobidzhan colonization project. Though many Jewish educational institutions were shut down, others succeeded for a while in carrying on an underground existence. The anti–Jewish campaign aimed at harassing Soviet Jewry in multiple fields, extending from the kosher slaughter of animals and fowl to the religious rite of circumcision and the Sabbath day as a day of rest.[70] It included special anti–religious agitation on the day of Yom Kippur, the day of Atonement, and the massive closing of the synagogues already in the 1920s.[71]

The suppression of Zionism and of the study of Hebrew underlines the special discrimination of Soviet Jewry and of Judaism, if compared to other denominations in the USSR such as the Greek Orthodox Russian Church, the Armenian, Georgian, and other churches. While in these churches worship was permitted in Slavonic, Georgian, and other languages, the virtual prohibition of the study of Hebrew in the Soviet Union has resulted in Soviet Jews not understanding the language of the prayer. Similarly, as one writer observed, other denominations could manufacture "sacred vessels, priestly cassocks, rosaries, crucifixes used in worship," while Jews were "forbidden to make prayer shawls, phylacteries, and mezuzahs."[72]

The Hebrew language became from the very start of the Bolshevik regime a major target selected for destruction. The language of Jewish prayer books, it became soon the hated object of Soviet atheism. Of course, Hebrew was a means of preserving Jewish culture, religion, and nationality, representing the tie with the Jewish past and present and with all countries where Jews lived. The survival of Hebrew was to prevent assimilation. The latter, the Soviets had decided, was the proper solution of the Jewish question. An indication of the widespread use and dissemination of Hebrew in Russia may be seen from the circumstance that in 1917–19[73] more than 180 books, pamphlets, and reviews appeared in Russia in the Hebrew language! Foremost among them were the publications *Ha–Am* and *Ha–Shiloach*. Due to Soviet repression of the Hebrew language, the majority of Hebrew authors left Russia hurriedly in the 1920s.

Both the Hebrew language and the Zionist movement blocked the striving toward assimilation of the Jews. In the summer of 1918 there was published in St. Petersburg a Yiddish pamphlet by Z. Grinberg, "The Zionists in the Jewish Street."[74] The assault against them had not yet the official support of the Commissariat of Jewish Affairs, though the latter soon adopted the sharp anti–Zionist line. Grinberg denounced Zionism as reactionary and as aiming to separate Russian Jewry from the Bolshevik Revolution. Actually, Russian Zionism treaded rather carefully to avoid any clash with the official communist ideology and its propagandists. When Zionist delegates assembled in Moscow in May 1918, they adopted a resolution proclaiming their "neutrality" on questions of internal Russian politics.[75] But a "neutral" position toward Communism was never fully satisfactory to the Bolsheviks.

Since early 1919 the Soviet–Jewish relationship began markedly to worsen. Following the closing down of Zionist offices and clubs and the repression of the Zionist press, the struggle against Zionism took on an increasingly hostile character. The Cheka carried out a policy of persecution of Jews. In 1920, at its Third Conference, Yevsektsiya proclaimed that there was "no longer a reason for any restraint in the struggle against Zionism." The Soviet government itself, however, as became evident in the conversation of a leading representative of the Zionist World Organization with the Soviet Commissar for Foreign Affairs, G. V. Chicherin, was still evasive in its attitude toward Zionism.

While in the wake of World War II Moscow unleashed an acrimonious campaign against Soviet Jewry and adopted most repressive measures, in foreign affairs Stalin continued to tread cautiously, pursuing the policy of non–interference in the Middle East. But after Stalin's demise, Krushchev adopted a more adventurous and "activist" policy in foreign affairs. In April 1955, *Izvestia* openly proclaimed Soviet interest in establishing "closer relations"[76] with the countries of the Middle East. In an address to the Supreme Soviet on December 19, 1955, Krushchev admonished Israel which had taken from the very first day of its existence an allegedly threatening position toward its neighbors,[77] asserting that behind Israel stood the Washington imperialists. In a conversation with Eleanor Roosevelt in October 1957, Krushchev reminded her that one million Jews in Israel faced eighty million Arabs and warned that a continuation of Israeli policy would bring about Israel's "annihilation."[78]

Jewish Emigration and other "Repatriations" from the USSR

Soviet policy on emigration of Jews was shaped both by internal and foreign–policy considerations. Since these frequently changed, the annual emigration quota too has varied considerably. But for many years emigration was virtually prohibited. Though Jew–hatred should have dictated to Moscow a liberal emigration policy, the screws have been frequently tightened due to sheer power policy and the desire to continue to hold Jews captive and submissive. In recent years the Soviets have often cited the "danger of brain drain." This would have been flattering to Jews if one would have disregarded their outright persecution, the bureaucratic arbitrariness, and dismissal from employment on grounds of political accusations such as the "crime of Zionism," the alleged fear of their revealing Soviet military "secrets" once abroad, and so–called economic misdeeds. Finally, economic policy, strongly motivated by the necessity of "catching up with the West" and even fear of falling further behind the U. S., the USSR was anxious for trade and technology and looked upon the Soviet Jews as a bargaining chip. Within limits it was prepared to trade some of its Jews for loans and technology.

The Soviets had virtually prohibited Jewish emigration in the 1920s and had again effectively curtailed it after World War II. This stance contradicted specific pledges that Jews had the freedom to emigrate. It is of course logical for any closed, especially a totalitarian society to firmly shut the gates of emigration. The multinational Soviet Empire holds its numerous second– and third–class nationalities virtual prisoners. Permitting one of them the freedom to leave the Soviet motherland, would have opened the Pandora box of the Soviet nationalities' flight from "Mother Russia" and destroyed the Soviet

myth of having solved the perennial nationality problem. It would
have virtually ended the great–power status of the USSR and threatened its survival. The right to emigration from the USSR was for
many decades denied not only to Soviet Jews but also to individuals
of other Soviet nationalities. But his policy has been modified.

It was largely conquest which in the course of centuries had
brought many different people into the Russian realm. Also, individuals from all over Europe had been invited by Russian rulers to
immigrate and colonize the vast Russian territory when their services
were needed. Conversely, in the wake of World War II individuals of
different ethnic stock were occasionally permitted to emigrate from
the USSR to return to their countries of origin. The permission given
to Soviet Jews to leave the USSR, apparently envied by some Soviet
nationalities, was by no means a unique and completely unprecedented Soviet policy. During the last decades, it has been allowed,
though on a smaller scale than the emigration of Jews.

In 1956 the Soviets permitted the repatriation of Spanish na-
tionals. During the Spanish Civil War the Spanish Republican Government had sent youngsters from its territory to the USSR. After
1956 a total of 1,899 Spanish adults in the Soviet Union were allowed
to be repatriated. While the Greek Civil War raged during and after
World War II many Greeks had fled to the USSR. They, along with de-
scendants of Greek settlers of earlier times were permitted to return
to Greece. During World War II the Japanese had sent thousands
of Koreans to Sakhalin. After the war seven thousand of them were
repatriated from Russian–occupied Sakhalin. Between 1971 and June
1, 1987, 38,000 ethnic Germans left the Soviet Union for Germany.
Prior to this time, between 1950 and 1969, 21,988 ethnic Germans—
among them about two–thirds former prisoners of war or Germans
from Lithuania (the Memel region)—were permitted to return to the
Germanies.[79]

German settlers had been invited to Russia by Peter the Great
and Catherine II, herself a German princess who came to Russia while
in her teens. The settlers received land, freedom from military service
and from paying taxes, but were confined to Western Russia. The
Baltic Germans in the West, an upper class, became Russian subjects
in the wake of Russia's expansion into the region in the eighteenth
century. During World War II they were expelled from the Baltic
region into the Reich.

As far as the Volga Germans were concerned, deportation from
Russia threatened them already in World War I. But it was during

World War II that about three-quarters of a million were deported
to Siberia, having been accused of carrying out espionage and sabotage at the approach of German troops. While in the postwar era
they were not permitted to return to the Volga region, the Germans
in Russian Asia achieved a favorable position. In many respects it
was more advantageous than that of the Jews in the USSR. They
were given the opportunity to preserve a national-cultural existence
of their own. While Soviet Jews were deprived of having facilities
to maintain their special national, religious, and cultural heritage,
Germans were permitted to develop their own schools, teachers' colleges and to possess their own clubs, libraries, and newspapers. The
Soviet interest in cultivating good relations with the German Democratic Republic (DDR) as well as their own interest in establishing
a positive relationship with the German Federal Republic influenced
substantially the improvement of the situation of the former Volga
Germans in their new Asian residences. Several German weeklies, a
literary journal ("Wochenschrift"), German language programs sent
from radio stations in Alma Ata, Frunze, and Omsk, while spreading
communist propaganda, strengthened German national identity. The
Germans in Soviet Asia were well supplied with books from the DDR.
No such links were permitted between Soviet Jewry and Jews abroad;
to the contrary, they were made subject to stiff penalties.

In the postwar period the Soviets staged a major campaign for
Armenians to immigrate into Soviet Armenia. Armenian "Zionism,"
the return of Armenians to their homeland in Soviet Armenia was pro-
pagandized and greatly encouraged by Soviet Communism. Moscow
did not consider such a movement, differently from that of Jews in
Palestine, as inspired by national "exclusiveness" or "separatism."
The Soviets facilitated similar "repatriation" efforts aimed at the
return of Russians, Ukrainians, and Byelorussians living in foreign
states. This "nationalism," in contrast to that of the Jews, was natural and legitimate. However, many Armenian "returnees" were unable
to adjust themselves to life under Soviet conditions, turned out to be
"unassimilable." and were permitted to leave the Soviet Union for
the country of their former residence.

After a Soviet-Polish Repatriation Agreement signed on March
25, 1957, the government of Poland, communist-ruled as the Soviet Union, permitted the return of about 14,000 Polish Jews from
Russia.[80] But when the Gomulka purge of 1968 ravaged the country,
the great majority of these Polish Jews emigrated to Israel. The Polish regime, just as the Romanian and Byelorussian and other East

European governments, but very differently from the Soviet Union, allowed many of its surviving Jews to leave these countries again. Despite their dependence on the USSR, the governments of these East European states granted their Jews freedom of choice and refused to hold them virtual prisoners as the Soviets did.

VII.   THE SOVIET NATIONALITY CRISIS. GORBACHEV, GLASNOST, AND THE JEWS

The Soviet Nationalities Problem Bursts Wide Open

After his election as General Secretary of the CPSU in March 1985, Gorbachev, zeroing in on the flagging economy first paid little attention to the nationalities problem in the USSR and made no significant pronouncements on it. In February 1986, at the 27th Party Congress, while making only a brief reference to the nationality situation, he followed the routine course of praising past Soviet nationality policy. Yegor Ligachev, then second in command, focussed on the need for exchange of cadres, which held out the prospect of greater central control over nationalities and state and local Party organizations. Perhaps to counter the impression that Gorbachev favored strengthening the center's power, he promoted Aleksandr Yakovlev, a critic of Russification, to the Politburo. There followed personnel shakeups in Central Asian Republics, in Uzbekistan, Kirghizstan, Turkmenistan, and Tadzhikistan.

The problems emerging in Kazakhistan and elsewhere in 1986 centered on Russian–national minorities relations. But there were also differences between various Soviet nationalities. Changing demography, based on internal immigration as well as emigration, on differences in the birth rate of Soviet nationalities, and unequal economic performance and productivity in the various Republics caused the flare–up of unrest among nationalities. Tartar demonstrations in the USSR were caused by their desire to return to the Crimea from which they had been ejected by Stalin during the Great Fatherlands War. But unprecedented mass demonstrations took place also in many other parts of the USSR in the course of 1987 and 1988.

The apparent objectives of the national minorities differed from area to area, depending on their history and their relations with Russians in the tsarist period, on their development and relative numerical strength, and on geography. In the Ukraine and Byelorussia linguistic issues, complaints about the decline of enrollment in Ukrainian and Byelorussian schools, figured most prominently. In the Baltic region the growing Russian population, a consequence of Russian colonization, caused both increasing concern of the indigenous population but may have also made the Soviets more amenable to making concessions[1] such as the formation of a "popular front" in Estonia, a "quasi–political group" and a potential competitor for the CPSU. In the Caucasus region Armenian mass demonstrations over the Nagorno–Karabakh issue and the killings of Armenians by Azerbaidjanis—a relationship complicated by Christian–Moslem dissensions—led first to Moscow's refusal in July 1988 to alter the boundaries of the two republics. Later, a different provisional arrangement by the Moscow authorities pointed to willingness to contemplate changes in nationality policy.

Gorbachev's speech to the CC of the CPSU on February 17, 1988, referring to the nationalities problem as a "crucially important vital question of our society"[2a] appears a year later to have been almost an understatement. Gorbachev asked then for "a very thorough review of our nationalities policy" "both in theory and practice."

Soviet national minorities were stirred up from the Baltic to the Black Sea, from the Asian East to the West. They felt that the era of Gorbachev's "new thinking" and proposed reforms, the open acknowledgement of economic and military errors and failures, especially in Afghanistan, the policy of attempting to reach some agreement on disarmament and to improve relations with the U. S., were likely to bring about a reexamination of Soviet nationality policy, decentralization and greater autonomy. The Soviet minorities raised their voices, displaying unprecedented courage and drive to take advantage of new opportunities, of the greater freedom of speech and action.

The goals of the various Soviet nationalities are by no means identical. Few aim at outright secession from the USSR. But their demands for genuine autonomy have grown at an alarming rate. The dissident movements have been greatly strengthened by continuous demonstrations and mass protests all over the USSR. These occurrences, widely observed, are most damaging to the Soviet Union's power and prestige. The challenge to its concept of sovereignty by the Baltic Republics has been without precedent.

Can the nationalities' unrest become a real threat to the integrity of the USSR? It is unquestionably taken most seriously by the Kremlin rulers. Though the improvement of Soviet–American relation has in Soviet eyes diminished the prospect of outside support, moral or otherwise, to the various Soviet nationalities by the U. S., the nationality situation for the USSR is one of immediate danger. Faced with searing economic problems and the resistance to Gorbachev's plan of reforms—"openness," "reconstruction," and "democratization"—the Soviet leadership will be compelled not only to give greatest attention to the demands of its national minorities, but also to make some major concessions to them. This new situation poses for the student of Soviet nationality problems and of Soviet Jewish policy in particular the question: Can a thorough reform of the nationality problems be undertaken without changing the Soviets' highly discriminatory policy toward Jews? Far–reaching changes of the Soviet nationalities' thought and action is likely to have an impact both on the ruling CP's nationality thinking as well as on that of Soviet Jews.

The "Single Stream" Idea of National Culture. Pro and Contra

Some of the Great Russian nationalists of recent years have clearly been out of step with Leninist thought, though they have never admitted it. In an article "The Russian Cultural Legacy: Two Views"[2b] in *Moskva*, 1986, Vladimir Kozhinov hailed the resurrection of Lenin's idea of national culture, claiming that it embraced the entire Russian legacy. In his view, Trotsky and Bucharin had wanted to destroy the bourgeois elements of Russian culture. Kozhinov went on to express satisfaction with the efforts being made to preserve "everything that is dear to the people's memory." He seconded for instance those who are raising their voices in alarm over the architectural "appearance of our glorious ancient cities."[3a] Speaking at the 27th Congress of the CPSU, Kozhinov's judgment was seconded by Ye. K. Ligachev who voiced the Party's endorsement of "the upsurge in patriotic feelings that we are all [!] experiencing and of the increased public interest in the history of the fatherland and in the wealth of our centuries–old multinational culture."

From the same congress rostrum Boris Yeltsin, likewise a most prominent Communist, emphasized that the question of the loss of Moscow's architectural distinctiveness had "moved into the category of political questions." Recalling Lenin's oratorical endeavors in 1918 to preserve and restore Kremlin buildings, the author referred to recent attempts to flagrantly distort Lenin's concept of national culture. It had been a bourgeois concept as long as the bourgeoisie held power, but after the October Revolution it became a "proletarian concept." "Whoever fails to understand this fundamental difference in the two different situations, will never understand either Leninism or the national question." Before the war, Lenin had also distinguished between democratic and socialist culture and had battled against he inclusion of bourgeois elements in the latter. But in 1919 he held the view: "We must build the entire [!] culture that capitalism left behind and build socialism from it." Some people, however, erroneously believed that Lenin's prerevolutionary view of Russian national culture remained unchanged after the Revolution. This remarkable change in the Party's attitude to nationalism, both the Great Russian variety and that of other Soviet nationalities, was unquestionably the Soviet leaders' response to the rise of nationalism among the masses, to the upsurge of what was previously considered a rightist, reactionary deviation. Yeltsin charged that Kozhinov ignored Lenin's class-based approach and encouraged undesirable ethnic nationalism.

In *Sovetskaya kultura*[36] Koltakhchyan in 1982 held that Lenin's ideas on the attitude toward the cultural legacy and

> patriotism are sometimes distorted and the slogans of restructuring are used not to move us forward but to push us back. . . . The 1960s saw an increased interest on the part of Soviet nations and nationalities in the past. But during these same years an alarming tendency also came to light, a tendency to regard the development of artistic culture as a "single stream."

There was talk about the "wholeness of each national culture" which was supposedly attributable to special "genetic information" and the "genetic memory" of each nation. Authors of other nationalities who share the foregoing point of view put their own nationality in place of the "Russian."

> They say that this "national soul" is something special, that it is superior to the course of centuries during which the Uzbeks remained Uzbeks and the Russians remained Russians. Evidently there is a spirit of peoples.

"Idealistic, psychological, and even religious–teleological 'arguments'," concluded Koltakhchyan, have been pressed into service to resuscitate the pre–Marxist theory of the "single stream." But he was selective: "Everything progressive from the past should pass through the present into the future. But only what is progressive." He concluded:

> The champions of the "single stream" also being quite a bit of confusion into Lenin's understanding of patriotism in

general. Lenin never talked about patriotism in general. On the contrary, he precisely distinguished proletarian, socialist patriotism from bourgeois and petit–bourgeois patriotism, regarding it as a historical and therefore developing category. . . . Patriotism is easily crowded out by ethnocentrism, from which it is but a step to an independently valuable nationalism.

On March 19, 1982, *Pravda* carried a brief article by S. Andreyev seconding Koltakchyan's attack on the 'single stream' view of national culture and, in particular, on Kozhinov's arguments in "Lessons of History."[4] The foregoing nationalist attitude of Kozhinov was scored by Koltakchyan and other advocates of the traditional Leninist concepts of nationalism and national culture. While Kozhinov confirmed the strong links between Russia's cultural past and present, emphasizing that a "single stream" of national culture bound them together, his numerous critics, harking back to the older Party view, castigated him because this new concept allegedly ignored, among other matters, the class approach to the nationality question and national culture.

Religion and Atheism

The Soviets are also alarmed at the deficiencies of their own communist education in general, including that of the Young Communist League (YCL), especially in some of the border republics and in regard to the nationalities question. In 1984, *Kommunist* was appalled at the "idleness among YCL members, their drunkenness, girls' smoking and at the survival of "religious traditions" among young people.[5] The YCL combatted in an ineffective manner "instances of the penetration of religious ceremonies into the daily lives of young people. The *Azerbaidjan Bakinsky Rabochy* wrote thus:

> We cannot tolerate the fact that certain party and YCL organizations, taking the role of detached observers, ignore instances in which young people are drawn into the performances of religious ceremonies, attend services in mosques and churches, and wear articles of religious symbolism. *Kommunist Tadzhikistana*[6] stressed the need of working people being "armed" with Marxist–Leninist theory and "atheistic ideas"!

Some religions in the USSR are now better treated than in earlier decades. But atheism continues its propagandistic activities which are favored by the Party and the shafts of which are directed against all religions. There is, however, no equality in the treatment of religions. Of the various religions, the Greek Orthodox Church, relatively speaking, is best treated, minority religions less so. Judaism is the most suppressed religion.

The Soviets are continually concerned about "the best way to teach atheism."[7] In an article in *Nauchny ateizm* A. J. Vinogradov admitted that religion was a "historic reality" and even socialist society retained objective and subjective "preconditions for the existence of superstitions, mysticisms, and religious prejudices." And a "certain number of Soviet citizens—young as well as old—are susceptible to them." Atheistic propaganda should not confine itself to simply negating religion and the idea of God. It should avoid topics that may evoke "an inward protest in people who do not accept atheistic arguments" and rather prefer less objectionable "attention–getting titles." The author conceded the many emotional attractions of religion. He revealed that often religion and nationality strengthened each other and that believers held that religion was part of the Soviet people's "cultural heritage," this especially in view of the approaching one–thousandth anniversary of the Christianization of Russia and the coming two–thousandth anniversary of the origins of Christianity.

Soviet Moslems

As far as Islam is concerned, a number of factors have produced a change to the better for its adherents in the USSR. Many of the Moslem people in the European part of the Soviet Union and especially in Central Asia are not only religiously but also nationally and linguistically distinct from the Great Russians and other Slavs of the USSR. While these nationalities are not the equals of the Russians, they enjoy a relatively privileged status as compared to Soviet Jews. A. Turnisiv in an article on Moslems in *Pravda* on January 16, 1987[8], urged no abandonment of atheistic propaganda, only a "restructuring" of it. The author considered both the "apologetic exaggeration of religion's role in the history of mankind" and the "vulgar sociological notion of it as a kind of counterculture" "insupportable." He found it impossible to agree with the ideologues of Islam who declared it to be a "civilizing religion." (Is there indeed any "civilizing religion" in the Soviet world view?) After all, Islam was originally implanted in Central Asia by fire and sword and systematically and intentionally "destroyed priceless landmarks of the culture and civilization of the peoples they conquered." Second, "the peoples of Central Asia and what is now Afghanistan and Iran began in the sixteenth century to lag in their development." The responsibility for it lay with Islam "which shrouded the whole region in a dense fog of superstition." The peoples of the USSR which have flourished in conditions of a largely atheistic society, disapproved of the ideology of Christianity, of Islam, and of other religions. On the other hand, "religious feeling is on the rise here and there in our country and not just among people who are not permanently employed but among young people as well."

Today it is realized that the earlier notion of a direct connection between the degree of religious feeling and the lower level of a person's education was an "oversimplification." There are after all known cases of members of the intelligentsia (including teachers) joining a religion, to say nothing of the "fascination with all sorts of occult sciences on the part of people with a higher education." Religion was not a thing of the past. "We cannot simply brush aside the obvious fact that the overwhelming majority of believers were born in an atheistic environment." The author came to a somewhat puzzling conclusion. It was necessary to "fundamentally restructure the system of atheistic propaganda [!]."

> The world's religions were able to win the hearts and minds of millions of the masses of dissimilar countries and continents, and they continue to do so. The number of followers of Islam . . . is increasing not only as a result of natural population growth, but via a huge number of converts (Islam is ceasing to be a purely Eastern phenomenon).

Belonging to the Moslem religion is "often associated" in the minds of believers with their belonging to a given ethno–religious community.

Though having itself invaded Moslem Afghanistan, the Soviet Union officially lamented the Iranian–Iraqui war, a war between two Moslem states. Among other matters, this war has also split the Arab world and delayed the "solution" of the Palestinian problem! In *Izvestia* Konstantin Gievandov deplored the Iran–Iraq "war of attrition."[9] "There was not one disputed problem that could not be solved by peaceful means at the negotiating table." The author complained that the Iranian regime which considered itself revolutionary finds itself "in the same foxhole as the most aggressive forces of imperialism on matters relating to counterrevolutionary activity that is being carried on year in and year out against democratic Afghanistan." The armed conflict between Iran and Iraq has done considerable damage to the unity and solidarity in the ranks of the Arab countries "and especially to their struggle for a just Middle East settlement and a solution of the Palestinian problem." Here is the gist of the Soviet thesis: Instead of fighting each other, Iraq and Iran should fight the real enemy—Zionism! The present war was "beneficial" only to the American–Israeli "strategic allies."

"The Anti–Zionist Committee of the Soviet Union"* and the Soviet Press

"Did Zionists collaborate with the Nazis?" This question was seriously dealt with in *Literaturnaya gazeta* on October 17, 1984.[10] The journal reported of a press conference held in Moscow on October 12 by the Anti–Zionist Committee of the Soviet Union, and in the press center of the USSR Ministry of Foreign Affairs! The place of the Conference gave the anti–Zionist and anti–Semitic activities in the USSR and the organization a great deal of publicity and a semi–official stamp of approval. It constituted an entirely new phase of anti–Semitic activity and testified both to the new assertive international role of the USSR, especially in the Mideast as well as the growth of anti–Zionist propaganda. The Soviet sponsorship of anti–Semitism recalled the Tsarist support for anti–Jewish propaganda before the October Revolution.

Among the participants of the conference were, to judge by their names, about one–third Jews and two–thirds gentiles. Three were non–Russians, one a Swede, another a Finn, both members of the "International Commission to Investigate Israel's Crimes against the Lebanese and Palestinian Peoples"—a name apparently chosen before the investigation was even started. According to *Literaturnaya gazeta*, the press conference was devoted to "exposing the Zionists' criminal collaboration with the Nazis, whose methods are being used by Israel's current rulers."

A leading member of the Anti–Zionist Committee, Colonel D. A. F. Dragunsky, of Jewish ancestry, claimed that it was the Soviet Union's victory that "saved" Jewish remnants in East and Central Europe from "complete extermination." He ignored that Soviet troops were intent on driving the enemy from Russian soil and defeating him rather than on "liberating" East European peoples and the remaining Jews. Colonel Dragunsky accused the Zionist leaders of minimizing the Soviet Union's "decisive role in the victory over fascism" and also

---

* According to the *Jerusalem Post*, 1988, there were rumors that Soviet authorities planned to dissolve the "Anti–Zionist Committee" some time in 1989.

of having actively joined the "crusade" against the USSR. He also charged that Zionist propaganda, "in defiance of historical truth," tried "to narrow the problem of Nazi crimes against mankind," apparently by drawing attention to the Nazi goal of total annihilation of the Jews as distinct from the mere selective killing of individuals of the Russian, Polish, and other nationalities on Soviet soil.

Other speakers, such as G. L. Bondarevsky, asserted that the Zionists were seeking an alliance with the Nazis already in the 1930s, without offering any evidence. The same holds true for Yu. A. Schulmeister and S. L. Zivs[11] who promulgated the "guilt" of Zionist leaders in the extermination of Jews during World War II! All speakers suppressed the known evidence of Moscow's collaboration with Berlin during the years 1939–1941, not to mention the non-aggression pact which unleashed World War II in the first place. No speaker dwelled on the mass murder of East European Jews which started with the outbreak of the war against Poland and Moscow's suppression of all news relating to the Holocaust. Two participating non–Russian speakers, Takman and Krupkin, further accused the Zionists of carrying out a policy of expulsion against the Palestinian people and pointed an accusing finger at the election of the Jewish extremist leader Kahane as proof of the extremism and racism of all of Israel, its people and government. Colonel Dragunsky finally gave assurances that the Committee never equated the concepts of 'Zionist' and 'Jew' in past or present. But his remarks on the latter were as defamatory as those about the former.

In journals which lean toward Russian or Soviet nationalism and seem 'right–wing" such as *Oktiabr* or *Zamia*—the latter the organ of the Defense Ministry—anti–Semitism was frequently voiced. *Novy Mir*, though having a liberal reputation in some matters, has also published anti–Zionist and anti–Semitic articles. Anti–Semitic materials appear also in large quantity in other journals, repeatedly in the authoritative dailies *Pravda* and *Izvestia*. Next to journalism, television shows, movies, and fiction arouse a great deal of anti–Jewish animosity. On account of the relatively large reading audience in the USSR, fiction has a far–reaching emotional impact. In essays, novels, and short stories the Jew is frequently pictured as a murderer, a mercenary, an aggressor and a spy. While in the prerevolutionary era he was painted as cowardly, in the last decades he is presented as a militant aggressor and exploiter. The picture of the Jew which emerges follows a well established stereotype, one which with only slight modifications is closely followed in all branches of Soviet communication, including movies. The Party and state communication networks take an active part in this sort of Soviet propaganda.

As Tsigelman sums it up[12]:

> Jewish Soviet citizens are presented by Soviet propaganda as inferior citizens. Their loyalty is suspect. They elbow their way everywhere, demoralizing the Soviet people, and most harmfully affect the intelligentsia and the youth. The Jewish Soviet citizens are suspect because they are Jews.

Based on this image of the Jew, Soviet propaganda has created the corresponding image of the Jewish state "as a militaristic and fascist state, a treacherous and ruthless enemy of all [!] peoples, a foe who especially hates Russia and the Russians as stronghold of communism."

According to Tiktina, another Soviet emigrant, this official anti–Semitic propaganda has been greatly escalated in the 1970s. In her judgment, the denunciation of the Jew is part and parcel of the Soviet struggle against "pluralism" which it wanted "to nip in the bud."[13] Also, the ruthlessness with which the fight against Soviet Jews is carried on can be explained fully only by the comprehension of Lenin's concept of polemics. According to Lenin, the purpose of the dispute with the political adversary is "not to influence the opponent," but "to destroy him."[14] While the Soviet anti–Semitic propaganda has made deep inroads among the Russian populace and among some members of the Soviet intelligentsia, it should be borne in mind that, for several decades prior to the Bolshevik Revolution and also since, other segments of the intelligentsia continue considering anti–Semitism dishonorable[15] and have rejected it as being not democratic and even immoral and indecent. Yet as twentieth century history demonstrates, a serious threat or mortal danger to Jews can emerge if a mere plurality comes to share these sentiments, attains power and single–mindedly pursues its sinister objective.

In the view of a professor who emigrated to Israel, the group of leading anti–Jewish propagandists consists not of respected intellectuals, but of "good–for–nothings,"[16] many of whom have a rather variegated career. Emel'ianov, for instance, worked one time in the Institute of Oriental Studies before being expelled. Skurlatov was once a "dissident," even a Nazi follower, associated with the University of the Young Marxist, distributing there instructional materials which were openly copied from Hitler's writings. Removed from his post in Komsomol, he was representative of underground nationalists in Russia who publish the magazine *Veche* and openly proclaim a nationalist ideology. These people could not operate without support from some highly placed officials in the Party, the state, or the KGB.

In the perennial power struggle between different Soviet factions anti–Semitism is simultaneously a mighty weapon, a strong motivating force, and a political objective. Several Russian Jewish scholars, having left for Israel, assert that anti–Semitism has become or was becoming "to some degree state ideology."[17a] Its adherents may display different tenets. There exists, for instance, an increasing tension between Russian nationalists and Soviet imperialists, with the latter being compelled to make concessions to the various national cultures of the Soviet nationalities. Whatever their differences on how to preserve the Soviet empire, both Russian nationalists and Soviet imperialists agree on upholding anti–Semitic doctrine.

The element of irrational anti–Semitism was well brought out by the observation of Professor Voronel. The nationalists, he held, "cannot allow the Jews to do anything that they want to. If the Jews want to leave, they must not be allowed to leave. If the Jews do not want to leave, they must be driven out."[17b] This irrational core of Soviet Jewish policy may be partly explained by the circumstance that "not all Russian politics is planned from above, in particular anti–Semitism."

There exists an anti–Semitism which is directly harmful even to Russian interests. It is the result of initiatives and pressures from below, the outgrowth of an anti–Semitic populist fanaticism. It is also the product of governmental anti–Semitic propaganda and policy extending almost over the entire Soviet spectrum. Voronel holds that the Jews in the Soviet Union live under the shadow of "the most dreadful danger."[18] Even the relatively moderate group of Party workers has only one path in the "struggle with the extreme right wings, the path of making concessions with regard to the Jews."

In the article "A Very Zionist Business" in *Ogonyok*, which in past years had frequently published anti–Semitic articles, the author charged that "international Zionism" has close ties with the American military–industrial complex and offered as proof a long list of Jewish and gentile individuals and of American corporations—which supposedly proved his accusations.[19] Though numerous individuals and countries, including the USSR, have been involved in the arms race, the writer focused exclusively on the "discriminatory role played by the Zionists" in this area. Former Defense Secretary Melvin Laird and presidential candidate Barry Goldwater had allegedly close ties with the "Jewish–Sicilian Mafia" and "Zionist nepotism." Since U. S. companies regrettably did not make public the race, religion, and national origin of company officials, it was "difficult," the writer conceded, to determine the amount of wealth owned by the Jewish bourgeoise and to show the extent to which "pro–Zionist capitalism" controlled the companies, but it was "undoubtedly [!] quite large." Zionism was seeking to get its hands on the military–industrial complex as the most profitable sphere of business. "Ever since the formation in the late nineteenth century, Zionism has been an enemy of peace and progress."

In the following issue of *Ogonyok*[20] Korneev tried to show that Israel was far from being a "Jewish paradise." Rather a place of hard labor for the working people. Israel, was, however, a "paradise for investors." It was actually "a form of colony" for the Lehmanns, Kuhns, Loebs, Rothschilds, and other financial magnates. This line, if not these very names, followed closely the pattern of the writings of the *Völkischer Beobachter* and other Nazi journals. As far as the West was concerned, it wished to transform Israel "into a military base for the world's reactionary forces."

In "Zionism Unmasked" V. Yemelianov, in *Nash sovremennik*[21] referred to Soviet anti–Zionist publications, among them one by Yu. Ivanov in 1969: "Since that time," Yemelianov wrote, "articles exposing Zionism have regularly [!] appeared in the Soviet press." Nevertheless, a recent book by V. Begun, *Unarmed Invasion*, presented "scientifically substantial conclusions." "Zionism was a complex, ramified, and well–organized system of organizations and associations, functioning in many countries, linked with Masonic lodges." The Masons have become a major target of the Soviets—as they were under the Third Reich. Like the Nazis, the Soviets have made a point of identifying Jews and Freemasons as heir "enemies."[22] Masonic lodges operated behind a center of philanthropy. But in truth, "not only the monopolies but also international Zionism and shock detachments of imperialists and reactionary forces" were extremely interested in Masonry.

The target of the article "Formula for Treason" by V. Aparin in *Izvestia* is the emigré Voronel, a "Zionist barker"[23] in behalf of Israel, the "promised land." The article was intended as an attack on both Judaism and Zionism, and the individual singled out was portrayed as an "ordinary parasite with a damaged reputation," blinded by hatred for Soviet people and his homeland. He was only an alleged scientist and an "undistinguished provacateur." Aparin spewed forth sarcasm, hatred, and contempt, presenting Voronel and his associated as contemptible traitors.

Soviet Cultural Policy and the Zionist Threat

In the article "The Indestructible Power of Soviet Culture" in *Izvestia*, December 24, 1976, K. Orlovsky and S. Polin praised the achievement of "great things in carrying out Lenin's nationalities policy."[24] It claimed that Jewish culture was actually thriving in the USSR. Contrary to assertions of the "enemies" of the Soviet Union, "of the imperialists and international reactionaries," Zionists sound an "especially hysterical note in the chorus of hostile anti–communist propaganda." The author referred to unspecified documents in the State Archive of the October Revolution which allegedly disclosed "the especially malicious nature of subversive [!] activity" that Zionism has launched against the Soviet people and particularly against Soviet Jews! Zionism was supposedly making attempts "to separate our country's nations and national groups and set them against one another." It was resorting to propaganda of open Russophobia. What especially infuriated the authors was the assertion that Soviet Jews were oppressed and that their rights were "infringed upon as compared to representatives of other nationalities." In past years Zionist propaganda has made efforts to "incite" Soviet Jews to leave their homeland and resettle in Israel. Their efforts had acquired "invariably anti–Soviet overtones."

The authors of the foregoing article made extensive claims about the mass printing of Yiddish books in the USSR and their translations into languages of other Soviet peoples. While ignoring the birth of Israel, they asserted that Biro–Birobidzhan represented "the first [Jewish] state formation in 2000 years"! In the field of culture as well as in others, Jews in the USSR have "absolutely the same rights as the representatives of all other nationalities inhabiting our country." But the Zionists were not interested in the "equality" of Russian Jews, but in their "exclusiveness," in "subversive" ideological propaganda aimed against Soviet nationality policy and that of other socialist countries. As was well known, no one in the USSR was forbidden to study any language, including Hebrew or Yiddish. And "no one interfered with religious Jews." The Soviet Constitution guaranteed the right to observe religious customs and ceremonies. But the Soviet public "cannot tolerate" that Jewish nationalists wanted to use Hebrew study groups for propagandizing Zionist ideology and nationality and cultivating a spirit of national exclusiveness and open racism.

Zionists want to establish direct and permanent ties between Jewish religious communities in the USSR and Zionist centers abroad—which was "downright impudence." The USSR will not allow "interference in its internal affairs." While anti–Semitism was prosecuted under the law, "this does not mean that the Soviet Union ;will permit Zionists to engage in racist [!] propaganda with impunity." Imperialism and Zionism were closely linked.

> Zionism has become one of the basic weapons used by world reaction in its struggle against the Soviet Union and the entire socialist commonwealth, against the Communist and workers' movement and against the national–liberation movement.

> International reaction and one of its leading detachments—Zionism—are striving to undermine the unity of a new historical community of people—the Soviet people.

The article, while vastly magnifying the alleged accomplishments of Soviet nationality policy and its policy toward Russian Jews in particular, paraded half–truths, vilified Zionism and Jewish national demands, and distorted them as being hostile and dangerous to Soviet existence. It considered Jewish criticism of Soviet discrimination as an attack upon the Soviet Union itself, reversing their actual relationship into one between a true aggressor, Israel, and its victim, the USSR. Moscow's placing of anti–Semitism and Zionism on the same plane and painting the latter as a mere instrument of "imperialism" distorted reality. The desire for Jewish independence and sovereignty is turned into "racism." By the same token European and world history would have to be rewritten and the national independence movement of the last two centuries in Europe and the world at large would have to be denounced as retrogressive. The USSR also proclaimed Zionism as the foe both of the world Communist movement as well as of the national liberation movement everywhere.

The reckless and senseless Soviet attitude toward Jews and Zionists leaves little room for any possible reconciliation between them. Nor are there any indications of any real change in Soviet domestic policy toward the Jews. Zionist ideology is declared unacceptable. Even taking full account of Soviet rhetoric regarding all of its "enemies," it appears doubtful that such ideological obstacles as piled up by Soviet propagandists over decades can be quickly overcome.

Human rights, foreign "interference," and subversion, aimed at weakening and at disintegrating the USSR, are in the Soviet mind inextricably intertwined. On March 15, 1977, Candidate of Medicine S. L. Lipavsky wrote the following *Open Letter to the Presidium of the USSR Supreme Soviet*[25-26] confessing to his earlier personal involvement in human rights issues. The author had been in contact with CIA members working surreptitiously in Moscow under cover of official posts.[27] He had concluded that anti–Soviet agitators were distorting the problem of civil liberties and human rights in the USSR. They aimed at slandering the Soviet system and the friendship of Soviet peoples. Theirs was the desire to boost emigration from the USSR and to "undermine the foundations of Soviet power."[28] The letter–writer criticized Jewish activities not only for their Zionist ideas and encouragement of emigration. Zionism was also accused of undermining Soviet nationality policy in its entirety and of aiming at overthrowing the Soviet regime itself!

The Soviets are concerned about accusations raised in the Western press against the USSR and the system of Soviet justice.[29] Western journalists had levelled vicious charges against Moscow on occasion of the case of one "Shtern," charging that his trial was totally unjustified.[30] An article about Shtern in the London *Times* showed that the Zionists had decided to inflate an ordinary swindling and bribe–taking case "to whip up national enmity [!] and to discredit socialist democracy."

V. Yugow, reviewing in *Pravda* a collective work by Soviet authors "exposing Zionism," wrote that *The Ideology and Practice of International Zionism* highlighted Zionism as "one of imperialism's shock troop detachments in its struggle against socialism, democracy, progress, and peace."[31] The authors, while focusing on international Zionism and its ideology of "a worldwide Jewish nation," stressed its activity against the USSR and the entire socialist commonwealth." They asserted that up to 80 percent of the Western news agencies and an extensive and ramified television and radio network as well were "under the infuence of international Zionist centers," which published more than 1,000 periodicals! No less than eighteen international Zionist associations were engaged in directly influencing citizens of "Jewish nationality" in socialist countries. This propaganda machine was also aimed at undermining the process of detente and at deteriorating the international climate. Thus Zionism threatened the peace of the world! The list of accusations against it grew steadily longer.

The West and Soviet Anti–Semitism

It has taken Soviet Jews and even more so Western public opinion a long time to fathom the depth of official and populist Soviet anti–Semitism. The reasons are rather obvious. Marxist–Leninist ideology and its language of internationalism, the apparent theoretical freedom of development of the native languages and national cultures in the USSR in general, and the struggle against fascism and for national equality at least in theory, have created the illusion of a deep–seated ideological opposition between the National Socialist credo and Communist faith and doctrine. Jews themselves, some segments of the Soviet population, and liberal friends of the USSR abroad have long suppressed their inner doubts and refused to acknowledge the distortion of socialism and democracy by Stalinism and its chauvinist tendencies. That the Soviet Union and its peoples battling the Nazi invader, would end up by adopting the Nazi creed of Jew–hatred, seemed incredible and rationally incomprehensible. That the Third Reich, smashed to its foundation, would obtain a posthumous victory by a rebirth of extreme nationalism and anti–Semitism on Russian soil appeared to many a mere figment of fear and wild imagination.

Liberal and socialist public opinion had always assumed that "progressivism" forbade national hatred and religious biases and persecution. They were convinced that Communism, despite inconsistencies in practice, promised national and racial brotherhood and religious tolerance. Indications that this prognosis rested on blind, uncritical "faith" in progress were largely ignored. Since the Enlightenment it was widely believed that progress toward brotherhood and freedom from bigotry was only threatened by ultraconservatism and reaction. The danger to these liberal concepts came only from the Right, never from the Left. The ideologies of the Left and of anti–Semitism were plainly irreconcilable. These widespread but illusionist preconceptions dominated the thought of most people in nineteenth century Europe and long thereafter, including Jewish thought.

There were, of course, distinctions between the Nazi and Soviet practices of Jew–hatred. While the former proudly displayed the banner of anti–Semitism, the Soviets denied sponsoring and supporting it. They thus revealed that it was something shameful rather than worthy of emulation and acknowledgement. Like Janus, they are two–faced, showing one side, the anti–Semitic one, to people at home, and the other, the nobly progressive one, to the world at large. Soviet "internationalism" seemed to run counter to the arrogant and murderous chauvinism of the Nazis. But in practice the Soviets have come close to the Nazis' demonstration of contempt of and discrimination against Jews, ascribing all evil to them and no good.

It also seemed unbelievable that after a victory over the Nazis the Soviets would permit Jew–hatred to penetrate their own ranks and their own peoples. The war and Nazi atrocities, one could have expected, would bring all Soviet citizens closer together rather than widen the national, religious, and cultural gulf between them. Could one reasonably assume that after the Holocaust the Soviets would be so callous as to oppose that the Jews build their own homeland and would adopt a threatening posture toward them? Could one assume that the champions of national self–determination all over the world would oppose national liberation and national independence only for the Jews?

After the Holocaust, the Jewish desire to gain freedom, to gather the remnants of their people, to lead a life free of Soviet second– or third–class citizenship burned brighter than ever. But after a fleeting moment of seeming Soviet support for Jewish national aspirations in Israel, came brutal Soviet suppression of Soviet Jewish cultural and religious endeavors and unremitting hostility to Zionism. This extreme hostility has never since ceased puzzling Soviet Jewry and Western public opinion.

Pamyat, Otechestvo, and the "Zionist–Masonic Plot"

On May 24, 1987, *Komsomolskaya pravda* offered a sharp denunciation of the "ultra–nationalist" and anti–Semitic Pamyat organization under the title "Where the leaders of the so–called Memory Association are heading?" by Ye. Lesoto: "Dragging behind us from out of the past is a patriarchal patriotism," are "totally illiterate peasants who had believed for centuries in God and Tsar and had for centuries ascribed all evil to devil and the infidel." Their patriotism was "based on land–holding, Greek Orthodoxy, and Russian national traits; it is pure nationalism. Touch the lighted match of anti–Semitism to it, and you will see *Memory*."[32a] Unscrupulously and ignorantly, they try to combine "Leninism" with the ideological platform of Memory, mixing it with clericalism and mysticism. The author castigated Moscow City's Lenin Borough Party Committee for assigning space for a meeting of *Memory*. Like other correspondents in other Soviet cities the foregoing reporter makes clear that speakers and organizers of these gatherings try, partially at least, to hide their ulterior purposes, including their anti–Semitic sentiments and thoughts, behind innocent–sounding phrases. But on occasion they incautiously show their colors. Among the culprits pronounced guilty for the destruction of venerable monuments are named exclusively Jews, such as "Lazar Moiseyevich Kaganovich," Yaroslavsky (originally Gubelmann), Chairman of the Union of Militant Atheists, and the architect Ginsburg. The audience responded at the naming of each of these Jews with "furor."

D. Vasilyev, journalist and photographic artist by profession, a prominent leader of *Pamyat*, in the attempt to reconcile the concept of Moscow as the "Third Rome" with "Leninism" to which he claimed loyally to adhere, thundered against the cosmopolitans and those who pledged allegiance to "Satan" and discoursed at length about Masonic and Zionist "symbols." He displayed a special dislike for visiting foreigners to Moscow who came "from overseas" by the thousands! "Away with them! We don't need them here."

As long as Vasilyev denounced "imperialism and Zionism" he followed the traditional Soviet approach. He accused both of placing agents in Russia and elaborated upon "Masonic–Zionist intrigues." He aimed his shafts primarily against non–Orthodox and non–Russians whom he accused of having destroyed "Orthodox monuments" in the Soviet Union. He and other speakers for *Memory* tried to frighten the audience with details of an alleged monstrous conspiracy "planned against the Russian people." Vasilyev referred to a prerevolutionary anti–Semitic publication *Freedom Fighters* (1907).

Needless to point out that the road of *Pamyat* has been paved not only by Tsarist anti–Semitic propaganda but also by the almost continuous official Soviet attacks against Zionists and Jews. Contemporary anti–Semitic propaganda in the Soviet Union used the most modern methods of propaganda, cassette tapes—which were also widely used in Iran, where Satan too was the target! *Ogonyok's* journalists doubt that *Pamyat's* speakers' orations can be discounted simply as "maniacal ravings."[32b] "But hundreds of people were listening to these tirades. And just think how many cassette tapes of Vasilyev's speeches have spread through the cities and villages." The journalists raised the question: "Can we offer a rostrum (in the name of that very openness, in the name of democracy) for instigation, lies, and dangers of social demogoguery?" Great vigilance was most urgent today. The correspondents found it "very painful that, in the process of restructuring, the voices of demagogues who are trying to hitch a ride on that process are heard so loudly." This weak reaction of the press and authorities to the reckless agitation and dangerous subversive activities of *Pamyat* was not likely to cut short the efforts of this nationalistic and anti–Semitic organization, actually aiming to disorganize and subvert restructuring and glasnost, while hypocritically pretending to support them. The latter view was also expressed in an interview by Albert Sirotkin with Doctor of Philosophy Anatoly Butenko of the USSR Academy of Sciences in *Moskovskaya Pravda.*

The national resurgence and simultaneously the reawakening of anti–Semitism have occurred in different parts of the Soviet empire, not only in the RSFSR but also in the outlying Soviet Republics. In either case this nationalism had xenophobic and in particular strong anti–Jewish and anti–Zionist overtones. Thus, whether primarily aimed against the Great Russians or against the "bourgeois nationalism" of the minority nationalities, whether directed at Soviet Jews and/or at Jews and Zionists abroad, its common denominator is anti–Semitism.

During the last years, especially since Gorbachev's glasnost, Soviet journalism has removed some of the traditional shackles to free expression. As noted, it has expressed concern about the meetings in various parts of the Soviet Union, which under the guise of openness have given vent to anti–Semitism and anti–Zionism. This appears for instance in an article by A. Maisenya in *Sovetskaya Byelorussia,*[32c] November 17, 1987, entitled "With the Measure of *Memory.*—Polemical notes on an event that took place in Minsk" on November 1, and reporting about an assembly of about 200 persons, including well-known poets and writers, scientists, artists, people from the theater, officials of the Party and of the Young Communist league, and many young people. Some in the audience were associated with *Tuteishiga,* an association of young writers, and the Talaka Club, around which "young people who on the whole are patriotic and have united and initiated the revival of this glorious tradition." The report is marked by ambivalence, part admiration and part critical distance from the Byelorussian participants at this gathering.

The meeting started with the reading of a poem by Yanka Kupala written in 1905, depicting "all the bitterness and sorrow of the difficult past of the Byelorrussian people, our ancestors, of their joyless existence, adversities and deprivations." The names of dozens of innocent people were listed who in the 1930s fell victims during the "dark days of the rampage or repression." The reporter was especially disturbed when one in the audience referred to the "genocide" in Byelorussia in the nineteen thirties practiced by the authorities. Despite the journalist's apparently critical attitude toward Stalinism and its excesses, this, in her judgment, went too far. After all, others such as Georgians, Ukrainians, and Russians suffered "much more during those somber years." It was just as dangerous to "ache with the past" as it was to ignore it. Still, the journalist despite many doubts considered the meeting a "success in terms of its frankness and sincerity" and its "openness."

While young participants at the meeting showed "boundless patriotism," there were intriguants trying to manipulate them and fighting for the "liberation of the Byelorussian people." The movement of which one need not be afraid, must, however, "purge itself, using its own forces." The following day, the reporter dropped in at a neighbor, the foreman of a plant who referred to a rumor that at the meeting which he himself had not attended, had taken place "some kind of Zionist escapade. . . . My heart sank." That notorious "Zionist—Masonic plot is making the rounds again." Decades after the Nazi invasion of Russia, after the mass murder of Jews and the killing of numerous prominent Soviet leaders, some Byelorussians gave apparently testimony to the effectiveness of Nazi propaganda and to Soviet permissiveness in regard to it—which hurt not only Jewish reputation and existence, but also the survival of the Soviet regime![33]

What was involved here was a national minority aspiration which had not only an anti–Russian point but also an anti–Semitic character. Characteristic of it was not only a greater daring and outspokenness against Great Russian nationalism, but also a strong resurfacing of Jew–hatred. Anti–Semitism in this case appeared as an ally of the nationalism of a small nationality! This link–up leaves the Soviet Union the choice of opposing both this Byelorussian nationalism and allied Jew–hatred, or sacrificing the Jews to the Byelorussians. The journalist of the foregoing piece clearly opposed support for the anti–Semitic stance.

The same opposition to anti–Semitism is expressed by the following reporter, though Jew–hatred in this case was apparently voiced by Great Russians in Leningrad. The piece in question demonstrated the intense anti–Semitism in some intellectual circles in Leningrad. It focussed on "overseas enemies," Jews and Zionists, rather than Western imperialism, on the activities of organizations such as *Pamyat* [Memory] and *Otechestvo* [Fatherland], apparently most active in the dissemination of an elaborate anti–Jewish propaganda—which clearly was also anti–Soviet. It aimed its shafts not only against "bureaucracy," an old enemy, but also against "Zionism and the Masons"— Nazi bugaboos which the Soviets in their official propaganda and So-

viet people at large have uncritically embraced. This particular progaganda was also aimed against Gorbachev's "restructuring." What
irony that Gorbachev and "Zionism" have become joint targets of
some of the Soviet Russian nationalist "opposition," of *Pamyat* and
Otechestvo![34]

According to Soviet journals, the theme "Russian Chauvinism
and Anti–Semitism" was aired on occasion of a scholarly conference
organized by the Leningrad University's Department of Russian Literature and the A. I. Herzen Teacher Training Institute.[35] But the pure
chord of filial concern for the homeland was "intermingled with extra-
neous motifs." The allegedly scholarly presentations were filled with
"insulting epithets, distortions, and misrepresentations", and "crude
attacks against hated colleagues," designed to "intimidate the audience by citing plots and sabotage by enemies of the Russian people
who allegedly are operating everywhere." One literary critic claimed:
"Somebody wants the national roots of culture and art to be alien."
Another scholar stressed "kinship with the people" rather than the
ideology of Marxism–Leninism. The reporter was taken aback by the
inflection in which non–Russian names were pronounced at this "scientific" [!] conference. Others, in "fiery speeches," called attention to
a lot of Russian intellectuals who had mysteriously died in the 1930s,
not at the hands of government but apparently by a band of criminals, and stirred up "dark passions" in the audience. One charged
that some "ministries and departments are directed by our overseas
enemies [!]"; the rejoinder hereto by an economist, M. Lemeschev,
was "vague and confused." Anonymous notes were passed up from
the audience. One of them read: "What is the role of the Jews in
the conspiracy against the Russian people?" But the speaker chose
as reply the following: "They don't leave their autographs."

Clearly, according to the reporter, a "special audience" had gathered there, apparently anticipating a scandal. "They even welcomed a
farce staged by V. Vasilyev, a leader of the *Pamyat* association. This
speaker had come from Moscow, had taken possession of the rostrum, and resorted to "theatrical gestures" and a demogogic speech.
He howled: "We can earn for somebody overseas [!] who is pumping
out our wealth." The reporter concluded that while the dissemination of democracy and openness was "extremely necessary," so was
responsibility in public speech.

On May 22, June 24, and On December 19, 1987, *Komsomolskaya
Pravda*[36] referred to attacks, spearheaded by *Pamyat*, against "Jew–
Bolsheviks" for ruining Russia. These gatherings were seen as a bid

to create a "neo–fascist opposition party." In the article in December 1987 by Ye. Losoto "Thinking about the Mail: Too much alike," the latter sounded off this way:

> I don't understand the newspaper's position: Who needed to shield the Yid–Masons and why? After all, any sensible person understands that the phenomenon of stagnation in public life and in the economy is the handiwork of "the sons of Israel."

The letter was signed I Ivanov, Russian, no address. Another letter–writer claimed that "our government" was made up of Masons and that the Party was leading the people into an impasse. Quoting and analyzing several of these letters, the journalist concluded that it was possible to grasp "the logic of these people . . . !" "Jew–Bolsheviks who hated Russia smashed and ruined everything that was primordially Russian." "Out of hatred for Russian foundations, it is said, they made the Revolution. The Party continued this poisonous work and is continuing it to this day."

Komsomolskaya Pravda, however, warned against Jew–hatred: "Anti–Semitism impels Jews to unite on the basis of 'blood'; it makes a nationalistic opposition out of them. Anti–Semitism is the dream of Zionism." Unfortunately, the writer continued,

> the mail shows that there are people in our country who have been made terrible fools of, who are going out of their minds calculating the 'percentage" of people's blood and tracking down those of neighbors or co–workers who have sold themselves to the Zionists.

> A whole bundle of letters came from Sverdlovsk. *Pamyat* [Memory] operated very actively there. It's called *Otechestvo* [Fatherland] there. It is headed, as it is in Moscow, by representatives of the creative intelligentsia whom no one knows.

Cassette recordings of a speech given by a *Memory* representative at a meeting with artists in Leningrad were circulated around Sverdlovsk. "Bureaucracy, restructuring, Zionism, Masons—everything has been fused into a single alloy . . ."

> One thought runs like a refrain through the speeches made by *Memory's* leaders while they were visiting Sverdlovsk." The age–old enemies of Russian culture, the destroyers of national self–awareness and the present–day opponents of

restructuring are the Masonic–Zionist circles, an enemy that must be ground to dust, against which people must be united in committees of distrust and committees to defend restructuring.

The paper concluded that these efforts are an "overt attempt to create embryos of an opposition party," of a "new neo–fascist party."

In the conditions of openness and democracy, some other, more curious

unofficial associations, have appeared. How do you like union of Monarchists (Soyuz monarkhistov), for example? They telephoned the editorial offices and threatened to blow them up for criticizing *Memory's* leaders. In my opinion, we have before us the buds of all kinds of unions and groupings. Given the appropriate conditions, they could blossom . . .

It is hardly surprising that the partisans of "reconstruction" accused their opponents such as *Pamyat* of wishing to form a "neo–fascist party." The terrorist–like threats against a Soviet paper, and the apparent Communist concern over the future harm of some of the new "unions" springing up in the USSR speak volumes.

There is no assurance that "glasnost" will have only a favorable impact on Soviet–Western relations or diminish the internal threat to the Soviet regime emanating from dissident domestic circles. Nor can there be certainty that glasnost will lessen either official or unofficial anti–Semitism.

Defenders and Critics of *Pamyat*

In an article in *Nash sovremennik* "Our Cultural Legacy and the Present Day: Sacrifice Yourself for the Truth," Valentin G. Rasputin pleaded the case for Historical Memory (the organization called *Pamyat*), charging that the "left–leaning press" treated *Pamyat* society unfairly.[37] Praising "national memory," he spoke of the "unbroken link between the living generations and the generations of the past and the future," and pointed to the formation of unofficial ("neformalny") societies and organizations in Moscow, Leningrad, Sverdlovsk, Novosibirsk and Tabolsk, which restored landmarks, collected money and combatted "illiteracy" in the fields of culture and history. Though not directly mentioning Zionist Jews, Rasputin obviously alluded to them as "people who betrayed Russia, ran off, and heaped filth on her." But then they failed to find the promised paradise elsewhere and were moved by self–interest to return to Russia. They were "treated practically as heroes in our country and have been granted indulgences for their mistake forever," while people earnestly concerned over the fate of the homeland are "hastily smeared with black political and nationalistic paint—also forever."

Shortly after this address, Vladimir Petrov counterattacked in *Pravda*[38] castigating *Pamyat* (not the concept but a reactionary organization exploiting this name) and *glasnost* and several other groups. Judging from letters to *Pravda's* editor, Petrov expressed the letter-writers' astonishment and his own surprise "that in some auditoriums extremist speeches are being made openly and national enmity is being stirred up. And all of this is being done under the guise of democracy and glasnost." Clearly, he concluded, there was reason for "alarm." All these groups were "noisy organizations that have ambitious aspirations and in some cases are utterly ill–disposed toward the Soviet regime and Party policies." They have become the "focus" of public attention and of various debates, not without help of the mass media." Mainly, passions are seething over the organization *Memory*. According to one point of view, *Memory* is preaching anti–Semitism and fighting for Great Russian chauvinism. According to another point of view it was time to "quit persecuting *Memory*." Evidently, *Memory* may not have numerous active supporters, but it has struck a responsive chord both with many Great Russians, especially with its partly open, partly shame–faced appeal to anti–Semitism.

Petrov traced the origin of the organization *Pamyat* back to the early 1980s when Moscow historians, scholars, engineers, workers, and students formed an association under the Ministry of the Aviation industry, coming to the defense of causes such as restoring historic buildings and of the preservation of cultural landmarks. These people were also concerned about the demographic situation in Russia, about the fact that many Russian villages had been designated as having no future, and they were distressed about widespread drunkenness. Yet since then a new leadership had taken over *Memory*. They are almost openly calling for extremes. In the so–called "Appeal to the Russian people" they urged it to "name hostile clandestine quarters," to hold demonstrations and referendums throughout the country and to "establish control over the mass media." The homeland was allegedly "in danger." Zionists and cosmopolitans and associates," claimed Petrov, were "trying to stir up anti–Semitic feelings among the Soviet people." Vasilyev was an "extremist" and it was regrettable that some people were hesitant to call a spade a spade and that they "mix everything up." "All of a sudden the name of Russian and Soviet writers were attached to Vasilyev's inflammatory slogans, creating the impression that they were acting in concert with the extremists." But Russians and people of other nationalities sense that "something is wrong" and that at present *Memory's* leadership threatens "the Revolution and friendship among peoples."

Only a few weeks later, *Izvestia*[39] ridiculed *Pamyat*. The latter assumed a "frightening respectability" by directing its recent "Appeal" to "patriots of all countries and nations" and demanding the reinstatement to the ranks of the CPSU of two of *Memory's* leaders who had been expelled from the Party. The members of *Memory* wore now black T–shirts—"so they've even got a uniform"—and also wanted to set up "people's tribunals." There were allusions that the organization appealed to great–power chauvinism among the Russians. They talk of a "treacherous enemy," aiming to corrupt and then destroy from within the Russian "chosen people," "the only people that is capable of resisting plans for establishing the worldwide supremacy of Zionists and Masons. Yet the leaders of *Memory* propose that everything that is happening be seen from precisely this point of view" and that is why the meetings of the association always take place "in an atmosphere of emotional outbursts, hysteria, maniacal suspicion and defamation of the people who are under suspicion."

Then, turning to authors who are well–known for their anti–Semitic views expressed in books and articles such as V. Yevseev, V. Begun, and A. Romanenko,[40] *Izvestia* continued, they were accused of propagandizing the concept of "conspiracy"; they indulge in "erroneous propositions and inaccuracies. They were anti–Semitic and essentially disorienting to readers but they were 'favorite lecturers' in *Memory*." Yevseev in turn accused *Sovetskaya Kultura* of "complicity in planned action by Zionist elements" and Romanenko charged the journal with "giving aid to the Zionists" in their political campaign against the USSR." They went as far as to resort to judicial proceedings against *Sovetskaya Kultura*, filling the courtroom with their supporters. On that occasion, Yemelyanov, author of an "incoherent and anti–Semitic samizdat opus," appeared in a T–shirt that read "Carry out de–Zionization." Romanenko at the start of the trial asked the members of the court to indicate their national affiliation. When they refused to do so, he left the courtroom.

At the request of the editors of *Sovetskaya Kultura*, noted Soviet scholars associated with the Academy of Sciences' Oriental Studies Institute had publicly stated that the three foregoing authors linked with *Paymyat* had indulged in exaggerations and distortions of quotations.[41] The scholars charged Begun in particular with voicing anti–Semitic views, replacing Marxist–Leninist concepts with them and reaching conclusions in harmony with Hitler's *Mein Kampf*, the bible of German fascism. *Pravda* regretted that V. G. Rasputin had stooped to defending *Pamyat* and had assailed several Soviet journals because they had dared criticizing *Pamyat*.

Only seldom do Soviet circles call for open battle against the *Pamyat* nationalists. But, on August 14, 1988, Leningrad scholars protested "the chauvinist, anti–Semitic propaganda of *Memory*" and attacked the city authorities who "condoned" it. *Izvestia* itself joined the chorus of calling *Pamyat's* actions "socially dangerous," hampering restructuring."[42] It thus declared the organization, rather than Soviet Jews, a threat to the government's reform plans and to the USSR.

The Leningrad scholars associated with the local division of the USSR Academy of Sciences' Institute of Oriental Studies denounced the "hysterical whipping up of hatred for the non–Russian nationalities." The Memory Front was distorting the history of the Soviet Union by

> ascribing to Jews, Latvians and other "non–Russians" most
> of the blame for the unwarranted repressions of the 1920s
> and 1930s and for violation of legality during the time of col-
> lectivization and for the destruction of monuments of Rus-
> sian culture.

Through its Leningrad activities *Memory* was publicly justifying "the disgraceful organization known as the League of the Russian People and Black Hundreds," the reactionary and anti–Semitic groups of the Tsarist period. *Pamyat's* ideologists also condemned marriages between members of different nationalities, recalled slogans of Nazism, and considered "socialist patriotism" and "internationalism" as "something discreditable." Putting much pressure on Jewish citizens as well as on active figures in restructuring belonging to other nationalities, they even called for "guerrilla actions" against them. Such agitation was in violation of specific articles of the USSR constitution which prohibited the preaching of national or racial discord. The Leningrad scholars called upon the city's Party and Soviet agencies who maintained silence in face of such vilification, to take effective action.

Izvestia's editors warned that *Pamyat's* ideologists and ringlead-

ers have "more in mind" than just struggle against "Jewish domination of Soviet science and culture." *Memory* was trying "to fragment"
the country's peoples "with national discord and to sow the seeds of
ruinous enmity," and, contrary to the proclamations of its leaders,
battle "against restructuring." In view of the nationality tensions
and clashes in some regions of the USSR, the stepped–up activity of
the *Memory* society was "provocative and socially dangerous." *Izvestia* thus linked *Pamyat's* anti–Semitic propaganda to anti–government
plans against restructuring. Its anti *Pamyat* stand should therefore
not necessarily be interpreted as a pro–Jewish gesture. In the end
Izvestia wondered whether the widespread propaganda activities of
Pamyat can and will be effectively combatted by the local authorities.

Roy Medvedev and the Future of Soviet Jewry

Criticism of the trials of Jews staged especially under Krushchev
in the 1960s have been uttered by some leading intellectual dissenters.
Foremost among them were two groups, the "legalists" (zakonniki),
comprising the Soviet Committee of Human Rights, and a broader
group dubbed "pragmatists." The principal organ of the latter was
the *Khronika teksobytiikh* [Chronicle of Current Events]. Since early
1968, it has been published six times a year, focussing both on trials against Soviet Jews and on Jewish protests against anti–Israeli
and anti–Semitic campaigns aimed against the Jewish national movement. Next to the legalists and pragmatists, there was a third group
among the intelligentsia greatly concerned with the Soviet Jews and
the Jewish question, the so–called "neo–Communists." They were
reminiscent of Dubcek's Czechoslovakian followers, bent on giving socialism a "human face."

A major figure in this group was Roy Medvedev. Like Lenin,
Medvedev looked upon assimilation of the Jews as "historically progressive." Though he opposed the policy of forcible assimilation,
which has been followed since the last years of Stalin, Roy Medvedev
recommended that Moscow return to the policy of the 1920s and
1930s when the state had given support to Jewish cultural institutions and Jewish schools. Estimating that the number of Jews who
wished to leave for Israel numbered only between 200,000 and 300,000,
he recommended that they be permitted to leave. He conceded that
a whole generation of young Jews had never experienced national
equality but only civil discrimination. It was this policy which has
held back genuine assimilation and has furthered ethnic consciousness

among Jews. Soviet leadership should "openly confess the mistakes and misrepresentations of the past years" and break with them. It should guarantee to Jews equality of rights in political, economic, and cultural affairs.

According to Medvedev, Jew–hatred was a perversion of Soviet history, and not an inherent part of Russian history. This analysis, however, did not take full account either of the long history of Jew–hatred and the repression of Jews in prerevolutionary Russia or of Soviet anti–Semitism which has a long tenacious history. The Soviet attitude toward Jews was one of outright hostility, not just of indifference or neutralism. Medvedev also overlooked that Lenin was hardly a judaeophile. He had wanted complete assimilation of the Jews, though a voluntary not a forcible one—an attitude, however, which can hardly be considered friendly. The Tsars too wanted the disappearance and elimination of the Jews as an ethnic and religious group and had encouraged "merger" and baptism, an attitude which did not spring from "friendship." Despite differences in their approaches, Tsarism's suppression of and discrimination against Jews and Lenin's insistence on legal and actual "equality" but also "amalgamation" and extinction of the Jews as a distinct national, religious, cultural, and linguistic group had much in common.

However, after the seizure of power the Communists made numerous concessions to the development of all national cultures, including that of the Soviet Jews. Despite serious limitations of these rights for Jews—the virtual prohibition of the study of the Hebrew language and culture and the repression of Zionism—the possibilities of developing Jewish national culture in some limited aspects had existed for several years. The authorities had permitted the formation of cultural institutions, schools, numerous Yiddish publications and a flourishing Yiddish theater, though the content of this culture was to be "socialist," narrowly confined. However, these institutions, it soon became clear, were intended to be only temporary, until such time that Stalin's full–blown forcible assimilation was to sweep away all Jewish cultural establishments. In the end, during the last years of his reign, brutal force was used to kill the foremost representatives of Jewish and Yiddish culture and even move toward expulsion of the Jews into Asia.

Soviet persecution of Jews, officially never admitted though ruthlessly practiced, defeated of course their policy of assimilation. Their repression only deepened Jewish ethnic consciousness and resistance. The Soviet persecution of Jews created new roadblocks to national

merger. By vilifying Soviet Jews and their heritage it made them
only shy away from "amalgamation" with their tormentors. It was
foolish to expect them to rush into the arms of their "big brother,"
the Great Russians who maltreated them. By making the designation
"Evrei" (Jews) in their internal passport, the door was swung wide
open to discrimination in employment, promotion, schooling, and in
many other areas of Soviet life and to facilitating anti–Semitic abuse.
The child of Jewish parents by age sixteen had no choice but to declare his or her nationality to be Jewish, as the domestic passport
disclosed. Even if the individual wished to change his other nationality at a later date, he or she was unable to do so. Whatever the
original motives of having the entry of "nationality" in one's passport when it was introduced in the early 1930s, it ran counter to the
professed goal of "assimilation" of the Jews.

Experts on the Jewish question in the USSR have parted ways
with Roy Medvedev about the depth of Soviet anti–Semitism. They
question that Soviet policy can be reversed to make equality and
voluntary assimilation plausible goals. A prominent Soviet Jew who
emigrated to Israel, Professor Mikhail Zand, in an unsigned document
The Jewish Question in the USSR (Theses)[43] has denied the likelihood of an autonomous Jewish existence even for a mere transition
period, as Roy Medvedev has suggested. As Zand pointed out, the
former communal structure of the Soviet Jews has been completely
destroyed. Its restoration appeared to him and other Soviet Jews
quite improbable, even if the government should suddenly want to
reverse its policies and course of action.

According to Medvedev, there exists a solution of the Jewish
problem for Soviet Jews: either total assimilation with the majority
population or emigration. (Jewish activists rather speak of "repatriation," probably expecting that this notion, familiar due to the Soviet
policy of the return of Russian citizens from Europe after World War
II, would encounter less resistance in government circles.) Zand questioned, however, whether the Soviets would abandon their past and
present policy of national discrimination and bigotry on racial and
religious grounds. Various groups, including Jewish dissenters, have
pointed to the survival of anti–Semitism, its intensity, and spread into
every corner of Soviet life.

Imitating the tactics of the democratic Russian and Soviet intelligentsia, Soviet Jews have copied its methods. They have addressed
petitions and letters to Soviet leaders as well as to organs of the
U.N., foreign statesmen, and prominent leaders. These tactics aside,

they have resorted to various demonstrations, sit–ins, and even long strikes. As long as these demonstrations fall short of violence, they are likely to win the favor of the Soviet intelligentsia, a segment of the Soviet population more likely to be favorably disposed to the Jews and sympathetic toward them on account of their persecution by the authorities.

During the last decades, Jewish "resistance" has grown in strength and has at various times led to direct confrontations with the authorities. Though the government is not insensitive to public opinion at home and abroad, the concessions made by it have so far been only temporary; they are also not substantive. They have not led to a decisive change of Soviet policy or tactics toward the Jews.

Glasnost, Admissions of Nationality Policy Errors, and Soviet Jews

In the wake of glasnost, an intellectual revolution has gripped Soviet life. A greater degree of free speech prevails today in the Soviet Union, which has affected political leaders, scholars and public opinion in general. The results are also apparent in the discussion of nationality and ethnic issues. The complete silence, which for decades reigned in regard to delicate problems such as nationality in the USSR, has given way to a willingness to admit past errors and to the recognition of the need for a change of nationality policy, at least of correcting its direction and course. However, this has not yet resulted in baring Soviet anti–Semitic policy, eliminating discrimination against Soviet Jews, and terminating their propagandistic vilification.[44]

In an interview with Soviet historians conducted by G. Melikyants[45] of *Izvestia* on March 22, 1988, one historian freely admitted that

we inherited quite a few little knots between nationalities. Most of the peoples who created their own republics had never had statehood before. Their pronounced national consciousness made the creation of several autonomous republics a necessity.

The very strength of nationalism was the major cause of creating a federal structure embracing several republics. The historian Yu. Poliakov acknowledged that Lenin had been in favor of ending national "isolation and national backwardness."[47] On the other hand, nationality problems still existed due to the intermingling of nationalities. He reminded the interviewer that, according to the 1979 census, only

60 percent of all Armenians lived in the Armenian Soviet Republic, and about 11 percent each in Azerbaidjan and Georgia, some in the Russian Federation. It is, it might be added, this very diaspora which is at the very root of the recent flare–up of the Azerbaidjani–Armenian national dispute.

Polyakov criticized that the provision of a quota in Soviet higher education "handed down from on high" was "harmful." But no mention was made that this critique justifiably applied to all nationalities of the USSR, including Soviet Jews. Another historian, L. Dobrizlava, referred to alien influx into Estonia and to emigration from this Republic, both of which pitted Russians against Estonians, economic developers against those wishing to preserve the ethnic character of many a Soviet Republic. Polyakov underlined the "duty" of Great Russians and other immigrants into Soviet Republics to learn the language of the Republic in which they live. There are national problems which are only "smoldering" at the moment. Some of the scholars interviewed stressed the importance of "ethnic psychology." After all, peoples are "different, we can't get away from that."

> Many [indigenous] students from the Caucasus, Chechen, Ingush, and Balkars, after receiving education in other regions of the USSR, go home to the land of their forefathers, and this is understandable. That's their tradition.

Such a policy, however, is blocked by a contrary Soviet nationality theory and practice relating to Soviet Jews and Israel!

Polyakov is fully aware that the members of the foregoing and other peoples were rejected and repressed by the government and that Soviet historians have "kept silent about this," after running into outright objections from some local Party and research institutions officials who feared "stirring up the past." "Unjustified repressions" have left a lasting imprint upon the psychology of hundreds of thousands of people of various generations and nationalities. It was important to fully comprehend this at a time when "national feelings" are strongly manifested. "Respect for one another's national feelings" was urgent. It is apparent that Polyakov's considerations apply in force to the entire Soviet Union and all its nationalities, including Soviet Jews, though politicians and Soviet nationality theoreticians following Lenin's and Stalin's paths have dwelled on the alleged differences between most Soviet nationalities and Soviet Jews, decreeing who shall live and who was doomed to cultural extinction.

In a report to the Board of the USSR Writers' Union on "improving nationality relations," V. V. Karpov in *Literaturnaya gazeta*, 1988, warned that "nationalism" was "becoming one of the primary dangers to the practical implication of restructuring." [48] While "nationalistic outbursts, excesses, and demonstrations" in the USSR have, in his view, often been inspired by "outside support," he freely conceded "our own fear of touching on real acute [nationality] problems" which have been hidden behind a shiny facade of official pronouncements. Karpov came out against special national privileges or restrictions of any kind and against any "compulsory measures." To abandon "the voluntary approach in parents' choice of their children's language of instruction would result in a violation of democratic principles in the nationality issue." It is quite evident, one might add, that no enlightened policy has in the past or present been applied to Soviet Jews. Jews have been denied linguistic–national rights on the most flimsy grounds.

In another speech to the Writers' Union Sergei Baruzhdin, editor of *Druzhba Narodov*, deplored the "pompous image" of Great Russians as the "older brother." This notion was just as "insulting" to the older brother as it was to the younger ones. After Lenin the Soviets forgot that "equal respect for every people [in the USSR], no matter how great or small," was imperative.

> Distortions in nationality policy began in the 1930s. On the one hand, there was sometimes a purely superficial display of national cultures and literatures, done for sake of effect; on the other hand, there was a forced, abrupt rush toward the merging [sliyanie] of peoples, nationalities, and languages.

Soviet scholars should abandon the "sloganeering postulate" that all peoples and nationalities "annexed themselves to Russia in a truly voluntary way." Some did so, "but others were forcibly annexed. Russia was a prison of peoples. . . . Why should history be forcibly rewritten?" The events of recent years, "Alma–Ata, the Baltic region, Yakuta, the Crimean Tartars, the problem that has come to a head in Nagorno–Karabakh—all these are disturbing phenomena." There was a "common responsibility" shared between the Soviet "ideological services," the Party leadership, and "our scholarship" for these nationality problems being in "a state of stagnation in our country." There was, admittedly, no precedence for such startling semi–official admissions of policy failure in the particular area of Soviet nationalities policy. But there was still a long way between the admission of error and remedial action, especially in regard to Soviet Jews.

Another crucial admission of theoretical failure has been made in this Moscow gathering by Nil Gilevich, apparently a Byelorussian who complained that in Minsk "we open one Byelorussian language first–grade class out of five first–grade classes." The speaker assailed furthermore the thesis that "convergence and mergers" of languages and cultures in the USSR was progressive. In reality this thesis was "groundless and unscientific" and plainly "absurd." It revealed a "global provincialism" which was characteristic of some "all–knowing and adamant comrades." In another address at the Moscow meeting Roman Lubvisky, a delegate from the Ukraine,[49] also recalled that only recently, in the 1960s, the "merging of languages" was spoken of "as something positive" and the concept of internationalism was "equated with the absence of national features." The present–day view on this very question was voiced by Armenian writer Rachy Ovanesyan[50] who, like other speakers, insisted that there was no Soviet people as such,

> but rather there are Soviet Russians, Soviet Uzbeks, and Soviet Moldavians; there are no Soviet languages in general, but there are the Armenian, Tadzhik, and Georgian languages. Each of the Soviet peoples had its own history, culture, language, character, and significantly distinctive traditions.

All the foregoing addresses clearly show how far the present USSR or at least its leading intelligentsia have moved away from the thesis of an early merger of Soviet nationalities and languages. The Soviet peoples, according to Ovanesyan, have created a distance between the present–day view of the nationality question with its theoretical recognition at least of national pluralism and the "accusations of nationalism" in the 1930s when nationalism had become the most common bugbear in the national republics of the USSR. But to return to Soviet Jews: To this moment they have become neither the beneficiaries of a pragmatic or even merely theoretical change in Soviet nationality policy pursued since the 1930s and during the postwar period.

At the foregoing Writers' Conference Maya Ganina,[51] a member of the Russian intelligentsia, asserted that she had always rejected "contempt" for any nationality. She regretted the decline of the number of kindergartens and schools run in the national languages of the Soviet Republics. But she also rejected the charge that Russian bureaucratic "scoundrels" were responsible for the Russification,

for wanting to change the national identity of people in the national
border republics. She held that "Russians too often were readily
blamed for the sins of the Georgian Stalin, the Georgian Beria, the
Jew Kaganovich, and the Russians Krushchev and Brezhnev." "No
single people . . . can be criminal."

The recent growth of nationalism in the USSR was blamed by
the opponents of restructuring on Gorbachev, to weaken his popular appeal and undermine his program. Janis Peters,[52] speaking to
the Writers' Union and referring to demographic changes in Latvia—
where according to the 1979 census only 53.7 percent of the population had declared themselves simply Letts—stressed that indigenous
people wanted to defend their language and preserve their nationality. The speaker rejected the accusation that self–preservation was
"nationalism" and saw in the nationality field no alternative but a
return to the Leninist tradition. The latter apparently was identified
by her as cultural and linguistic pluralism.

In the case of Jews, however, the will to "preserve" national culture and nationality, has been consistently denounced by the Soviets
as "nationalism." It is therefore of some interest that a recent notice in *Pravda* about "Shalom," a new society of Jewish culture in
Moscow, struck a positive note.

A New Beginning?

On November 12, 1988, N. Michina in *Pravda* reported that
"Shalom," "a society of Jewish Culture was being created in Moscow."[53]
A theater had been opened which is going to play an "active part in
the process that is taking place across the country concerning the
restoration, strengthening, and development of national cultures."
The writer made a point of picturing the event as part of a nationwide
policy, in apparent response to the stirrings of nationality movements
all over the USSR.

According to the interview of the theater's artistic director, A.
Levenbuk, it all began "with a desire to organize a cultural center
within our walls." The plan was welcomed by a large number of
supporters and was warmly responded to on the part of prominent
figures in art and science. This led to the creation not merely of a
theater but also of a society with by–laws and various subdivisions.

> Until recently there was nowhere to see a Jewish show. Where
> can one watch a Jewish film today? Only one magazine is
> published in Yiddish and it has a pitiful circulation. It would

> appear that Yiddish courses are given somewhere, but no-
> body knows where. Getting records or sheet music of Jewish
> songs is a difficult matter. There is only one library open
> and it's self–run. And for all of that, we are dealing here
> with a people of a very ancient culture. The main task of
> the society is to gather up, bit by bit, whatever has been
> preserved, to restore what has been lost.

It might be added what has been "lost" has actually been destroyed
by the Soviet government.

Anyone, the interview continued, irrespective of nationality, may
join the center if he is prepared to pay annual dues.

> There will be courses in modern Hebrew [!], Yiddish, and his-
> torical, philosophic–religious, theatrical and club sections, as
> well as youth and sport associations, health groups, and a
> cafe with national cuisine. We intend to publish our own
> newsletter.

It remains to be seen whether these plans will materialize. But
there can be no denial that their very announcement in the pages of
Pravda is bound to raise hopes for a breakthrough in Soviet cultural
policy toward the Jews. The artistic director of the theater also reported that people called from Kiev and Odessa proposing to set up
branches or departments of the new society in those cities. A "flood"
of inquiries, calls and letters, had also come from other places. One
will have to refrain from any judgment until it is proven that the
report is correct, in order to ascertain whether it will be followed by
meaningful deeds and whether the example will be emulated wherever
in the USSR Jews reside.

In the article "Rebirth of a Culture?" in the *Jerusalem Post* (International Edition) of March 25, 1989, Charles Hoffman[54] reported
of a bus tour through Moscow provided by Intourist, the official Soviet
tourism agency, to see "Jewish Moscow." The guide was Anna Gold-
stein, an activist in the Jewish Cultural Association. Such a tour,
according to the writer, was not only impossible a few years ago, but
was simply "inconceivable." Yet in the last weeks "one barrier after another fell in a concentrated effort to encourage the revival of
Jewish cultural and religious life in the Cultural Center in Moscow."
The latter is to be opened as a joint venture between local Jewish
activists, the Jewish Musical Theater of Moscow—the Jewish Agency
and Diaspora Jewry acting through the World Jewish Congress. The
opening of the Cultural center in Moscow was attended by Jewish

leaders and intellectuals from Israel and the Diaspora.

The readiness of the Soviet authorities to suddenly tolerate the open expression of Jewish national aspirations and political controversy has encouraged many young Soviet Jews, but has also generated great caution on the part of others. In the pre–glasnost era there existed semi–legal organizations like *Gesher*, which were neither prohibited nor permitted. But membership in such organizations always carried certain risks. The attendance, however, at a series of concerts in Moscow and Leningrad, growing out of a cultural exchange program between Australian Jewry and the Jewish Cultural Theater of Moscow, as accompanying for instance the recent opening of the Mikhoels Center brought out more conservative Jewish groups. They heard Israeli singers who performed before an audience of thousands. But the reporter who expected that the concerts would open the floodgates of suppressed Jewish feelings was disappointed at the lack of a more positive reaction and by the restraint, whatever its motivation, by the Leningrad audience of elderly Jews. They were in his view plainly fearful and intimidated, apparently recalling Stalin's fury against Jewish intellectuals and the flower of the Jewish stage. Yet a Moscow audience responded quite differently, standing up and clapping enthusiastically, despite the apparent presence of KGB personnel.

A different message, according to the journalist of the *Jerusalem Post*, was reported for a much smaller group of Orthodox activists, pointing to the possible revival of traditional Tora study and serious Jewish learning. In an elegant hall provided by the Soviet Academy of Sciences Rabbi Adin Steinsalz of Jerusalem, an eminent Talmud scholar, proclaiming the opening of a Jewish Studies Center, in Moscow under his direction, that would train rabbis and scholars for the remnant of Soviet Jewry. The center is sponsored by the Academy of World Civilizations in Moscow having the blessing of the Soviet government. Only a few weeks before two dozen young men enrolled in the yeshiva programme of the Center, with an additional eighty men and women taking part in general Judaica courses. The teachers at the Center come from Israel and the U. S. One young student from Leningrad remarked that no one could have foreseen such a development only a short time ago. "Things are definitely changing. It could eventually be far worse, but we hope it is for the best." Clearly hope springs forth, but it is not unmixed with caution and fear of a relapse, the result of bitter Jewish experiences in the past.

A major event during the unofficial Moscow "Jewish Culture

Week" occurred, according to Hoffman, the evening before the opening of the new Mikhoels Center when a film on the Holocaust called
"Genocide," produced by the Simon Wiesenthal center of Los Ange-
les, was screened for a select audience of actors and professionals in
the film industry and several dozen Jewish activists. True, the event
was not publicized in the Soviet press. But in view of the deliberate
and willful suppression of any news in the past about the Holocaust
this was no insignificant occurrence, but perhaps a beginning in the
rewriting of Soviet Jewish history. As Hoffman put it: "One cannot
talk about an authentic revival of Jewish culture in the Soviet Union
unless this missing chapter in [Jewish] collective consciousness is restored." The showing of "Genocide," held under the auspices of the
Soviet Actor's Guild, was provided with a simultaneous translation
into Russian and also mentioned the Swedish diplomat Raoul Wal-
lenberg, a gentile, who saved thousands of Hungarian Jews. Mention
was made that he was "kidnapped" by the Russians and may still be
"rotting away in prison."

At the following private gathering of some of those who saw the
movie, leaders from Moscow, Vilna, Riga, and Leningrad as well as
from more remote areas such as Rostov, Chernovtsy, Lvov, Tiblisi,
Perm, and Samarkand were present. The gathering took place in the
friendly setting of a Jewish-owned restaurant without fear of police
raids. The group publishes a bi-weekly pamphlet on Soviet Jewish
affairs that first appeared in 1987. Four hundred copies of each issue
are sent from Moscow to fifty cities throughout the USSR. Those who
started the publication have largely emigrated to Israel. The purpose
of the bulletin is to demonstrate the Soviet Jews' interest in maintaining their culture, in emigrating, in the dissemination of the truth
about Israel, and to right the distortions printed about Israel in the
official press. The group has not received official permission for publishing, yet as one activist expressed it, "no one stops us." It is not
yet officially recognized, as is for instance *Sovietish Heimland*, which
reaches only a few hundred people. There still prevails an atmosphere
of fear and anxiety next to one of hope for lasting improvements of
the cultural situation of Soviet Jews. Even the activists are unsure
of the success of their undertakings. The reporter Charles Hoffman
concludes that "if all goes reasonably well—and there is a very big
"if"—"there will be more Hebrew lessons, Jewish books, musical per-
formances, journals, films, lectures, and courses on Jewish subjects,
museums, and art exhibits available for hundreds of thousands of Jews
in the large cities." But at present it was impossible to say how many

Jews would respond to the new opportunities for cultural expression. "Some will come out of the closet once they are convinced that such behavior is acceptable in the eyes of the authorities." But others may still be afraid or may not want to do anything to deflect themselves and their children from assimilating into the dominant Russian culture.

VIII.   CONCLUSION

From their beginnings the Soviets have stressed the multinational character of their polyglot realm. Nationality in their thought is an integral part os Soviet citizenship and has far–reaching political and cultural consequences. At every turn of their history the Soviets have emphasized not only the national and cultural diversity of their realm, but also underlined the contrast between the past and the present, the tsarist Empire and the Communist–ruled state. In feudal and capitalist Russia nationalities were repressed, while in the Soviet state the nationality problem has been allegedly solved.

In reality, the problems of the Soviet multinational state have grown more acute than they were. Despite recently admitted short-comings the Soviet structure has been held out by Moscow as a model in economic, social, cultural as well as administrative respects, especially in regard to the nationality problem. Soviet policy toward nationalities and also religious groups has in reality been repressive and Soviet policy toward the Jewish minority has continued to be especially discriminatory. In the Russian "prison house," as Lenin called it, the Jews, have remained one of the most oppressed national–religious groups. Contradictions of Soviet policy in regard to Jews are more pronounced than those about any other ethnic or religious group. With exception of a trickle, Soviet Jews have not been permitted to emigrate, have been maltreated for indications of their wishes to do so, and been treated like hostages.[1]

Jews constitute a national–cultural and also a religious group. While religion is the perennial target of atheistic communists, nationality, though generally accepted in Leninist theory, is still considered a rival of Soviet communism in practice. Loyalty to the Soviet system and development of an independent national–religious culture are considered irreconcilable. Whatever temporary theoretical and practical concessions have been made to nationalism in the USSR, they have only a transitory character. At the end winks the unchanging goal of national merger and "amalgamation" into a single nationality and a single language.

There are special reasons for the phenomenon of anti–Semitism in the USSR. In contradistinction to other Soviet minorities, Soviet Jews are dispersed throughout the USSR. They are not territorially concentrated and do not have a Soviet Republic or autonomous republic of their own as compared to many other Soviet national groupings. They are thus deprived of a more effective legal protection which self–determination provides. The lack of self–determination prevents the preservation of the Soviet Jews as a distinct national, cultural, and religious group and speeds the process of forcible assimilation. Soviet Jews are the scapegoat of Russian and non–Russian popular anti–Semitism, which in turn is rooted in differences of nationality, religion, culture, language, and a different socio–economic structure. It is repeatedly fostered by Party and Government for their own dubious purposes. There is, last but not least, the traumatic Nazi experience which made an indelible impression both upon the Soviet peoples as well as their rulers. The Nazi holocaust and the inadequate Soviet response demonstrated to the peoples of the USSR how vulnerable and expendable Jews are.

As far as nationality is concerned, Soviet policy from its beginnings was plagued by outright contradictions. In many respects, the Jewish community has been accorded the legal status of a nationality, though Lenin had tried to minimize Jewish ties as being merely those of a caste.

Just before the outbreak of World War I, in March 1914, Lenin drafted a bill on nationality, spelling out the future legal status of Jews in Russia. The bill was to eliminate all restrictions on Jews and all those based on an individual's nationality or descent. In 1919, after the seizure of power, Lenin urged the Great Russians, Ukrainians, and Poles to show particular sensitivity to the national feelings of formerly oppressed nationalities such as Jews and Bashkirs[2] as well as support for their equality and for the development of the language and literature of the working people of all oppressed nationalities. Similarly a Communist Party resolution adopted at the Tenth Congress of the CP in 1921[3] emphasized the right of national minorities to free national development and specifically listed the Jews in this context.[4] Most importantly, a consequence of the recognition of the legal status of a Jewish nationality, was the creation of a Commissariat for Jewish national affairs within the framework of the People's Commissariat for National Affairs (Narkomats). The latter was created the very day after the Bolsheviks seized power and headed by Josef Stalin. According to the official proclamation, it was designated to initiate Soviet legislation on the national question and "in particular the economic and cultural uplifting of the nationalities." It promised not just maintaining the national status quo, but pledged the nationalities' cultural development.

But in the case of the Jews the major purpose of the Commissariat for National Affairs was quite different from that of other Soviet nationalities. The task of the Commissariat for Jewish national affairs was to win adherents to the Bolshevik cause and to achieve the abolition of existing Jewish autonomous institutions. The Jewish Sections (Yevsektsii) were to carry out propaganda in Yiddish among the toiling masses and to prepare the way for the total and forcible assimilation, aiming at the disappearance of the Jewish nationality in the Soviet Union. Until the dissolution of the Jewish Sections in January 1930, and even thereafter, Soviet Jews were considered a nationality, though one doomed by "history" to die. The death certificate was written by the Bolshevik party soon after it came to power, though the date was not yet inserted.

For the moment, however, and for an indeterminate period, the Jews of the USSR were, and still are, considered a nationality, though one of a unique type and one only of a transitory character. It had also a legal identity. The Hebrew language was discriminated against on religious grounds and also because it was the language chosen by the competitors in Jewish affairs, the Zionists. The Yiddish language, however, was given some deference, at least for the next few decades. The Byelorussian Republic acknowledged Yiddish, next to three other languages, to be one of the official languages of government.

The Soviets had long ago decided that assimilation of Soviet Jews should be the goal of Soviet policy. It was not the Jews of the USSR but the Communist Party of the Soviet Union (CPSU) that made this crucial decision, in violation of the much touted national self–determination. At no time have the Soviets retreated from this capricious negativist decision on the centuries–old Jewish tradition and preservation of their unique national and religious culture. Unwilling to concede the errors, the one–sidedness, and the injustice of their policy, they have exaggerated the extent, speed, and genuineness of the assimilation process. Soviet Jewish experts and Jewish public opinion, while nor denying the threatening decline of interest in religion and the speed–up of cultural and national assimilation, have pointed out that extensive Soviet claims in this regard have been greatly overstated.

The war years have witnessed both a strengthening of Soviet "patriotism" as well as one of Russian nationalism. In view of the ethnic composition of the USSR, the latter was not only directed against nationalities across the Soviet borders but, by implication, also against the non–Great Russian nationalities within the Soviet Union. The non–Russian nationalities were assigned a somewhat lower status as "younger brothers," but were promised broader cultural and administrative development. Yet against several Soviet nationalities, a number of small Caucasian ethnic units, the Tartars of the Crimea, and the Germans of the Volga region, Stalin's wrath, allegedly caused by their traitorous activities, came down like lightening. They were brutally expelled from their abode and banished to Asia. Rarely in history have peoples been equally maltreated, and never by a regime boasting of international brotherhood. During the war, Russian Jew–hatred was deepened by Nazi atrocities, the demonstration of Jewish vulnerability, and total Soviet silence about the Nazis' mass murder of Jews. During the Cold War period, however, Jews were no longer looked upon as a trusted nationality group, but turned into a hostile domestic target. In a world divided between East and West, Soviet Jews were considered a pro–Western element and potentially dangerous to the Soviet regime. Their religious, national, and ideological ties with the West made them suspect in the eyes of Moscow. Their loyalty to the USSR began to be questioned. In the heated Zhdanovite atmosphere of Soviet isolationism, fear of encirclement, and feverish claims of national achievement, the Soviet official attitude to its Jewry and to Zionism worsened.

Ties between Soviet Jews and Jews abroad were not suddenly severed when the war against Hitlerite fascism ended. When Palestinian rabbis appealed to Jewish communities the world over to declare a day of fasting in memory of millions of Jews murdered by the Nazis, the Moscow Jewish community responded. Notables such as the Jewish wives of Foreign Minister Molotov, of Marshal Aleksei Antonov and of General David Dragunsky gathered for prayer and to demonstrate their solidarity with Soviet Jewry.

When the state of Israel was proclaimed, the Jewish Anti–Fascist Committee (JAC) sent a congratulatory telegram to President Chaim Weizmann. Soon thereafter, however, the JAC ceased all contacts with Jews abroad. Even in the telegram the members had been cautious enough to express the hope that "the brilliant example of Stalinist friendship among peoples set by the USSR would inspire the workers of Palestine."[4]

In this early postwar period, the Soviet government tried to revive the interests of Soviet Jews, not to mention those of foreign Jews, in the Birobidzhan settlement project. The new postwar Soviet propaganda in behalf of Birobidzhan virtually coincided with its vigorous though short-lived defense of Zionist aspirations in the U. N. Clearly, Zionism was for Jews in the West and for some Jews from prewar Eastern Europe, Birobidzhan for those Soviet Jews who wished to preserve their national heritage. According to Andrei Gromyko, Soviet Jews demonstrated no interest in emigration to Palestine. The USSR thus sharply distinguished between its support of Jewish endeavors in Palestine and the separate character of the Jewish question in the Soviet Union. Soviet Jews, Moscow claimed, were not linked either by nationality, ideology, or aspirations to Palestine's Jewry and other Western Jews. For the latter, Zionism may then have been "acceptable," since, by Soviet standards, a Jewish problem existed in the capitalist West. But as far as the USSR was concerned, the socialist example of "brotherhood" made the return of Jews to their historic homeland superfluous. Would Jewish emigration from the USSR not necessarily be followed by emigration of other Soviet national groups? What would this tell about the success story of Soviet nationality policy in general?

While the elimination of Soviet Jewish culture was soft-pedaled by the Soviet media, if not entirely repressed, the attack against Jewish "cosmopolitanism" and Jewish Zionism, rather contrary if not incompatible phenomena, was in full swing. In April 1949, Moscow intensified its anti-cosmopolitan and anti-Jewish campaign. In early May, Harrison Salisbury of the *New York Times* observed that the drive against "cosmopolitanism" seemed to be over—which proved to be mistaken. So were, he continued, the "open attacks" on Jews "after a conference of editors of the Soviet main press organs that was called by the party Central Committee."[5] There was no doubt that both the start of the distinct anti-Jewish propaganda as well as its cessation was orchestrated by the highest central authorities. The anti-cosmopolitan campaign was designed to pin the blame for Moscow's postwar foreign policy disappointments on Western and Israeli Jewry. The Soviets had first looked upon this alien Jewry as a "democratizing" force in the world, hoping that it would at least neutralize the growing East-West conflict. But Moscow had exaggerated its power and influence.

The frenzied attacks on Soviet Jewry were bound to incite only more anti–Semitism in the USSR. To it must be added the hardly disguised discrimination against Jews in employment and public life and the rising populist aversion against them during the last years of Stalin's regime. At the same time any mention of the existence of a Jewish nationality virtually disappeared from the Soviet media. Emigration of Russian Jews to Israel remained forbidden. On May 21, 1950, Prime Minister Ben Gurion appealed to Soviet authorities to give permission to Soviet Jews to emigrate to Israel. Later in the year Vyshinskii replied negatively: allowing Jewish emigration from the USSR would contradict Soviet general policy on emigration of any national minority. The Soviets feared opening a Pandora's box. Concessions to Jews would necessarily have to be followed by concessions to other minorities and would lead to a mass flight from the USSR, and it would have most adverse consequences for the Soviet Union.

While most Soviet nationalities and ethnic groups, after expurgation of so–called nationalist and anti–socialist prejudices, have been permitted to develop their own culture, language, and national tradition, the Jewish survivors of Nazi oppression and extermination, virtually alone among Soviet nationalities, have been targeted for complete obliteration and elimination. It can hardly be questioned that traditional Russian anti–Semitism, first tolerated and then increasingly endorsed by Soviet authorities, had played a major role in the formulation of this discrimatory Soviet policy which violates all pledges and programs of internationalism. Other nationalties may have their libraries, theaters, and museums, but the Jews were destined for disappearance! Jewish assimilation was largely a forcible phenomenon, the result of Soviet political decisions. The Soviet aim was to deprive the Jews from preserving their culture and languages and to speed the process of their merging with the Russian people. The Communist regime has used all means to impose its will upon Soviet Jewry. The purges in the late 1930s, though affecting all Soviet nationalities, struck the most deadly blow at Soviet Jewry. Ironically, leading Soviet Jewish cadres, partly responsible for devising, surely implementing, the Soviet policy of forcible assimilation of Jews, fell as first victims to Stalin's murderous policy. They were the former leaders of the Jewish Sections and prime instruments of Soviet Jewish policy. Of greatest importance in the struggle against Jewish survival was the virtual elimination of Jewish communal institutions, the destruction of the entire cultural–national infrastructure of the Jewish community.

Though some Jewish cultural institutions were restored during World War II, in the postwar period Jewish communal life fell again victim to Stalin's rage. Jewish papers were shut down, the Jewish State Theater in Moscow and other professional theaters were closed and other Jewish institutions permanently destroyed. Most prominent members of the Jewish Anti-Fascist Committee were murdered and the Committee itself dissolved. During the last years of Stalin's life, between 1949–1953, the Jewish leadership in the USSR, outstanding literary figures and activists were eliminated, being accused among other matters of wishing to sever the Crimea from the USSR and to create there a Zionist-bourgeois republic! It was a body blow aimed against Jewish ethnic survival, designed to kill the leaders and to cow their following into submission.

Soviet nationality policy in regard to Jews was always negative, and more hostile than toward other Soviet nationalities. In a noted speech at the Communist University of Toilers in the East in May 1925, Stalin had promised the Party's aid and support to "national culture."[6] National cultures must be given an opportunity to establish the conditions "for their fusion into a single common culture with a single common language." It is of interest to note the inherent contradiction in Stalin's and the Soviets' position. In the same sentence in which Stalin made seemingly broad pledges of free cultural development of nationalities he clearly revealed the Communist goal of ultimate "fusion" of nationalities and national cultures! Simultaneously he held out the promise of national-cultural development and of national-cultural death! Marxist-Leninists have tried to bury the contradiction in the sea of Marxian "dialectics."

A major source of anti-Semitism in Russia has been the Greek-Orthodox Church which has a long history of anti-Jewish teachings and practices. In addition to age-old religious and doctrinal roots—which made hostility to Jews also flourish in Catholic and Protestant Europe—it was extreme nationalism, and partly conscious racism, which made it grow in a rampant fashion in Russia. Soon after the October Revolution, a deepening nationalism overcame Lenin's early internationalism. The ambition of rapidly developing the Soviet economy and of achieving "socialism in one country" was dictated by ideological as well as nationalist considerations. The fear of a worldwide conflagration and of actual Russian involvement in such a war had aroused strong national feelings. Later, toward the end of World War II, Stalin had praised the "Russian people" as the "most outstanding of all nations of the Soviet Union." It was in this climate that sprouted the seeds of populist anti–Semitism which the Bolshevik Revolution had never aimed at completely uprooting.

Jew–hatred was also linked with the establishment of a full–blown totalitarian system. The independent national development of any minority was anathema to the growth of totalitarianism. The latter permitted neither corporate nor individual autonomy. The growth of the cult of the individual placed absolute power into the hands of one man whatever his prejudices and shortcomings. He thus obtained unfettered control over the fate of individuals, nationalities, all aspects of life and future prospects. The strengthened totalitarian structure enabled Party *apparatchiks* serving the *Vozhd* to amass power to intimidate independent–minded individuals, to break down opposition on political, national, religious, and other grounds, and magnify or invent alleged threats to the security and well–being of the Soviet Union.

Will Gorbachev's "new thinking"—"openness," "reconstruction," "democratization," and the improvement of Soviet relations with the U. S.—lead to a new Soviet nationality policy, to greater tolerance toward religion and in particular to a change, perhaps a reversal, of Soviet Jewish policy? Even if Gorbachev should consider making major changes in this policy, there are formidable obstacles blocking the road to "normalcy" between the Soviet government and Soviet Jewry. With only brief interruptions Soviet policy from the October Revolution on has been marked by hostility to the concepts of Judaism as a religion, to the Jewish people as a nationality, and its desire to return to its country of origin, to Palestine. For very short periods only have Communists combatted anti–Semitism, during the first years after the October Revolution and during the Civil War. Most of the time the Soviets have closed tight the gates of emigration to Jews and given material, diplomatic, propagandistic, and military support in form of equipment and advice to the many Arab enemies of Israel.

There are indications, however, that an improvement of Soviet–Israeli relations and some improvement of Soviet policy toward Soviet Jews is not beyond all possibility. A growing number of contacts between Soviet diplomats and leading Israelis have been reported during the past year. Israeli political leaders have talked about the feasibility under certain conditions of a peace conference under U. N. auspices, including the Soviet Union. Emigration of Jews from the USSR has been increased and is likely to continue. According to the *Jerusalem Post* rabbis from the Soviet Union have been permitted to travel to

Israel and closer contacts have been established with Jews abroad. Rumors that the Anti–Zionist Committee of the Soviet Union is to be dissolved in 1989 have circulated abroad. Criticism in leading Soviet dailies of anti–Semitic and anti–Zionist organizations which have broadened their activities during the last years, such as *Pamyat* and *Otechestvo*, has grown, though any sort of Judaeophilism should be excluded. If true, recent reports of the Soviets permitting Jewish cultural activities, among them the study of Jewish history, Jewish national culture and religion, of Yiddish and even of Hebrew, would of course signify a new policy. But after more than two–thirds of a century of Soviet repression and negativism toward Jews, toward their religious and national culture, and toward Zionism—leaving aside the earlier repression of Russian Jews—one should guard against an overly optimistic outlook on the Soviet–Jewish relationship.

NOTES

Notes to Preface

[1] Yanai, Y., (ed.), *Anti-Semitism in the Soviet Union. Its Roots and Consequences*, Jerusalem, 1979, I, 191.

[2] *Ibid.*, S. Ettinger, (ed.), III, 42.

[3] Lenin, "About the Pogromist Agitation against the Jews," in Fetscher, I., *Marxisten gegen Antisemitismus*, 1974, p. 170.

[4] *Pravda*, July 19, 1965.

[5] Lawrence, G., *Three Million More*, p. 9.

[6] Howe, I., (ed.), *Basic Writings of Trotsky*, "Thermidor and Anti-Semitism," pp. 206–7.

[7] Statement, Appendix A. in Schechtmann, *Star in Eclipse . . .*, pp. 243–8.

Notes to Introduction

[1] Censusses were held in the years 1920, 1923, 1939, 1959, 1970, and 1979. Alec Nove and Newth, ch. 7 in Kochan, L. (ed.), *The Jews, Soviet Russia since 1917*, p. 152 and 126–53. Data on language and nationality in the 1979 census were published in *Vestnik statistiki*, Nos. 7–10, 1980. For the census results in 1959 and 1970 respectively, see *Pravda*, Feb. 4, 1960 and *Izvestia*, Apr. 17, 1971.

[2] Schwarz, S., *Jews in the Soviet Union*, p. 138.

[3] Cang, *The Silent Millions*, p. 179.

[4] See Baron, *The Russian Jew under Tsars and Soviets*, p. 330.

[5] Souvarine, Boris, "Gorky, Censorship, and the Jews," *Dissent*, Winter 1965, p. 83.

[6] *Ibid.*

[7] Deutscher, I., *Trotsky Armed, 1879–1921*, 1954, pp. 325–6.

[8a] *Izvestia*, Decree, July 27, 1918; see also Korey, W., *The Soviet Cage*, p. 65.

[8b] *Pravda*, Feb., 19, 1929.

[9] Trotsky's letter to Bucharin, *Pravda*, Feb. 19, 1929.

[10] *Pravda*, Nov. 30, 1936.

[11] Gilboa, Y., *The Black Years of Soviet Jewry*, pp. 229f.

[12] *Ibid.*, chap. 6.

[13] Low., A. D., *Lenin on the Question of Nationality*, pp. 55–8.

[14] *Réalités*, Paris, No. 136, May 6, 1957.

[15] About the Yiddish language in the interwar period, see Schwarz, S. M., *Jews in the Soviet Union*, p. 137; about Yiddish literature, see Mark, J., Aronson, G., et al., (eds.), *Russian Jewry, 1917–1967*, 1969.

[16] Slutzki, J., "The Fate of Hebrew in Soviet Russia," in *Russian Jewry 1917–1967*, Aronson, G. (ed.).

[17] Deutscher, I., *Stalin*, p. 604.

[18] *Pravda*, V. Blishuklin, Apr. 6, 1971; Zionism is repeatedly called "the main enemy."

[19] Nudelmann, R., *Social Progress*, 1970 (Moscow); also Sawyer, *The Jewish Minority in the Soviet Union*, p. 166.

[20] *Ibid.*

Notes to Chapter II

[1a] S. Ettinger, (ed.), *Soviet Anti–Semitism after the Six–Day War*, vol. III (Jerusalem, 1985), Introduction, pp. 11–24.

[1b] Kokovstev, N., *Memoirs* (Paris, 1933), pp. 92–3.

[2] See 1a.

[3] *Ibid.*

[4] Cohn, N., *Warrant for Genocide* (1966–67), "The Protocols in Russia," pp. 108–25.

[5] *Ibid.*; also ch. XI.

[6] Tolstoy, L., private letter, 1910, in S. W. Baron, *The Russian Jew under Tsars and Soviets*, p. 164.

[7] Souvarine, *Dissent*, 1965, pp. 81–3.

[8] Korolenko, V. K., *Yom Kipur*.

[9] Marx, K., *Zur Judefrage*; also A. D. Low, *The Jews in the Eyes of the Germans*, pp. 285–6.

[10] Low, *Lenin*, pp. 25–6.

[11] See Rafes, M., *Ocherki po istorii Bunda* (1923); also Lenin quoted in Sawyer, *The Jewish Minority in the Soviet Union*, p. 13.

[12] About the Bund, see also Gitelman, *The Jewish Nationality and Soviet Politics*, 1972, pp. 33–66.

[13] Low, *Lenin*, pp. 55-6.

[14] *Ibid.*, p. 58.
[15] Gitelman, *op. cit.*, p. 109.
[16] Krupskaya, N., *Reminiscences of Lenin*, p. 148.
[17] Low, *Lenin.* Lenin's essays on nationality are listed on pp. 181–5.
[18] Lenin, *Soch*, 2nd ed. (1924), XVII, 291.
[19] *Ibid.*
[20] Low, *Lenin*, p. 14.
[21] Medem, V., "Der moderne Antisemitismus in Russland," *Neue Zeit*, 1910–11, Bd. 1; about Medem, see also Gitelman, *op. cit.*, pp. 55f, 107, 256–63.
[22] *Ibid.*
[23] Low, *op. cit.*, p. 70.
[24] *Ibid.*, p. 26.
[25] Cang, J., *The Silent Millions*, p. 54; Stalin, *Marxism and the National Question* (New York, 1942), p. 157.
[26] Ulam, A., *Stalin*, p. 120.
[27] Stalin, *op. cit.*, p. 41.
[28] Low, A. D., *The Sino-Soviet Dispute*, pp. 53 and 155.
[29] Lenin, *Soch.*, 2nd ed., XVII, 66; Low, *Lenin*, p. 56.
[30] Lenin, *Soch., Critical Remarks*, XVII, 141 and 143; Low, *Lenin*, p. 59.
[31] Carr, E. H., *The Bolshevik Revolution 1917–32*, I, 420.
[32] Trotsky, L., *The History of the Russian Revolution*, I, 650.
[33] Deprecatory designation for Jews.
[34] Reprinted in *Pravda*, Nov. 30, 1936.
[35] Lenin, *Soch*, 3rd ed., (Moscow, 1937); see also *Iskra*, No. 51, Oct. 22, 1903.
[36] Declaration of the Rights of Peoples, Nov. 15, 1917, in Bunyan, J. and H. H. Fischer, *The Bolshevik Revolution 1917–18. Documents and Materials*, 1961, pp. 282–3.
[37] Soviet ratification of UNESCO, Aug. 1962.
[38] Stalin, Univ. of Toilers of the East, May 19, 1952; also Low, *Lenin*, p. 173.
[39] *Pravda*, Nov. 2, 1961; also Low, "Soviet Nationality Policy and the New Program of the CPSU." *The Russian Review*, vol. 22, No. 1, pp. 3–29.
[40] Dzusinov, H. S., *Soviet Sociology*, vol. I, No. 2, pp. 10–28.
[41] Pipes, R., "The Forces of Nationalism," *Problems of Communism*, Jan.–Feb. 1964, pp. 10–28.
[42] Kantor, Y. in *Bleter far Geschichte* (Warsaw, pp. 10–28, Yiddish), vol. 15, p. 146f.

[43] *Manchester Guardian,* June 25, 1956.
[44] Greenberg, Louis, *The Jews in Russia,* II, 158.
[45] Cang, *op. cit.,* p. 64.
[46] *Ibid.,* p. 66.
[47] The Study of Discrimination in the Matter of Religious Rights and Practices, Conference on Paper No. 351 and Manifestations of Racial Prejudices and Religious Intolerance (Doc. A/5473/Add. 1).
[48] Curtiss, J., *Religion in the Soviet Union,* 1961; Rothenburg, J., *The Jewish Religion in the Soviet Union,* 1971, and Kolarz, W., *Religion . . . in the USSR,* p. 388.
[49] Also Lawrence, G., *Three Million More,* pp. 98f., and Rothenberg, *op. cit.,* pp. 529f.
[50] According to press reports of early 1989, there are indications of a change of Soviet policy to the better, though this remains to be seen.
[51] Schechtman, J. B., *Star in Eclipse. Russian Jewry Revisited,* p. 152.
[52] Pinkus, *op. cit.,* pp. 313–14f.
[53] *Ibid.,* p. 316; see also 49.
[54] See 49.

Notes to Chapter III

[1] Kalinin, M., *The Jewish Question and the Resettlement of Jews in the Crimea,* (Moscow, 1926).
[2] Larin, Y., *Yevreii antisemitizm v SSSR* [Jews and anti–Semitism in the USSR], (Moscow, 1929).
[3] Lunacharsky, *Ob Antisemitizma,* 1929, p. 64.
[4] Kochan, L., *The Jews, Soviet Russia Since 1917,* p. 68.
[5] Chemerisky in Cang, *The Silent Millions,* pp. 69–70.
[6] *Yevrei i Antisemitism v SSSR,* 1929, pp. 187–90, 306–7.
[7] Lenin, "Critical Remarks," *Soch.,* 2nd ed., XVII, 158.
[8] See 1.
[9] See 1.
[10] Stalin, "On the Draft Constitution of the USSR," Nov. 25, 1936.
[11] Howe, ed., *Trotsky,* p. 209.
[12] *Ibid.,* pp. 208–9.
[13] *Ibid.,* pp. 214, 212.
[14] *Ibid.,* pp. 206–7.

[15] Trotsky letter, Oct. 7, 1938 in Fetscher, *Marxisten gegen Antisemitismus*, 1974, p. 178.

[16] *Ibid.*, p. 211.

[17] *Ibid.*

[18] *Pravda*, Molotov, Nov. 30, 1936.

[19] Litvinov, M., *Notes for a Journal*, p. 27.

[20] *Ibid.*, pp. 53–5.

[21] Schwarz, S., *op. cit.*, pp. 354f and 364; also Alliluieva, *Only One Year*, pp. 52–3.

[22] Trotsky, "Imperialism and Anti–Semitism," May 1940, from Manifesto of the Emergency Conference of the Fourth International, first published in *Socialist Appeal*, June 29, 1940.

[23] Ainsztein, R., "Soviet Jewry in the Second World War," Kochan, L., (ed.), *The Jews in Soviet Russia*, p. 269.

[24] *Bezboshnik*, May 1940; also Fetscher, *op. cit.*, pp. 270–1.

[25] *Novy mir*, Gallai, Mark, Sept. 1966, No. 9.

[26] *Pravda*, Aug. 24 and 25, 1941.

[27] Kochan, *op. cit.*, pp. 282–3.

[28] *Ibid.*

[29] *Ibid.*, p. 281.

[30] *Ibid.*, pp. 304–6.

[31] *Black Book*, Ehrenburg, I. and V. Grossman. (eds.), Holocaust Publications, 1981.

[32] Yevtushenko, *Autobiography*, (London, 1964), pp. 104–06; also Pinkus, *op. cit.*, doc. 32, pp. 104–06.

Notes to Chapter IV

[1] Schwarz, S., *The Jews in the Soviet Union*, 1951, pp. 274–5.

[2] *Great Soviet Encyclopedia* III (1926), p. 68.

[3] *The Small Soviet Encyclopedia*, I, 441–2.

[4] *Harvard Projection the Soviet Social System.*

[5] Pinkus, B., *The Soviet Government and the Jews 1948–67*, Documents, 99–100, pp. 103–4; also *Conquest, Power and Policy*, pp. 79–80; for the following: Léneman, *La tragédie des juifs . . .*, p. 167, and Crankshaw, *Krushchev. A Career*, pp. 78 and 160–2.

[6] Djilas, M., *Conversations with Stalin*, 1962, pp. 154, 170–1.

[7] Pinkus, *op. cit.*, Doc. 33, p. 106–8; also *Krushchev Remembers*, 1970, pp. 260–3.

[8] *Krushchev Remembers, ibid.*

[9] Alliluieva, *Twenty Letters to a Friend*, 1967, pp. 173–83.

[10] *Ibid.*

[11] *Ibid.*, p. 181.

[12] *Ibid.*, pp. 186–7, 189.

[13] *Ibid.*, p. 69.

[14] *Ibid.*, p. 67; also pp. 193, 197–8, 206, 217.

[15] *Ibid.*, p. 53.

[16] Marx, K., *Zur Judenfrage*, 1843.

[17] Krushchev's oration, Feb. 24 and 24, 1956, at the Twentieth Party Congress.

[18a] Litvinov, *op. cit.*, p. 7.

[18b] Ulam, A., *Stalin*, p. 680.

[19] Ehrenburg, *Memoirs*, p. 310; also Goldberg, Anatol, *Ilya Ehrenburg* (London, 1984), pp. 226–50.

[20] Crankshaw, E., *Russia without Stalin*, 1956, pp. 71–87.

[21] Carr, E. H., *The Bolshevik Revolution 1917–1923*, I, 377.

[22] *Borba*, Belgrade, Dec. 14, 1952, Djilas, p. 162.

[23] Lenin, *Soch*, 4th ed., vol. 20, p. 10.

[24] *Izvestia*, May 25, 1945.

[25] Mazour, A. G., *Russia, Tsarist and Communist*, 1962, p. 676.

[26] Krushchev's interview in *Le Figaro*, Apr. 9, 1958.

[27] Namir, M. to Sharett, Israel, Oct. 1949, *A Mission to Moscow*.

[28] For background, see Gilboa, *op. cit.*, chap. 8.

[29] Redlich, Sh., *Propaganda and Nationalism in Wartime Russia*, about Einstein and the JAC, pp. 113–5.

[30] Ehrenburg, I., *Memoirs*, and Cang, *op. cit.*, p. 98.

[31] *Ibid.* pp. 98–9.

[32] Gromyko, U. N., May 14, 1947, and R. I. Ruben, *The Unredeemed*, 1968, pp. 207–9.

[33] Gromyko in the U. N., Nov. 26, 1947.

[34] *For a Lasting Peace . . .*, Mikunis, Oct. 1948.

[35] Radio Moscow, May 1948.

[36] *New Times*. D. Zaslavski, June 17, 1948; also Pinkus, *op. cit.*, p. 239.

[37] Ehrenburg's interview in A. Werth, *Hopes and Fears*, 1962.

[38] About Czechoslovakia's help, see also Pinkus, *op. cit.*, p. 233.

[39] *Foreign Relations, U.S.*, L. Steinhardt, Dec. 1949, vol. V, 381, and James Penfield, early Dec. 1949.

[40] *For a Lasting Peace*, June–July 1948.

[41] Tarasenko, in U. N. Security Council, May 1948.

[42] J. Malik, Aug. 18, 1948; compare this speech with his rabidly anti–Semitic outburst in the Security Council, Provisional Verbatim Record, Sept. 25, 1971.

[43] *Voprosy istorii*, Dec. 1948.

[44] "Toady of American Aggressors," *New Times*, 422, 1948.

[45] C. Abramsky, "The Birobidzhan Project," ch. 4 in L. Kochan's *The Jews in Soviet Russia*, and Cang, *op. cit.*, pp. 138f.

[46] *Figaro*, Paris, Apr. 9, 1958.

[47] Cang, *op. cit.*, pp. 96–8, 134f.

[48] Larin, *Jews and Anti–Semitism*, and Gilboa, *op. cit.* p. 229.

[49] Cang, *op. cit.*, p. 136.

[50] *Literaturnaya gazeta*, March 9, 1949.

[51] Gilboa, *op. cit.*, p. 191.

[52] *Great Soviet Encyclopedia*, 2nd ed., see Weimann.

[53] Gilboa, *op. cit.*, p. 217.

[54] *Ibid.*, p. 229.

[55] Cang, *op. cit.*, p. 103.

[56] *Unser Stimme* (Yiddish), Paris, May–Dec. 7, 1957.

[57] Krushchev revealed their fate on Feb. 24 and 25, 1956.

[58] *Krushchev Remembers*; also Cang, *op. cit.*, pp. 101–3.

[59] *Ibid.*

[60] Tass, Jan. 13, 1953.

[61] *Pravda*, Jan 13, 1953, p. 1; also *Trud*, Jan 13, p. 1.

[62] *Novoya vremya*, end Jan. 1953.

[63] *Krokodil*, Feb. 20, 1953.

[64] *Meditsinsky rabotnik*, Jan. 13, 1953; also Jan 27, p. 1, and Feb. 13, p. 4.

[65] *Pravda* and *Izvestia*, Feb. 12, 1953, p. 3.

[66] *Pravda Ukrainy*, Feb. 13, 1953, p. 4.

[67] *Literaturnaya gazeta*, Feb. 17, 1953; O. Prudkov (see *Current Digest of the Soviet Press* (CDSP), 1953, No. 5, pp. 11–13. Many of the quotes from the Soviet press and journals since the early post–World War II period have been taken from the CDSP. See "Acknowledgement" of this study.

[68] Cang, *op. cit.*, p. 110.

[69] Lendvai, P., *Anti–Semitism without Jews*, pp. 243–58.

[70] Gilboa, *op. cit.*, pp. 331–2; also *New York Times*, June 8, 1957, and *London Times*, Apr. 16, 1956.

[71] Gilboa, *op. cit.*, p. 332.

[72] *Times*, London, Sept. 8, 1959.

[73] See 71.

[74] *Pravda* and *Izvestia*, April 3, 1953, p. 4.
[75] Yevtushenko, Y., *Precocious Autobiography*, 1963, pp. 89–90.
[76] Gilboa, *op. cit.*, pp. 324–5, 327.
[77] *Pravda*, Apr. 6, 1953.
[78] *Ibid.*
[79] *Ibid.*, July 24, 1954.
[80] Ulam, *op. cit.*, p. 737.
[81] *Pravda*, Apr. 7, 1953.
[82] Ulam, *op. cit.*, p. 678f.

Notes to Chapter V

[1] Treadgold, D., *Twentieth Century Russia*, 1976, ch. 29.
[2] Medvedev, R., *Krushchev. The Years in Power*, and Cang, J., *op. cit.*, chap. 7.
[3] Cang, *op. cit.*, p. 123.
[4] *Folksztyme*, Warsaw, 1956, p. 4; about Krushchev's lengthy interview with a delegation, including the Canadian Jewish communist Salzberg. See the latter's articles in the pro–communist *Morgen Freiheit* which were sharply critical of Krushchev's attitude toward Jewish issues, New York, Nov.–Dec. 1956. Also *Le Figaro*, Paris, Apr. 9, 1958.
[5] Pinkus, *The Soviet Government and the Jews.* p. 92.
[6] *Le Figaro*, Paris, Apr. 9, 1958.
[7] U. N. General Assembly, Official Records, New York, Vyshinsky, Apr. 13, 1953.
[8] "Entretiens entre Moscou et les Socialistes Français," *Les Réalités*, May 1957, No. 136.
[9] *Ibid.*
[10] *Le Figaro*, No. 136, May 1957, p. 104.
[11] Krushchev, Dec. 19, 1966.
[12] *Kommunist*, June 1963.
[13] Pinkus, *op. cit.*, Tables 23 and 24, pp. 350–2.
[14] *Ibid.*, Tables 21 and 22, pp. 346–7.
[15] Sakharov, A., *Progress, Coexistence, and Intellectual Freedom*, pp. 65–6.
[16] Medvedev, R. A samizdat document in *Survey*, vol. 17, No. 2, spring 1971, pp. 185–201.
[17] De Witt, N., *Education and Professional Employment in the USSR*, 1961, pp. 358–60.

[18] *Pravda*, Sept. 5, 1971.

[19] *Pravda*, July 16, 1971.

[20] Memorandum by A. Sakharov, A. V. F. Turchin, and R. Medvedev, March 19, 1971.

[21] *Pravda*, Sept. 5, 1965.

[22] *Ibid.*

[23] Lenin, *Soch,* 3rd ed. (1937), XIX, pp. 354–55.

[24] *Vechernaia Moskva,* May 31, 1960.

[25] Korey, *op. cit.,* chap. 6.

[26] Korey, "Reporting the Eichmann Case," *Survey,* Dec. 1961, pp. 17f.

[27] Nekrasov, V., *Literaturnaya gazeta,* Oct. 10, 1959.

[28] Yevtushenko, Y., *L'Express,* Paris, Sept. 1961, and *Precocious Augobiography,* 1963, pp. 116–21.

[29] *Literaturnaya gazeta,* Oct. 14, 1961, Starykov.

[30] Kremlin Conference of Writers, March 7–8, 1962, Korey, *op. cit.,* 111; also *Literaturnaya gazeta,* Aug. 9, 1966, letter by the literary critic Ariadna Gromova about a novel by A. Gavrutto. The latter had directed attention to an interpreter of Marshall von Paulus, a fictitious Kogan.

[31] *Yunost,* Aug. 1966, A. Kuznetsov, the novel *Babi Yar;* also Kuznetsov, in *Sputnik,* Apr. 1967.

[32] Samizdat material in M. Decter, *The Tower and Fate of Boris Kochubigowsky,* New York, 1970.

[33] Okuneva, R., "The Position of the Jews in the Soviet School Syllabus of World and Russian History," in Ettinger, S., *Soviet Anti-Semitism . . .,* 1985, III, 51–93.

[34] *Ibid.,* p. 57; thereafter p. 59, 65–6.

[35] Arthur Miller, "In Russia," *Harper's,* Sept. 1969, pp. 37–8.

[36] See the endless harangues by Soviet delegates in the U. N. since the passing of "Zionism is Racism" resolution in 1975.

[37] *Journal of the International Commission of Jurists,* "Economic Crimes in the Soviet Union," summer 1964, pp. 3–47.

[38] Bertrand Russell to Krushchev, *Jewish Chronicle,* Apr. 6, 1962, and March 1, 1963; also the Jewish Telegraphic Agency Bulletin, No. 101, Feb. 26, 1963.

[39] Russells' reply, *Times,* London, Apr. 6, 1963.

[40] *Krushchev Remembers,* pp. 178–79.

[41] *Ibid.,* p. 180.

[42] *Ibid.,* pp. 186 and 383–5.

[43] *Ibid.,* pp. 343–6.

Notes to Chapter VI

1 Gromyko's address to the U. N. General Assembly, May 1947. See also his speeches to the Security Council, May 21 and July 14, 1948.

2 Ehrenburg, I, in *Pravda*, Sept. 21, 1948.

3 *Krasnaya Zvezda*, March 13, 1970.

4 *Trud*, July 17, 1960.

5 *Ibid.*

6 A. Werth, *op. cit.*, p. 247.

7 *New York Times*, May 16, 1947.

8 *Pravda* and *Izvestia*, June 6, 1967.

9 Statement; also *Izvestia*, June 9, 1967.

10 *Pravda*, Zhukov, June 12, 1967, p. 5.

11 *Izvestia*, V. Petrov, Jan. 13, 1968, p. 5.

12 *Izvestia*, June 15 and June 16, 1968, p. 1.

13 *Pravda*, Kolesnichevski, June 28, 1948, p.5.

14 *Izvestia*, Yu. Ivanov, July 2, 1948, pp. 4–5.

15 Fedorenko, U. N. Security Council Official Records, 22nd year, S/PV 1352 and S/PV 1353, June 9, 1967.

16 Korey, *op. cit.*, pp. 133–40. The author is indebted to Korey for the following references to East European and communist reaction in the U. N. to the Arab–Israeli war, which differ from the official Soviet propaganda. Valuable sources for the divergence from the sharp anti–Israeli and anti–Semitic Soviet line are also to be found in "Soviet Reactions to the Middle East Crisis" (Aug. 18, 1967), deposited in the Archives of the Institute of Jewish Affairs, London, in Zev Katz, "Aftermath of the June War. Soviet Propaganda Offensive against Israel and World Jewry," *Bulletin on Soviet Jewish Affairs*, No. 1, 1969, and in M. Decter, "Soviet Anti–Semitism—An Instrument of Policy in Eastern Europe," Academic Committee on Soviet Jewry, New York, 1968.

17 Quoted by Korey, *op. cit.*, p. 130.

18 U. N. General Assembly, June 23, 1967.

19 *New Statesman*, Castro interview by K. Karol, June 16 and 23, 1967.

20 *New York Times*, Feb. 18, 1968.

21 *Rude Pravo*, quoted by Korey, *op. cit.*, 136.

22 *Ekonomika Politika*, Belgrade, July 10, 1967.

23 *De Wahrheid* (Netherlands), July 28, 1967.

24 *Weg und Ziel*, Vienna, several articles, November 1967.

[25] *Paese Sera*, May 29, 1967.

[26] *Presse Nouvelle*, May 30, 1967, and after the commencement of the war, letters in *L'Humanité*.

[27] Sakharov, *op. cit.*, p. 39.

[28] Medvedev, R., samizdat document, *Survey*, vol. 17, No. 2 (spring 1971) pp. 185–202.

[29] *New York Times*, Aug. 22, 1971.

[30] Yuri Ivanov, "What is Zionism?" *Khronika*, Aug. 31, 1969, appeared in many provincial journals; see for the following Korey, *op. cit.*, pp. 144f.

[31] *Ibid.*

[32] *Komsomolskaya Pravda*, Oct. 4, 1967.

[33] Saleh Daluki and Omar Amin (the latter actually Johannes von Leers, a prominent Nazi), *America—a Zionist Colony*, Cairo, 1957.

[34] *Komsomolskaya Pravda*, Oct. 4, 1967.

[35] Kichko, T., *Judaism and Zionism*, 1968.

[36] A. Low, *The Sino–Soviet Confrontation*, pp. 191, 340–42.

[37] Smolar B., *Soviet Jewry Today*, pp. 203–9, and Lawrence, G., *Three Million More*, 1970, p. 180.

[38] Lawrence, *op. cit.*

[39] *Ibid.*, pp. 182 and 184.

[40] *Ibid.*, p. 188.

[41] *Mezhdunarodnaya zhizn*, K. Ivanov, June 1968.

[42] *Krasnaya zvezda*, Aug. 17, 1968, and *Komsomolskaya Pravda*, Aug. 13, 1968.

[43] *About Events in Czechoslovakia*, The Press Group of Soviet Journalists, Moscow, 1968.

[44] A. D. Low, "The Soviet Nationality Policy and the New Program of the CPSU," *Russian Review*, vol. 22, No. 1, pp. 3–29.

[45] Twenty–Fourth Party Congress; also Sawyer, *op. cit.*, p. 155.

[46] Yevgeny Yevseev, *Fascsism under the Blue Star*, Moscow, 1971, p. 160, and V. Begun, *The Creeping Counterrevolution*, Minsk, 1972, pp. 57 and 74–80.

[47] Skurlatov, V. S., *Zionism and Apartheid*, 1975, p. 120.

[48] *Izvestia*, Apr. 5, 1964, review of Kichko's book.

[49] Ivanov,Y., *Beware Zionism* (1961), p. 259.

[50] Donetsky, M. in *Vechernaia Odessa*, June 23 and 24, 1973, pp. 266–76.

[51] Review by Yemeleganov Y., *Nash sovremennik*, No. 6, 1978, pp. 188–91.

52 *Molodaya Gvardiya*, on Yevseev, *Fascism under the Blue Stars*, 1971.

53 Kichko, T., *Judaism and Zionism*, 1968, p. 267.

54 V. Begun, *Creeping Counterrevolution*, 1972.

55 See 47.

56 *Jews in the USSR*, No. 13, 1976, G. Shimanov.

57 *Veche*, No. 3, 1971, in Ettinger, (ed.), *Anti-Semitism in the Soviet Union*, III, 349.

58 *Ibid.*, No. 3, Jan. 10. 1971, p. 350.

59 Ettinger, (ed.), *op. cit.*, III, 29–30.

60 *Ibid.*; for the following pp. 39, 102, 23–24, 24–30, 21.

61 *Saturday Review*, Sept. 18, 1971, p. 31.

62 Medvedev, R., samizdat document, see Zand, "The Jewish Question in the USSR," in St. Cohen, *An End to Silence*.

63 *Ibid.*

64 Kapto, A., "Question of Theory . . . Internationalism and Patriotism," *Pravda*, Aug. 23, 1985, pp. 1–2 (*CDSP*, XXXVII, No. 34, pp. 7–8).

65 *Ibid.*, p. 7.

66 *Pravda*, Feb. 17. 1987, "Questions of Theory . . . Achievements and Problems," (*CDSP* XXXIX, No. 7, March 18, 1987, pp. 1–2).

67 *Pravda*, Yesilbayev, Feb. 11, 1987, p. 2.

68 *CDSP*, XXXIX, No. 4, 1987, pp. 8–9; also Alimov, Feb. 21, pp. 3–4, Speeches, *Kommunist Tadzhikistana*, Feb. 22, p. 2 (*CDSP*, XXXIX, 1987, pp. 87, 90).

69 *Pravda*, Bagramov, E., Dec. 28, 1985, pp. 2–3 (*CDSP*, XXXVII, 1985, No. 51, p. 2).

70 Gershon Swet, "Jewish Religion in the Soviet Union," 1961.

71 Also Kolarz, W., *Religion in the Soviet Union*, 1961.

72 Slutzki, Yehuda, *The Fate of Hebrew in Soviet Schools*, pp. 396–405.

73 *Ibid.*, p. 397.

74 *Ibid.*

75 *Ibid.*

76 *Izvestia*, Apr. 17, 1955.

77 *Pravda*, Dec. 30, 1955.

78 *New York Times*, letter by Joseph Lasch about Mrs. Roosevelt, Dec. 17, 1970.

79 Cang, *op. cit.*, pp. 187–92.

[80] *Ibid.*; *Réalités*, No. 136 (May 1957) p. 67, and Cang, *op. cit.*, pp. 79–80.

Notes to Chapter VII

[1] *Current History*, Oct. 1988, "The Nationalities Problem in the Soviet Union," pp. 347, 325–27, 352.

[2a] *Pravda*, Feb. 18, 1988.

[2b] *Moskva*, No. 11, 1986, pp. 183–98, V. Koshinov, "The Russian Cultural Legacy. Two Views," *Ibid.*, "On Lenin's Conception of National Culture."

[3a] *CDSP* XXXVIII, 1986, No. 10, Kozhinov; also No. 9.

[3b] *Sovetskaya kultura*, March 17, 1982, p. 6, Koltakhchyan.

[4] *Pravda*, S. Andreyev, March 19, 1982, p. 2.

[5] *Kommunist*, Sept. 25, 1984, pp. 1–4, No. 43, pp. 13–15, pp. 2–3.

[6] *Kommunist Tadzhikistana*, Oct. 19, 1984, pp.2–3 and *Azerbaidjan Bakinsky Rabochy*

[7] Vinogradov, A. I., *Nauchny ateizm*, No. 6, June 1985, pp. 3-62, (*CDSP*, XXXVII, No. 38, pp. 4–5, 22).

[8] *Pravda*, Jan 16, 1987, A. Turnisiv: also Yusupov E., *Sovietskaya kultura*, Dec. 18, 1983, p. 3, "On National Traditions and the Prejudices of Islam."

[9] *Izvestia*, Aug. 26, 1985, Gievandov (*CDSP*, XXXVI, No. 34, p. 11).

[10] *Literatwinaya gazeta*, Oct. 17, 1984 (*CDSP*, XXXVII, No. 34, p. 11).

[11] *Ibid.*

[12] Tsigelman "The Concept of the Universal Jewish Conspiracy," in Ettinger, (ed.), *Soviet Anti-Semitism*, III, 3–50.

[13] *Ibid.*, I, 84.

[14] About Lenin's operational code, see Meyer, A. G., *Leninism*, 1957, pp. 80–81.

[15] *Anti-Semitism in the Soviet Union*, I, 111.

[16] *Ibid.*, p. 102.

[17ab] *Ibid.*, I, 104.

[18] *Ibid.*, I, 107.

[19] *Ogonyok*, No. 28, 1978, pp. 22-4, Abstract (*CDSP*).

[20] *Ibid.*, Korneev, No.29, July, pp. 22–28.

[21] Yemelianov, V., "Zionism Unmasked," *Nash sovremennik*, No. 8, 1978, pp. 188–91, (Abstract, *CDSP*, XXX, No. 45, pp. 5–6).

[22] About Freemasons, see also Pilazhaev, V., *Komsomolskaya Pravda*, Sept. 13, p. 3, Abstracts, p. 6.

[23] *Izvestia*, Aparin, (*CDSP*, XXVIII, 1976, No. 23, p. 12), *Izvestia*, Dec. 24, 1976.

[24] K. Orlovsky and S. Polin, "The Indestructible Power of Soviet Culture," (*CDSP*, XXVIII, 1976, No. 51, p. 1), *Izvestia*, Dec. 24, 1976.

[25] *Izvestia*, March 5, 1977, "Open letter . . . "

[26] *Ibid.*

[27] *Ibid.*, p. 6.

[28] *CDSP*, XXIX, March 30, 1977, No. 35, p. 9.

[29] *Ibid.*, No. 35, p. 6.

[30] Antonov B., *Chelobek i zakon*, No. 6, June 1977, p. 28, in *Abstract* (*CDSP*, XXIX).

[31] *Pravda*, Jan. 14, 1979, p. 4, Yugov (*CDSP*, XXXI).

[32a] *Komsomolskaya Pravda*, May 24, 1987, p. 1–4.

[32b] *Ogonyok*, 1987, No. 21, A. Golovkov and A. Pavlov, May, pp. 4–5 (*CDSP*, No. 21, 1987, pp. 4–5); see also inverview of Dr. A. Butenko and A. Sirotkin in *Moskovskaya Pravda*, May 7, p. 3.

[32c] *Sovetskaya Byelorussia*, Nov. 17, 1987, p. 3, "With the Measure of Memory, Polemical Notes . . ."

[33] See also Pepelyayev, V., *ibid.*, Dec. 29, 1987.

[34] According to the *Jerusalem Post*, international edition, June 1988, p. 5, Gorbachev is pictured as "extremely concerned" about *Pamyat.*

[35] *CDSP*, XL, No. 1, 1988, pp. 10–12.

[36] *Komsomolskaya Pravda*, May 22,, June 24, and Dec. 19, 1987 (*CDSP*, XXXIX, 1987, No. 2, pp. 1–4, No. 30, pp. 5–6).

[37] Rasputin, G., "Our Cultural Legacy . . .," *Nash sovremennik*, Jan. 1988, pp. 169–72.

[38] *Pravda*, Feb. 1, 1988, p. 4, and *CDSP*, XL, Nov. 12, 1988, pp. 13–14.

[39] *Izvestia*, Feb. 27, 1988, p. 3; (*CDSP*, XL, No. 12, 1988, p. 14.

[40] *Ibid.*

[41] *Izvestia*, Aug. 14, 1988.

[42] *Ibid.*

[43] *Ibid.*, Zand, "The Jewish Question in the USSR," in Ettinger, *Soviet Anti-Semitism . . .*, vol. III.

[44] *CDSP*, XL, No. 11, Apr. 13, 1988.

[45] Interview with Soviet historians, G. Melikyants, *Izvestia*, March 22, 1988, p. 3.

[46] Karpov, V. V., *Literaturnaya gazeta*, No. 10, March 9, 1988, pp. 2–3 (*CDSP*, XL, No. 11, 1988, pp. 5–6).

[47] *Ibid.*, Poliakov Yu.

[48] *Literaturnaya gazeta*, No. 10, Mar. 9, 1988, p. 4; *ibid.*, p. 6.

[49] *Ibid.* p. 7.

[50] *Ibid.*, p. 4.

[51] *Ibid.*

[52] *Ibid.*

[53] *Pravda*, Michin, N., (*CDSP*, No. 45, 1988, p. 22).

[54] *Jerusalem Post*, International Edition, March 25, 1989, pp. 9–10, 12.

Notes to Conclusion

[1] This view is widely shared by both Soviet Jews and gentiles. See Elkind in Yanai, Y., (ed.), *Soviet Anti-Semitism . . .*, part I, p. 198.

[2] Lenin, *Soch*, 3rd ed., 1931, vol. 24, p. 96.

[3] Tenth Congress, *CPSU*, 1921.

[4] Pinkus, *op. cit.*, p. 234.

[5] *New York Times*, early May 1949, H. Salisbury.

[6] Stalin, University of Toilers, May 19, 1925.

SELECT BIBLIOGRAPHY

Books and Articles

Not all books or journals listed throughout this study are included here. Samizdat are writings that have not received official approval for publication and are only privately circulated.

Adorno, Theodore, et al. *The Authoritarian Personality*, New York, 1950.

Ainsztein, R. "Soviet Jewry in the Second World War," in *The Jews in Soviet Russia Since 1917*, L. Kochan (ed.), Oxford, 1970.

Alliluieva, Svetliana. "Jewish Predicament," *Midstream*, Jan. 1971.

———. *Only One Year*, New York, 1969.

———. *Twenty Letters to a Friend*, New York, 1967.

Altschuler, Mordecai, (ed.). *Russian Publications on Jews and Judaism in the Soviet Union*, Jerusalem, 1970.

Amalrik, Andrei. *Will the Soviet Union Survive until 1984?* New York, 1970.

American Jewish Year Book, yearly editions, New York.

Arendt, Hannah. *The Origins of Totalitarianism*, New York, 1962.

Anti-Semitism in the Soviet Union. Its Roots and Consequences, Vol. I,, Yakov Yanai (ed.), Jerusalem, 1979.

———. Vol. 2, J. M. Kelman (ed.), 1980.

———. Vol. 3, S. Ettinger (ed.), 1983.

———. Th. Freedman (ed.), New York, 1984 (espec. pts. III and V).

Anti-Semitism in Eastern Europe. A Socialist International Publication, London, n.d.

Anti-Semitism—A Tool of Soviet Policy. Yaakov Moriah, Tel-Aviv, n.d.

Armstrong, J. *The Soviet Bureaucratic Elite: A Case Study of the Ukrainian Apparatus*, New York, 1959.

———. "Soviet Foreign Policy and Anti-Semitism," in *Perspectives On Soviet Jewry*, New York, 1971.

Aspaturian, V. V. "Non–Russian Nationalities," in A. Kassof (ed.), *Prospects of Soviet Society*, New York, 1968, pp. 143–200.

Azrael, Jeremy R. (ed.). *Soviet Nationality Policies and Practices*, New York, 1978.

Barghoorn, F. C. *Soviet Foreign Propaganda*, Princeton, 1964.

Baron, Salo W. *The Russian Jew under Tsars and Soviets*, New York, 1964.

Bauer, Otto. *Die Nationalitätenfrage und die Sozialdemokratie*, Vienna, 1907 (1924).

Bedell, Smith W. *My Three Years in Moscow*, New York, 1950.

Bennisgsen, Alexandre. "Soviet Minority Nationalism in Historic Perspective," in R. Conquest, *The Last Empire*, Stanford, 1986.

Bibichkova, N. "A List of Anti–Israeli and Anti–Semitic Books Published in the USSR in 1979–1981," pp. 369–374, in *Anti–Semitism in the Soviet Union*, vol. 3, S. Ettinger (ed.).

——. 'Anti–Semitic and Anti–Israeli Publications in the USSR, 1960–81," *ibid.*, pp. 629–645.

——. "Soviet Foreign Policy and Anti–Semitism," in *Perspectives On Soviet Jewry*, New York, 1971.

——. *The Politics of Totalitarianism*, New York, 1961.

Biographical Dictionary of Dissidents in the Soviet Union 1956–1975, compiled and edited by S. P. de Boer, e. J. Driessen, and H. L. Verhaer.

Bolshakov, V. *Zionism in the Service of Anti–Semitism*, Moscow, 1972.

Bunyan, J. and H. H. Fischer. *The Bolshevik Revolution 1917–1918. Documents and Materials*, Stanford, 1961.

Cang, Joel. *The Silent Millions*, New York, 1969.

Chalidze, V. *To Defend These Rights: Human Rights and the Soviet Union*, New York, 1975.

Chernov, F. *Proletarskii Internatsionalizm i Burshaznyi Kosmopolitanizm* [Proletarian Internationalism and Bourgeois Nationism], Moscow, 1951.

The Chronicle of Current Events, a samizdat publication.

Cohen, Richard (ed.), *Let My People Go!* New York, 1971, in *Ishkod*, No. 1, 212–17.

Cohen, Stephen F. (ed.) *An End to Silence*, from R. Medvedev's Underground Magazine, *Political Diary*, New York and London.

Cohn, Norman. *Warrant for Genocide. The Elders of Zion*, New York, 1966–67.

Commentary, Dec. 1963, "Russian Art and Anti–Semitism: Two

Documents."

Conquest, Robert (ed.) *The Great Terror. Stalin's Purges in the Thirties,* London and New York, 1968.

———. *The Last Empire, Nationality and Soviet Future,* Stanford, 1986.

The Council of Europe on the Jews in the Soviet Union, World Jewish Congress, London.

Crankshaw, Edward (ed.) *Krushchev Remembers,* trans. by Strobe Talbott, Boston, 1970.

Curtis, John. *Religion in the Soviet Union,* 1961.

Dawidowicz, Lucy (ed.) *The Golden Tradition,* New York, 1967.

Decter, Moche (ed.) *Redemption! Jewish Freedom Letters from Russia,* New York, 1970.

———. *A Hero for Our Times. The Trial and Fate of Kochubigewsky,* New York, 1970.

Deutscher, Isaac. *Stalin,* 2nd ed., New York, 1967.

———. *Prophet Unarmed. Trotsky 1929-1940,* New York, 1965.

———. *Prophet Outcast. Trotsky 1929-1940,* New York, 1965.

———. *The Non-Jewish Jew and Other Essays,* Tamara Deutscher (ed.), London and New York, 1968.

DeWitt, N. *Education and Professional Employment in the USSR,* Washington, D. C., 1970.

———. *Status of Jews in Soviet Education* (mimeographed), American Jewish Congress, 1964.

Dimanshtein, S. M. (ed.) *Revoliutsiia i Natsional'nyi Vopros* [The Revolution and the National Question], Moscow, 1930.

Dissent, N. Wyzeimoblo, "Was Lenin's Mother Jewish?" April 1971, pp. 141-44.

Djilas, Milovan. *Conversations with Stalin,* New York, 1962.

———. "Eastern Europe within the Soviet Empire," in R. Conquest, *The Last Empire,* 1986.

Domalskii, J. *Russian Jews. Yesterday and Today,* Jerusalem, 1975.

Dunlop, J. B. *The Faces of Contemporary Russian Nationalism,* Princeton, 1983.

Eckman, L. S. *Soviet Policy towards Jews and Israel 1917-74,* New York, 1974.

D'Encausse, H. H. C. *Decline of an Empire,* New York, 1979.

Engelmann, B. *Germany without Jews,* New York, 1984.

Ehrenburg, Ilya. *The Post-War Years 1945-54,* Cleveland and New York, 1967.

———. *People and Life 1891-1921,* New York, 1962.

———— and Vasily Grossman. *The Black Book*, Holocaust Library, New York, 1980.

Ettinger, S. (ed.) "Excerpts from Soviet Publications and Samizdat," in *Anti-Semitism in the Soviet Union*, vol. 3, Jerusalem, 1983, pp. 197–368.

Fainsod, Merle. *Smolensk under Soviet Rule*, Cambridge, Mass., 1958.

Fetscher, Irving (ed.) *Marxisten gegen Antisemitismus*, 1974.

Fischer, George. *The Soviet System and Modern Society*, New York, 1968.

"Mr. Solzhenitsyn and His Critics," *Foreign Affairs*, 1980, pp. 187–210.

Freedman, R. O (ed.) *Soviet Jewry in the Decisive Decade 1971–1980*, Durham, N.C., 1984.

Friedberg, Maurice. *The Jew in Post–Stalin Literature*, Washington, D.C., 1970.

Frumkin, J. B., Goldenweiser, A. (eds.) *Russian Jewry (1860–1917)*, So. Brunswick, N. J., 1966 (also 1969).

Gilbert, Martin. *The Jews of Russia. Their History in Maps and Photographs*, London, 1976.

Gilboa, Yehoshua. *The Black Years of Soviet Jewry*, Boston, 1971.

Gitelman, Zvi, *A Century of Ambivalence. The Jews of Russia and the Soviet Union, 1881 to the Present*, New York, 1988.

————. *Jewish Nationality and Soviet Politics. The Jewish Sections of the CPSU, 1917–1930*, Princeton, 1972.

Glazov, Yurii. *Narrow Gates. The Resurrection of the Russian Intelligentsia*, 1973.

Goldberg, Anatol. *Ilya Ehrenburg*, London, 1984.

Goldberg, B. Z. *The Jewish Problem in the Soviet Union*, New York, 1961.

Goldhagen, E. (ed.) *Ethnic Minorities in the Soviet Union*, New York, 1968.

Goldmann, Nahum. *Memories*, London, 1969.

Gorev, Mikhail. *Protiv antisemitov* [Against the Anti–Semites], Moscow, 1928.

Gouzenko, Igor. *The Iron Curtain*, New York, 1948.

Greenberg, Louis. *The Jews of Russia 1773–1917*, 2 vols in one, London, 1944–51.

Grose, Peter. "The Kremlin and the Jews," in *The Anatomy of the Soviet Union*, (Staff members of the *New York Times*), New York, 1968.

Harvard Project on the Soviet Social System, Cambridge, Mass.

Hindus, Maurice. "Jew–Russia's Stepson," in *House without a Roof*, Garden City, N.Y., 1961.

Howe, Irving. *The Basic Writings of Trotsky*, Vintage Books, 1963.

Ianov Ivaniana. *Kontinent*, No. 9–10, 1976.

Inglés, Jose D. *Study of Discrimination*, United Nations, 1963.

Israel, Gérard. *The Jews in Russia*, trans. by S. L. Chernoff, New York, 1975.

Istoria sovetskoi konstitutsii v dokumentakh 1917–1956, [The History of Soviet Constitutions in Documents], Moscow, 1956.

Jews in Eastern Europe, vol. III, No. 7 (Nov. 1967), London.

Katz, Zev. *The New Nationalism in the USSR: Its Impact on the Jews*, Cambridge, Nov. 1972.

Kelly, D. R. (ed.) *Soviet Politics in the Brezhnev Era*, New York, n.d.

Kochan, Lionel. *The Jews, Soviet Russia since 1917*, London, 1970.

Kolarz, Walter. *Religion in the Soviet Union*, New York, 1961.

Kon, I. "Psychology of Prejudice," *Novy Mir*, No. 9, Sept. 1966.

Korey, William. *The Soviet Cage. Anti-Semitism in Russia*, Viking Press, New York, 1973.

———. "The Legal Position of the Jewish Community in the Soviet Union," in E. Goldhagen, *The Ethnic Minorities in the Soviet Union*, Praeger, 1968.

Kosygin, A. *New York Times*, June 27, 1967.

———. *Pravda*, July 19, 1965.

Kuznetsov, Anatoly. *Babi Yar. A Documentary Novel*, trans. by Jacob Guralsky, New York, 1967.

Larin, Yuri. *Yevrei i antisemitizm v SSSR* [Jews and Anti-Semitism in the USSR], Moscow, 1927.

Lawrence, Gunther. *Three Million More?* Garden City, New York, 1970.

Lendvai, Paul. *Anti-Semitism without Jews*, New York, 1971.

Lestschinsky, J. *Dos Sovetische Identum* (Yiddish), New York, 1941.

Lewis, Bernard. *Semites and Anti-Semites,* New York and London, 1986.

Low, A. D. *Jews in the Eyes of the Germans. From the Enlightenment to Imperial Germany*, Philadelphia, 1979.

———. *Lenin on the Question of Nationality*, New York, 1958.

———. "Soviet Nationality Policy and the New Program of the CPSU," *Russian Review*, Jan. 1961.

Lumer, Hyman. *Soviet Anti-Semitism—A Cold War Myth?* New York, 1964.

_____. *Zionism. Its Role in World Politics*, New York, 1973.

Lunacharsky, Anatoly V. *Ob antisemitizma* [About Anti–Semitism], Moscow, 1929.

Mann, Thomas. *Sieben Manifeste zur jüdischen Frage, 1936–1948*, Darmstadt, 1966.

Maor, Y. *The Jewish Question in the Liberal and Revolutionary Movement in Russia* (Hebrew), Jerusalem, 1968.

Medem, Z.B.W. *Sotsialdemokratiia i Natsional'nyi Voppros*, [Social Democracy and the National Question], St. Petersburg, 1901.

Medvedev, Roy A. *Survey*, Vol. 17, No. 2, Spring 1971, pp. 185–201 (translated from Samizdat).

_____. *An End to Silence*, St. F. Cohen (ed.), from Samizdat, London.

_____. *Blishnevostochnii conflict i yevreiski vopros v SSSR* [The Near–eastern Conflict and the Jewish Question in the USSR], Moscow, May 1970 (a samizdat [self–published] document).

_____. *Krushchev, The Years in Power*, 1976.

_____. *Let History Judge*, New York, 1971.

_____. *On Socialist Democracy*, New York, 1975.

_____, and Zhores A. Medvedev. *A Question of Madness*, New York, 1971.

Meerson–Aksenov and Boris Shrogin, (eds.) *The Political, Social, and Religious Thought of Russian Samizdat*, Belmont, Mass., 1977.

Meir, Golda. *My Life*, Jerusalem and Tel–Aviv, 1975.

Meyer, P., et al. *The Jews in the Soviet Satellites*, Syracuse, 1953.

Miller, Arthur. "In Russia," *Harper's*, Sept. 1969, pp. 37–38.

Millman, Ivor J. *Soviet Jewry in the Census of 1970*, No. 21, London, 1971.

Minski E. L. (ed.) *The National Question in the Russian Duma*, London, 1915.

Mishin, V. *Social Progress*, Moscow, 1970.

Mitin, M. B., et al. *Zionist Theory and Practice*, n.d.

Moynihan, Daniel. *Dangerous Place*, Boston and New York, 1978.

Muhlen, Norbert. *The Survivors*, New York, 1962.

Namir, Mordecai. *A Mission to Moscow*, (Hebrew), Tel–Aviv, 1971.

Nudelman, R. *Social Progress*, Moscow, 1970.

Patterns of Prejudice, vol. I, No. 2 (March–April 1967).

Pelikan, Jiři (ed.) *Czechoslovak Political Trials 1950–59*, The Suppressed Report of the Dubcek Government's Commission of Inquiry, 1968.

Perspectives on Soviet Jewry, J. A. Armstrong, "Soviet Foreign Policy and Anti–Semitism," New York, 1971.

Pinkus, Benjamin. *The Soviet Government and the Jews 1948–1967*, A Documented Study, Cambridge and Israeli Academy of Sciences, 1984.

Pinson, Koppel. *Essays on Anti–Semitism.* New York 1946.

Pipes, Richard. "The Forces of Nationalism," *Problems of Communism*, Jan.–Feb. 1964.

Poliakov, Léon. *History of Anti–Semitism*, Vol. IV, *Suicidal Europe. 1870–1933*, New York, 1977 (1985).

Pommer, H. Jörg. *Antisemitismus in der USSR und in den Satellitenstaaten*, Bern, 1963.

Rabinbach, A. (ed.) and J. Zipes. *Germans and Jews since the Holocaust.*

Rafes, M. *Ockerki po Istorii "Bunda"* [Essays on the History of the Bund], Moscow, 1923.

Redlich, Sh. *Propaganda and Nationalism in Wartime Russia, East European Quarterly*, 1982.

Reitlinger, Gerald. *The Final Solution*, London, 1961.

Riasanovsky, N. V. *A History of Russia*, New York and Oxford, 1984.

Rigby, T. H. *Communist Party Membership in the USSR 1911–1967*, Princeton, 1968.

Rogger, Hans. "The Beilis Case: Anti–Semitism and Politics in the Reign of Nicholas II," *Slavic Review*, Vol. 25, (Dec. 1966), pp. 45–51.

Ro'i, Yaacov. *Soviet Decision–Making in Practice. The USSR and Israel, 1947–54*, London.

Rothenberg, Joshua. *The Jewish Religion in the Soviet Union*, New York, 1971.

————. *An Annotated Bibliography of Writings on Judaism in the Soviet Union, 1960–65*, Waltham, Mass., 1969.

Rubinstein, Joshua. *Soviet Dissidents. Their Struggle for Human Rights*, Boston, 1980.

Rubin, R. I. (ed.) *The Unredeemed. Anti–Semitism in the Soviet Union*, Chicago, 1968.

Rukadze, Avtandil. *Jews in the USSR. Figures, Facts, Comments*, Moscow, 1978.

Rywkin, Michael. *Moscow's Muslim Challenge*, Armonk, 1982.

Sakharov, Andrei D. *Progress, Coexistence, and Intellectual Freedom*, New York, 1970.

Salisbury, H. F. *Moscow Journal*, Chicago, 1961.

Samuel, Maurice. *Blood Accusation*, New York, 1966.

Schapiro, Leonard. "Nationalism in the Soviet Empire. The Anti-Semitic Component," in Conquest, R., *The Last Empire*, 1986.

Shaffer, Harry G. *The Soviet Treatment of Jews*, London and Washington, 1974.

Schwarz, Solomon M. *The Jews in the Soviet Union*, Syracuse, 1951.

Schechtmann, J. B. *Star in Eclipse. Russian Jewry Revisited*, New York, 1961.

Simmonds, G. W. (ed.) *Nationalism in the USSR and Eastern Europe in the Era of Brezhnev and Kosygin*, Detroit, 1977.

Solhenitsyn, A. *The Gulag Archipelago, 1918-1956*, Pts. 3-4, New York, 1975.

Souvarine, Boris. "Gorky, Censorship, and the Jews," *Dissent*, Winter, 1965.

_____. *Stalin*, New York, 1939.

Soviet Jewish Affairs, "USSR and Politics of Polish Anti-Semitism 1956-58," No. 1 (June 1971) and No. 2 (Nov. 1971), pp. 3-25.

Skurlatov, V. *Sionism i apartheid* [Zionism and Apartheid], Kiev, 1975.

Smolar, Boris. *Soviet Jewry Today and Tomorrow*, New York, 1971.

Soviet Jewry Today, Vol. 1, No. 1 (Nov. 1971).

Stalin, J. *Marksizm i natsional'no kolonialnyi Vopros* [Marxism and the National-Colonial Question], Moscow, 1937.

Tartakower, Arieh. "The Jewish Problem in the Soviet Union," *Jewish Social Studies* (33), 1971, pp. 285-306.

Teller, Judd L. *Ideology and History of Soviet Jewish Policy*, New York, 1964.

Trainin, J. "National and Multinational State in the Works of Comrade Stalin," *Sovetskoe Gosudarstvo i Pravo*, No. 6 (1939), pp. 25-47.

Treadgold, D. W. "Nationalism in the USSR and Its Implications for the World," in R. Conquest, *The Last Empire*, Stanford, 1986.

_____. *Twentieth Century Russia*, 1976 (also later editions).

Trials of War Criminals. Before the Nürnberg Military Tribunals, No. 10, Green Series, Washington, D.C., 1950, vol. IV.

Trotsky, L. *The History of the Russian Revolution*. New York, 1932, 3 vols.

_____. *Stalin*, New York, 1941.

Ulam, Adam B. *Expansion and Coexistence*, New York, 1969.

_____. *Stalin, the Man and His Era*, New York, 1973.

U. N. General Assembly Official Record, Fifth Emergency Special Session, June-July 1967.

U. N. Security Council Official Record, 22nd year, S/PV 1352 and S/PV 1353, June 9, 1967.

Vargo Bela and Mosse G. L. (eds.) *Jews and Non-Jews in Eastern Europe 1918-1945*, New York, 1974.

Velikovskii M. and Lenin, I. (eds.) *Natsional'nyi Vopros. Chrestomatiia* [The Nationality Problem], Moscow, 1931.

Vergelis, Aron. In *Druzhba narodov*, No. 4 (April 1971), pp. 204-21.

Voronel, Aleksandr and Yakhot, Victor. *I Am a Jew. Essays on Jewish Identity in the Soviet Union*, New York, 1973.

Voprosy filosofii. "Against the Bourgeois Ideology of Cosmpolitanism", 3 (1948), pp. 14-29.

Werth, Alexander. *Russia, Hopes, and Fears*, New York, 1969.

Weinryb, B. D. "Anti-Semitism in Soviet Russia," in L. Kochan, *The Jews in Soviet Russia 1917*, London, 1970.

———. *Jews in the Soviet Satellites*, Syracuse, 1953.

Whitney, Thomas P. *The Communist Blueprint for the Future*, New York, 1962.

Wiesel, Elie. *The Jews of Silence. A Personal Report on Soviet Jewry*, New York, 1966.

Yanov, Alexander. *The Russian New Right*, Berkeley, 1978.

Yevtushenko, Y. *A Precocious Autobiography*, New York, 1963.

Zaslavsky, V. and R. j. Brym. *Soviet Jewish Emigration and Soviet Nationality Policy*, New York, 1983.

Other Newspapers and Journals

Aynikait

Bulletin on Soviet and East European Jewish Affairs

Canadian Review of Studies in Nationalism (CRSN)

Current Digest of the Soviet Press (CDSP)

Druzhba narodov

Folksshimme (Warsaw)

For a Lasting Peace, for People's Democracy

Foreign Affairs

Jerusalem Post, International Edition

Izvestia

Jewish Social Studies

Jews in Eastern Europe, quarterly, London

Jewish Chronicle, quarterly, London

Khronika Tekushchikh sobytii [Chronicle of Current Events]

Kommunist

Komsomolskaya pravda

Krasnaya zvezda
Kultura i zhizn'
Literaturnaya gazeta
Mezhdunarodnaia zhizn
Moskovskaya pravda
Neues Leben (USSR)
New Republic
New York Times
New Times [Novoe vremia]
Novy mir
Pravda
Pravda Ukrainy
Russian Review
Sovetskoe gosudarstvo i pravo
Soviet Jewish Affairs
Soviet Jewry Today
Soviet News
Spiegel, Der
Trud
Ukrainian Academy of Arts and Sciences in the U.S.
Vechernaia Moskva
Voprosy istorii
Voprosy filosofii
Washington Post
Zvezda

INDEX